MADSTONE

The True Tale of World War I Conscientious Objectors
Alfred and Charlie Fattig and Their Oregon Wilderness Hideout

PAUL FATTIG

HELLGATE PRESS   ASHLAND, OREGON

Hellgate Press • PO Box 3531 • Ashland, OR 97520
For Information: *sales@hellgatepress.com*

Library of Congress Cataloging-in-Publication Data

Names: Fattig, Paul, author.
Title: Madstone : the true tale of World War I conscientious objectors Alfred
  and Charlie Fattig and their Oregon wilderness hideout / Paul Fattig.
Other titles: True tale of World War I conscientious objectors Alfred and
  Charlie Fattig and their Oregon wilderness hideout
Description: Ashland, OR : Hellgate Press, [2017] | Includes bibliographical
  references and index.
Identifiers: LCCN 2017059289 (print) | LCCN 2017038887 (ebook) | ISBN
  9781555718787 (ebook) | ISBN 9781555718770 (alk. paper)
Subjects: LCSH: Fattig, Alfred, 1892-1990. | Conscientious
  objectors--Oregon--Biography. | Fattig, Charles, 1889-1967. | World War,
  1914-1918--Conscientious objectors--United States. | World War,
  1914-1918--Oregon. | Frontier and pioneer life--Oregon--Chetco River
  Watershed. | Kalmiopsis Wilderness (Or.)--History--20th century. | Fattig,
  Paul,--Childhood and youth. | Brothers--United States--Biography. |
  Oregon--Rural conditions--20th century.
Classification: LCC UB344.O7 (print) | LCC UB344.O7 F37 2017 (ebook) | DDC
  940.3/16092273 [B] --dc23
LC record available at https://lccn.loc.gov/2017059289

ISBN: 978-1-55571-877-0

Also by Paul Fattig: *Up Sterling Creek Without a Paddle: Confessions of a Recovering Journalist* (Hellgate Press/2016)

Cover and interior design: L. Redding
Cover photo: Jim Craven

Printed and bound in the United States of America
First edition 10 9 8 7 6 5 4 3 2 1

Praise for Madstone

"Paul Fattig's fascinating MADSTONE proves on a larger stage a fact long known to readers of his deep and varied journalism: that he is 'an extraordinary teller of tales' (words he applies to his father's unfulfilled ambition to write). This remarkable book combines memoir, history, naturalist sketches, and the story of two uncles who fled to the Southern Oregon wilderness and lived like mountain men in order to avoid the draft of 1917-1918. We owe Fattig a debt of gratitude for resurrecting an alternative history, that of a forgotten resistance in rural America to the Johnny-get-your-gun jingoism of World War I."

—**Russell Working**, journalist and short story writer whose work has appeared in the *New York Times*, *The Atlantic Monthly*, *The Paris Review*, the *Chicago Tribune*, the *Boston Globe* and many others

"In this compelling and spirited account, the author tells the extraordinary story of two courageous men: two brothers who refused to fight, Unquestionably, our history books are filled with 'war heroes,' but what we really need to see today, more than ever, is nonviolence and peace heroes: men and women who had and have the fortitude to say no to war and bloodshed. This intriguing story does just that. Mr. Fattig's work is worthy of so much more praise than one can give in a few lines. I highly recommend it."

—**Flamur Vehapi**, author of *Peace and Conflict Resolution in Islam*

"There is a kind of madness that sweeps through Paul Fattig's towering tale of two draft-dodging uncles, who engage in their own personal war in the wilds of Southern Oregon. Against the backdrop of World War I, MADSTONE gives a rich account of the struggles of these constantly feuding relatives, who find themselves grudgingly united in their pacifism and ability to survive in the wilderness. The tension between the uncles is set against the serene, detailed descriptions of an Appalachian-like countryside that Paul Fattig knows so well and describes so lovingly...[It] takes the reader on a journey into a madness that has its own peculiar beauty."

—**Damian Mann**, journalist and author of *Shooters, Heels & Heroes: The Life and Times of Rico Valentino*

"I read MADSTONE in one sitting. It's fun to read and Fattig has a way with words that captures southern Oregon's stunning beauty and the fierce independence of its citizens...On a deeper level, the book describes the hard-scrabble hillbilly life that has shaped the outlook on life in many parts of this country, one unknown to today's college-educated, hi-tech city dwellers. To anyone who wants to understand the polarization in our country today, Madstone is a must read."

—**Nancy Tappan**, editor, *The New Pioneer* magazine"

"Madstone is an Oregon original. Told with insight and humor, it is the story of the author's two uncles, who spent years in the most remote, rugged parts of the Siskiyou Mountains evading military conscription during World War One. It is also a memoir of the author's own hardscrabble post-World War Two childhood in rural Josephine County. Fattig evokes the distinctive way of life of a region that is among the least-known but most distinctive sections of the state."

—**Jeff LaLande**, historian

CONTENTS

ACKNOWLEDGMENTS

LIKE MOST SAGAS, THE MADSTONE STORY WOULD not have been written had it not been for others helping to guide the author along the way.

Chief among them was my uncle Alfred Fattig who patiently and good-naturedly answered my barrage of questions just before the last leaves fell from his tree of life. His youthful decision based on his religious convictions to oppose the military draft during World War I was not a popular choice a century ago, anymore than it would be today if military conscription once again became the law of the land. He was ostracized by the very society from which he had formed his values. In defense of those who took issue with his evading the draft, many had sons who answered the call of duty, knowing full well their chances of survival on the bloody front lines were slim. Yet I respect my uncle for sticking to his religious guns, so to speak.

I am also indebted to my siblings—Jim, Charles, Delores and George—for offering their perspective when it came to our family history, from our hardscrabble childhood to our paternal uncles who refused to wear a military uniform. In particular, Charles, a history buff and the brightest fellow in our midst, broke the ice with our estranged uncle by beginning a letter-writing correspondence with him decades before the elderly gentleman passed away. With regard to my siblings, our memories generally mesh, and where they differ I accept full responsibility. Of course, any misrepresentations on my part should be placed squarely on the fact I was stuck in the head with an arrow while still a pup.

I appreciate that Oregon newspapers, namely the *Grants Pass Daily Courier,* the *Medford Mail Tribune* and the *Oregonian* in Portland, among others, were around before and during my uncles' anti-war escapade to capture the life and times of those fascinating years. It was while writing for the *Courier* in the late 1980s that I first began interviewing old-timers for the Madstone chronicle, and traveled to Texas to chat with Alfred about his draft-dodging days. Over the ensuing decades I gathered more information about my notorious uncles and their shadowy escapade.

As always, I thank my wife Maureen for putting up with my grousing and grumbling as I battle daily with the English language. Her patience and kindness would have impressed Mother Teresa.

PROLOGUE

T HEY CALLED IT THE WAR TO END ALL WARS. They were dead wrong, of course, as history clearly demonstrates. But there is no question that World War I changed the course of human kind on the planet. It was known as the Great War because of its immense scope and massive bloodshed. Some historians argue convincingly that its impact still reverberates today, particularly in the Middle East where it caused political upheaval and forced realignments whose cultural and religious ramifications continue to fuel smoldering resentment. But we'll leave that global labyrinth for others to disentangle.

On the surface, Madstone is a simple story about my uncle, Alfred Fattig, and his refusal based on his strong religious convictions to fight in WWI. Accompanied by his elder brother and fellow draft dodger, Charles Savannah Fattig, he hid out in the southwestern Oregon mountains for three years, then surrendered to Uncle Sam and was sentenced to nine months behind bars for his trouble. But if you peek under the surface, you will find a strange tale about a very peculiar family living in an extraordinary time and unique place. Yet it is also the quintessential story of someone listening to his conscience while rejecting the popular drumbeat of war.

When I began research for this project in the 1980s, Uncle Alfred, the youngest of my father's two older brothers, was still alive as were some of those who knew him. I was also able to interview soldiers who fought in WWI, including those who joined or were drafted in southern Oregon in 1917. And I've pored over countless yellowed newspaper clippings reporting on the conflict.

They are all gone now, the doughboys of the first global war. Had I waited even a few years, Madstone would have lacked the gravitas the subject deserved since most of the principal characters would have no longer been around to toss in their two bits. To a man, the WWI veterans I met over the years were remarkable folks who deserved our respect. In Madstone, you will meet several genuine WWI heroes from southwestern Oregon whose courage was conspicuous. Contrary to what some well-intentioned folks may have insisted in recent years, not everyone in a military uniform is a hero. Truth be told, many veterans like me fought nothing more than hangovers during our uneventful tours of duty. There is no shame in that, providing you served honorably while in uniform. The shame is in lying about your exploits. Anyone falsifying his or her military history steals the honor from the deserving folks in uniform who risked their lives for others or gave their full measure for their country.

Fought in Western Europe, WWI began in 1914 and ended four years later with roughly ten million soldiers killed. The armistice was signed on Nov. 11, 1918—precisely on the 11th hour of the 11th day of the 11th month. The day was celebrated as Armistice Day until it morphed into Veterans Day in 1954 to honor all who once wore a military uniform.

Obviously, some wars are bloodier than others. WWI was a war's war. Consider this: the U.S., which declared war on Germany in April of 1917 but didn't fire a shot until that October, lost some 116,500 Americans in uniform in the war. Some were mowed down by machine guns. Others died an agonizing death from gas poisoning. Many others succumbed to diseases that ran rampant in the rat-infested trenches. While it is true that a soldier dying on any battlefield is just as dead re-gardless of where or when the battle was joined, WWI was a brutal conflict which required being on full alert and a bit of luck to survive each day. It was a bloody, muddy hell.

In this book, I focus on what was happening in southwest Oregon in the years leading up to World War I and the period immediately following the armistice. The towns you will come to know are places like Grants Pass, Medford, Jacksonville and Kerby, all in southwest Oregon. The region, the people and the local newspapers unflinchingly reflected country life when our nation went to war a century ago. Southwest Oregon was a microcosm of rural America during the Great War.

You will notice that Alfred Fattig's quotes are often grammatically challenged. I purposefully did not change his manner of speaking because his earthy but spoken-from-the heart approach to our mother tongue told volumes about the man. Besides, it wasn't until I was a high school senior that I learned grammar wasn't my maternal grandmother. I have also discovered over the years that simply because a person uses poor grammar means he or she is a dullard, any more than a learned person employing proper grammar reflects brilliance. Being well acquainted with both college graduates—I are one—and fence posts, I am sometimes in awe of the intellectual similarities. Yet I have also been mightily impressed by the brain power and depth of knowledge of degreed folks.

To get the proper Madstone perspective, you will need to plunge into the family gene pool with all its odd characters to get the full flavor of the narrative. Otherwise, you will keep shaking your head and muttering to yourself, "My God, how could anyone live like that?" Not an unreasonable question. In answer, I've included several chapters about my family and it's extremely rustic lifestyle, chapters which may make the squeamish squirm even more. Those chapters illustrate that for Alfred and Charlie Fattig, already accustomed to an extremely roughshod lifestyle, the Madstone cabin era would be a mere extension of that rustic existence. In some respects, it could have even have been considered a bit of a reprieve.

Like most families, ours has never been too keen about inviting outsiders to peek into the family closet. We may have been raised in poverty, but we are rich in pride. Dragging two felonious Fattigs out into the light of day may not sit well with some family members, past and present. But I figure the strange yet fascinating tale of our two jailbirds is worth shaking the family tree. Besides, we're not talking about vicious criminal kith and kin preying on society. The draft-dodging Fattig brothers were two strong-willed individuals simply opposing war as a solution to global problems when they refused to be drafted into WWI. What's more, having spent decades asking people questions as a journalist, it seems only fair that I be willing to sit down and study my own family's belly button. It should come as no surprise that, like all navels, it is downright unsightly once you pluck the lint.

By the by, I become a journalist because nothing seemed more appealing than spending my adult life visiting people and hearing their life story. I've always enjoyed talking to folks in the autumn of their life who had followed the Robert Frost road, the one less traveled. Uncle Alfred would turn out to be one of the most fascinating people I would interview in some forty years of journalism.

The obvious question that comes up when folks refuse to fight for their country is whether they are driven by cowardice or conscience. As the reader, you be the judge.

ONE

The Killing Shot

T HE HUNTER TOOK A DEEP BREATH, HOLDING IT for a few seconds before slowly letting it out in an attempt to steady his .40-65 Winchester as he pulled down on the deer. The young man was tired and hungry. He desperately wanted a clean kill following unrelenting lean days in which a skinny squirrel was considered a veritable feast.

With its long octagon barrel, the model 1886 rifle weighed heavy in his weary arms. But this was the first deer he had seen in several weeks. He could ill afford to miss the opportunity. A good shot would reward him with fresh venison; a miss meant prolonging his hunger pains.

Earlier that morning he had waded across shallow rapids below a crystal-clear pool in the Chetco River deep in what is now the 180,000-acre Kalmiopsis Wilderness tucked away in Oregon's rugged southwest corner. Even today, it is unforgiving rugged country known to take the life of those who venture into it not fully prepared.

Hiking along a rocky stream flowing from the west into the river, the hunter had startled the young buck nibbling on the tender green leaves of the streamside brush.

After bouncing a short distance on spring-loaded legs, the buck began tiptoeing through the wild azaleas whose pink blossoms filled the canyon with an airy perfume worth a mint in Manhattan if you could figure out a way to bottle it. Halting in mid-step, the deer peeked through the foliage at the man who had come for breakfast.

His chest no longer heaving from his exertions and the rising sun warming his back, the hunter snugged his cheek against the rifle's wooden stock. Sighting along the top of the barrel with his right eye, he carefully aligned the tip of the tiny steel post mounted on the far end with the bottom of the "V" in the rear sight. He lined them both up with the deer's head and gently pulled the trigger.

"It was standing there, a forked horn, looking at me through the brush," the man would recall some seventy years later. "I shot him right between the eyes."

And nearly blew off the top of the young buck's head when the 260-grain bullet slammed into its target. The rifle belched a puff of black-powder smoke as the sound of the blast echoed up the narrow canyon that early summer morning in 1918.

Walking over to his fallen prey, the man drew his hunting knife, one kept sharp enough to shave a cat if you could hold the feline still during its hissy fit, and swiftly slit the dead deer's throat. Blood gushed out onto the rocky soil before eventually slowing to a trickle. Working with the efficiency of a hunter who had bloodied his knife countless times before, he cut into its tender underbelly, slicing from the genitals to the throat, spilling its bowels out onto the ground. He took great care not to puncture the bladder, knowing the deer's strong urine would contaminate the valuable meat.

"We was real hungry," stressed the man who spoke with the parlance of someone little acquainted with formal education. This fine morning would feature venison for breakfast, a tasty treat for any omnivore, let alone two brothers working hard to build a cabin in these rugged mountains before the snow flew.

Yet the hunter was not so ravenous that he didn't take a few minutes to cut open its fore stomach. It was there he discovered a curious-looking stone the size of an acorn. At last, he had found the prize he had long sought—a madstone.

"I had begun to look for madstones after meeting a man in the woods

2

years before I got that one," he said in an interview seventy years after he shot the buck. "He told me how he got his, finding it in the stomach. I didn't kill any more deer after that but what I didn't cut the guts open and went to looking for one. What causes them, some people say, is a deer licking himself in fly time, getting that stone going in his stomach."

"I carried that madstone in my pocket for a good many years," he added. "Don't know if it brought me luck, but I was mighty proud of it. It's a beautiful thing, that stone."

The man speaking was Alfred Fattig, my uncle. Despite having blood on his hands that morning, he was a World War I draft dodger on the run, one who steadfastly refused to kill for Uncle Sam. He was a devout pacifist, at least when it came to shooting men between the eyes. He and his older brother, Charles "Charlie" Savannah Fattig, were hiding out from the long arm of the law in the remote mountains.

After three years on the lam and growing ever more lonely and melancholy by mountain life, Alfred hiked out and surrendered to authorities. He was tried in federal court in Portland and sentenced to a relatively light punishment of nine months behind bars. The two brothers had parted company the last year in hiding because they could no longer tolerate each other's company. However, the elder sibling also gave himself up a year later, receiving the same punishment.

The man who shot the madstone-carrying buck in Oregon's Chetco River drainage back in 1918 would dub the stream where he made the killing Madstone Creek. The rustic dwelling he and his older brother, Charlie, were building across the river became known as the Madstone cabin. The cabin is long gone today but the historic cabin site is marked on the Rogue River-Siskiyou National Forest map at roughly 2,200 feet elevation above sea level. Just across the Chetco River from the cabin site is the confluence of Madstone Creek, the name chosen by the two brothers.

After field dressing the deer, Alfred lifted up a foreleg, then cut the skin around the ankle and sliced the tendon. With a snap, he broke the ankle bone and cut off the hoof. He quickly repeated the procedure on the other three legs. Following that, he cut through the fur around the neck at the base of the skull, slicing down to the vertebrae. Grasping the horns at their base, he gave the head a sharp twist, hearing the telltale snap of a broken neck. Picking up the knife once more, he quickly cut through the remaining tendons to decapitate the animal. He tossed the head and hooves onto the pile of guts which would soon be consumed by scavengers. But the heart and liver were tucked back inside the chest cavity. While he did not want to carry any unnecessary weight, he would not waste any precious meat. After all, there was no corner meat market nearby to pick up a few steaks when their supplies ran low.

Draping the carcass over his shoulder in a fireman's carry, he trudged slowly back to the cabin site, stopping periodically to rest. Upon reaching the cabin site, he would hang the deer carcass in the shade of a nearby cedar tree to cure.

Having washed his hands in the river as clear as holy water, he prepared a hasty meal, cooking slabs of the heart muscle in an iron frying pan on a campfire. His hunger satiated, he later picked up an ax, hewed a crude board out of a soft cedar log and began carving letters into the rough wood with a knife. Written on that crude slab of wood he placed over the door were the words "Madstone cabin." At least those were his intended words. The spelling may have been a mite off.

TWO

A Short Madstone Primer

B EFORE PROCEEDING ANY FURTHER INTO the tale of the two draft-dodging brothers in Oregon, we need to examine the reddish-brown madstone Alfred Fattig found in the soft underbelly of a buck back that summer morning of 1918. About the size of a bantam chicken egg, it looks like a polished agate you would find in a lapidary shop along Route 66 in Arizona. But this was obviously no rock formed in the belly of the earth. A close inspection reveals granulated material with light-brown rings at each end, indicating it was created in concentric layers.

It is an enterolith, a mineral concretion of mostly calcium which develops in the gastrointestinal tract of some ruminants. Like a pearl, the stone is created when a foreign object, perhaps hair as the hunter suggested, becomes lodged in the gastrointestinal system. Over time, it becomes coated with layers of mineral, forming a stone.

Some North American Indians, believing such stones had healing powers, called them "medicine stones." To the Euro-Americans who roamed the southwest Oregon mountains in search of venison, they were also considered good luck charms. Certainly finding one meant venison was on the menu for a hungry hunter.

In American mythology, some of our forefathers—and foremothers—also subscribed to the belief a madstone was a talisman whose principal powers included the ability to heal. Some insisted it was so powerful it could even cure rabies. Moreover, a madstone was believed to be particularly strong if it came from the gut of a white deer. Since a madstone in any deer is a rare thing and finding an albino deer is rarer still, it stands to reason such a madstone would have the most powerful medicinal powers, so went the thinking of those believing in the madstone myth. Just why they would believe such twaddle has been lost in time but it is arguably less delusional than much of the internet drivel one finds orbiting in cyberspace today. No matter your perspective on the power of the stones, they were a conversation piece around a camp fire or hearth.

Madstone is obviously an unusual name with a hint of mystery. Some folks say the moniker was derived from the practice of using the stone for medicinal purposes in the belief it could cure someone gone mad after being bitten by a rabid animals. Since many of those foaming at the mouth are dogs, often called mad dog, the talisman became known as a madstone. According to folklore, the stone could be used to draw poison from the unfortunate person who developed hydrophobia.

You will notice when I refer to madstone as an irritant in a deer's tummy, I use the lowercase but bump it up to upper case when referring to the Madstone cabin or Madstone country. My rationale is the latter deserves proper noun status. It is also a tip of the hat to those who built the cabin and explored those rugged mountains.

Madstones are mentioned in passing in a few pieces of American literature. One that stands out is *The Heart of the Alleghenies*, a book published in 1883. Penned by Wilbur Gleason Zeigler and Ben S. Grosscup, it flows with an interesting journalistic prose not often demonstrated in that era. The madstone pops up when the authors interview a veteran hunter named Ben Lester who is described as the epitome of a backwoods hunter with a rifle as long as his short, stocky body. They asked their version of Natty Bumppo if he had heard tales of a stone being found in a deer.

"Yes, the madstone," Lester responded on page 158. "People believe it will cure snakebites and hydrophobia."

With that, Lester produced a madstone which the authors described as smooth and red with a flat, white side. It was about the size of a man's thumb, they noted.

"It was found in the paunch of a white deer I shot this fall…mind you, the deer with a madstone in him is twice as hard to kill as one of ordinary kind," Lester told them. "Five bullets were put in the buck that carried this one."

While there is nothing to suggest the deer slayer was not a skilled hunter or that the buck was not tougher than rawhide, I submit Mr. Lester's aim may have been off a bit that day. Either that, or the madstone's magical powers were at work warding off bullets. Although Zeigler and Grosscup didn't question the hunter's ability, perhaps owing to the fact he was armed with the large weapon when they met, they clearly dismiss the madstone's reputed powers.

"The peculiar properties attributed to it are, in all probability, visionary," they wrote diplomatically. "The idea of it being a life preserver for the deer which carries it savors of superstition." In other words, unadulterated horse hooey.

Back in southern Oregon, the only person I had ever met who had a madstone was A. Donley Barnes, former Josephine County sheriff and one of our dad's lifelong friends who will pop up again in this tale. He carried a reddish-brown madstone in a small leather pouch. A little smaller than a fifty-cent piece, it was given to him by pioneer Sam Bunch who lived in the Illinois Valley all his long life.

"That's the only one I've ever seen," Barnes said as he carefully took it out of the pouch as though he was about to reveal a rare jewel. "An old Indian fellow gave it to Sam when Sam was twenty years old. When Sam was seventy-five, he gave it to me. He told me he hoped it would do as well for me as it did for him. He was ninety-seven when he died."

In fact, Sam Bunch was pushing ninety-eight when he died on July 9, 1984. He was born July 24, 1886.

"Indians always said it would keep you in good health and contribute to your longevity," Barnes said as he gently returned the stone to its worn pouch. "Might be something to that."

Could be. Not only did Sam Bunch live a long life but Barnes was ninety when he died on Oct. 19, 1995. What's more, Uncle Alfred, also a longtime carrier of a madstone, lived until he was ninety-seven. On the other hand, a medical doctor would suggest that genetics and healthy lifestyles, not magical stones, were the major contributing factors in the longevity of all three.

Shortly after killing the deer with the madstone, Alfred met a grizzled hunter who told him he had once killed a deer which carried a madstone. The fellow hunter told him he had cracked open the stone and found a small ball of deer hair inside.

"If that's so, it must be that it's caused from the deer licking himself and swallowing the hair," Alfred said, noting that hair isn't digestible. "It just stayed there until, you might say, it petrifies. It's just as hard as any other stone."

Upon examining the madstone Alfred had found in the forked horn buck, Dr. Walt Krebs, a longtime veterinarian in Grants Pass, had a more scientific explanation when I interviewed him in 1989. The veterinarian had practiced on domestic and wild animals in Southern Oregon for half a century, the latter at Wildlife Images, a local wildlife rehabilitation center which has earned acclaim throughout the Pacific Northwest.

Such a stone forms in the reticulum of ruminants, Krebs explained, noting the reticulum is also known as the fore stomach.

"Heavy things, such as bits of rock or sand, are forced over a little ridge into the reticulum," he told me. "Humans refer to that lining as tripe. You can buy it in local butcher shops."

The heavy objects settle in the waffle-like reticulum where they may become covered with minerals over the years, he said.

"Yes, this was probably formed in the reticulum," he said as he rolled it between a thumb and forefinger while examining it. "Once these solid objects get in there, they'll remain there. They don't come out."

Like a cow, when a deer begins chewing its cud, the action causes its four stomachs to activate, from the larger rumen to the reticulum, he said.

"The fact it is this shape, that indicates it had rolled around in there for a long time, like a tumbler effect," he said.

Yet Krebs, a life-long hunter, had never found a stone in any of his prey. "I'm going to start opening up the reticulum and look for them," he said. "I've never seen one of these before. Fascinating."

As to whether a madstone brings anyone good luck, he just shrugged. "Now that I couldn't tell you," he said.

Meanwhile, anyone hoping to fine one in a deer should be prepared to look long and hard, Alfred Fattig cautioned.

"Them stones are about the most rarest things on earth with no value," he said.

MADSTONE

THREE

Mystery Man

O UR LATE FATHER'S SOLE REMAINING SIBLING was ninety-six years
old when my elder brother, Jim, and I visited him in Gainesville,
Texas in late September of 1988. Alfred Fattig would die peacefully a
little over a year later, taking with him the last living memories of the
years he and his brother spent evading the WWI draft by hiding out in
the rugged Oregon mountains.

It would be the only time we spent with what my wildly imaginative
childhood brain always thought of as the mystery man. I half expected
to meet an ogre, an evil character who would reflect the tales I had heard
of him when I was young. In my childhood mind, Alfred was a dark and
sinister shadow about whom I had only heard scary snippets during my
formative years. When I read Wuthering Heights as a teenager, the
Heathcliff I imagined was Uncle Alfred who, like Emily Bronte's very
strange central character, was both hero and villain. I saw our family's
Heathcliff as a bold fellow for braving the wild mountains of Oregon
largely alone yet a shady scoundrel for his draft dodging ways and his
permanent departure from the family in the late 1920s. I would discover
decades later the only assumption I had right was his bravery in the
mountains.

As children, we seldom heard our enigmatic uncle's name without it
being mentioned as a potential threat. Our father slept with a loaded .38

caliber revolver in the event his big brother Alfred paid a nocturnal visit, our mother told us. Dad never said this, mind you, but it was something we kids understood to be bona fide. His pistol was reputedly kept under his pillow but that sounds too wacky to me, even for our peculiar family. We don't need to go into the safety problem of sleeping with a loaded gun near your ear, let alone how uncomfortable a pistol pillow would be. As for the pistol itself, it was allegedly taken from a lawman having made the grave mistake of venturing into the Madstone country alone in search of the scofflaw brothers. He never lived to see the civilized world again, so went the story. Although clearly bogus, the tale of the pistol's origins fed my childhood imagination that Uncle Alfred was the boogie man lurking in the dark corner.

Just why Dad's older brother would be a threat was never explained, although I discovered a likely explanation which we'll explore at the end of this book. As children, we didn't dare ask our father about Alfred. Dad believed in the silly notion that young offspring should be seen and not heard. Obviously, that approach doesn't lend itself well to educating youngsters, a goal that obviously should be foremost in parental minds. Let's hope that few parents today subscribe to such backward beliefs which frown upon curious children asking legitimate questions regarding the world about them.

Imagine my surprise when the man we met in Texas was a genial fellow with a quick laugh and a fine sense of humor. Moreover, he was glad to see his nephews and eagerly shook our hands.

"I always liked Paul—he was a good kid," he said of our father who was nearly fourteen years his junior. It was the first—and only—time I had heard anyone refer to our invariably solemn patriarch as a kid.

No, the Alfred Fattig we met was nothing like the bad boy I had antic-ipated. He was a simple man with no airs. A teetotaler, he had taken care of himself, although he smoked and chewed tobacco, preferably Mail Pouch, for forty years before giving it up. He was quick to demonstrate his fitness by nimbly jumping up and reaching down to touch his toes without bending his knees. I confessed it was a feat I could not duplicate.

"Well, maybe you'll be able to do that when you're my age," he quipped with a wide smile.

Yet Alfred was obviously well beyond his prime as he approached the century mark. Although photographs of him when he wore a younger man's clothes reveal a fellow who looked like he could have wrestled a bear to a draw, his sight through ninety-six-year-old eyes was failing. His hearing was dulled by the passage of time. Long missing were the strong teeth that once made short work of venison jerky while he hunkered on a mountainside, watching his back trail.

"My teeth, they have been gone so long that I don't know where they went," he said with a Walter Brennan chuckle and offered a wide grin to show his toothless gums. He didn't wear false teeth during our visit, apparently figuring they were nothing more than geegaws. He preferred to chew food with his gums, although he magnanimously spared us a demonstration. Presumably, tough venison jerky wasn't on his Texas menu.

He lacked formal education, speaking with the parlance of a fellow who had spent a lifetime working the land. Yet he was no cretin. He was obviously intelligent, having taught himself how to read and write. His writing often resorted to phonetic spelling. In a meandering yet interesting nearly 300-page manifesto of his philosophy written in longhand when he was in his mid-eighties, night is spelled "nite," right is "rite" and tough becomes "tuf."

"What I know about school I learned myself," he explained in the interview. "The school that I knew wasn't a school house. It was just where I happened to be. Sometimes it was out in the woods where the wild animals howled."

The homespun education created a fascinating philosophy, one blending his spiritual thoughts against war with his endless battle to account for his actions. The events and environment molding that philosophy, causing him to answer his conscience rather than the call of Uncle Sam, are a far cry from the world today. When we met, more than seven decades had passed since the world first went to war. His life began in the era of Winchesters and covered wagons, evolving into the age of nuclear weapons and rocket ships. When I brought out a small tape recorder with microcassettes to capture portions on the interview, he watched with fascination as the spinning tape caught each word. I've long since replaced the tape recorder with a digital version but even the taped one impressed him mightily.

"Well, I'll be dogged," he said, uttering a folksy phrase he commonly used to express amazement. "That's a new rig to me. Been a lot of inventions since them days we're talking about. It's a lot different now than it was when I was a kid. Pretty near unbelievable, the jumps they've made."

One jump he never made was riding in an airplane. "I always made up my mind that soon as I got on board, why, it wouldn't stay up there," he said. Parenthetically, as one who has flown a bit, including over both the Atlantic and Pacific oceans, I submit he didn't miss much. Flying, particularly these days, is akin to riding on a bus with over-zealous hall monitors and no stops to stretch your legs. Sadly, whatever fun there was in flying has flown the coop.

Upon meeting Uncle Alfred, my struggle to understand them and the circumstances that led them to defy the military draft and go to jail was just beginning. Obviously, you aren't going to get to know someone very well during a week-long visit. Come to think of it, I can't honestly say I know my own four siblings well, including my twin brother, despite having known them for sixty-five years. Dahna, a very smart friend who counsels people for a living, suggests the lack of sibling communications is directly tied to struggling to survive a challenging childhood in which you never let your guard down. She could be right, although big brother Jim insists we never had a childhood. Actually, they may both be onto something.

Alfred Fattig would seem to be a most unlikely candidate to challenge the authority of Uncle Sam. This was no political activist bent on undermining the state, no anarchist intent on taking down the power elite. We found a man with no political ax to grind, no delusions of grandeur. He preferred to leave the slippery world of politics to politicians on both sides of the aisle. He wanted only to be left alone to peacefully live his own life.

It would be incorrect to portray him as unpatriotic. He loved his motherland but his religious convictions didn't allow for killing fellow humans. Shooting deer or bear was one thing; plugging bipeds was quite another.

"I think we have a good government," Alfred wrote in scrawling longhand to my brother Charles in 1981 during the beginning of a long correspondence between them. "We get a few men in the government sometimes that make trouble but they are not the government."

Like those who settled the West, he placed a great emphasis on the pioneer spirit and independent thinking. In essence, he was born a century too late.

True, the old man with the piercing dark eyes edged by crow's feet would be perceived by many today as more than a little eccentric. But that is a charge he would have shrugged off. Despite his lack of a classroom education, his was a fascinating outlook that was both wise and whimsical, often simultaneously.

"There is just as much to learn if you are going to the mountains to live as there is if you live among people," he reasoned. "There is a good, happy way to live in the mountains."

He was, in short, a fellow worth getting to know. What's more, the intriguing fellow was the last living family member who could answer questions about what was to me a mysterious period that is the Madstone saga.

After his stint in jail, Alfred returned for a time to southern Oregon but could not abide the shunning by local residents who could have given lessons to devout members of the Amish faith turning their backs on a reprobate. He left the state in 1927, never to return. He initially wandered north to Alaska before heading south to Texas where he settled permanently after marrying a young woman named Leota Titus and raising as his own her six children from a previous marriage. Like his father before him, he was a farmer, working hard to support the ready-made family he had embraced and who embraced him. By most any measurement, his Texas years reflected a successful life which included a marriage lasting more than half a century. Born Dec. 4, 1892, he died at age ninety-seven on Feb. 22, 1990, and now rests for eternity beside his life's partner in the New Hope Cemetery just south of Gainesville. Leota, born on Feb. 16, 1899, died Nov. 11, 1995.

Alfred Fattig never returned to Oregon. Save for his sister Laura back on the West Coast who maintained a letter-writing correspondence with him for roughly half a century, he had no contact with his other siblings, including his beloved kid brother Paul. Whether Alfred communicated with his parents via letters after he left the state is unknown, although it is likely he did.

Following his own short stint in Alaska after his incarceration, Charlie Fattig headed back to southern Oregon where he continued his solitary lifestyle. Always somewhat of a misanthrope, the man I knew as Uncle Charlie lived in a tiny cabin on our property but kept to himself like a monastic monk, albeit one who was a devoted atheist with an ability to cuss that would impress a seasoned bartender. He passed away in 1967 at seventy-eight without revealing any thoughts on his draft evasion experience to his nephews or niece.

For the two brothers, their battle with those who would have them kill other human beings in war has long been over.

FOUR

Questioning a Legend

W HEN IT CAME TO UNCLE ALFRED, I HOPED to find answers to questions about his life and times that had puzzled me ever since I could walk upright. Finding out what happened and why would shed much needed light on my family and its decidedly curious ways, including what caused the schism between Alfred and his brothers that was as deep as the Grand Canyon. Incidentally, I am just as quirky as the rest, perhaps even more so. But I have had neither the inclination nor the pluck to take on the federal government.

By my reasoning, Alfred demonstrated courage by braving the wilds of the mountains. There was no doubt in my mind it took gumption to defy the federal government and social norms. Yet it was also clear to me that retreating from the authorities was not an act of bravery. In the back of my mind was the niggling thought it was a cowardly act to not face the penalty for draft evasion at the outset, and that not stepping up to serve your country was wrong. So I was facing major cognitive dissonance: he was courageous, yet cowardly. Could he be both? But it wasn't just the answer to that complex and seemingly contradictory question that I was seeking. Were they simply contrarians opposed to government service? Did they just not want to bother with the invitation to take up arms in the planet's first world-wide war? How were they treated by society during the post war period? Did they have any regrets?

My questions also went beyond the philosophical. I wanted to know what life was like in that wild country a century ago. What did they eat? What did they talk about around the campfire? What triggered their surrender? I needed to explore his early life, the era leading up to and past WWI. I wanted to get to know on a first name basis the people who lived during that turbulent time.

As one interested in all his ancestral footprints, warts and all, I sought to put flesh on those skeletons in the family closet. To anyone who knew us, it was clear the spirit of independence—some purists call it bullheadedness—was the bedrock of our family's genetic makeup. We tend to do things our own way at our own pace. The result can be humorous or hazardous, sometimes both. I would freely admit that none of us, including myself, is your typical humanoid. But that difference is generally in a good way. We do walk upright for the most part.

To be candid, the fact I was a journalist and this was a compelling story also drove me to discover what happened those many years ago. Truth be told, the idea for a book about two of Oregon's thirty WWI draft evaders who were imprisoned was on the back shelf of my mind since my college days. But it would take three decades to complete because life kept getting in the way and the answers were stubbornly reticent to step forth. The manuscript I started would have to wait until I became a recovering journalist which is somewhat like a recovering alcoholic, the difference being the delirium tremors are much more severe.

Admittedly, I am no brainiac. If you were to ask me about quantum physics, I could hazard a wild ass guess about atoms and photons feuding that would have made Albert Einstein cringe and cause Darwinists to reconsider whether humans were truly evolving. But I could function well enough in the Fourth Estate since my role was largely to ask questions and write down the answers in a somewhat coherent fashion. It was my interest in trying to understand our world that led to my career in journalism, that and the fact I probably couldn't hold down a real job.

Upon meeting our uncle, I explained my interest in writing about the Madstone cabin and his years hiding out from the law. Sitting on the edge of his bed in the comfortable room he shared with his wife in a

Texas senior center, he studied me for a moment. It was a cool day yet I could feel beads of sweat trickling down my back. But I matched his gaze, waiting for his response.

Alfred Fattig glanced out the window at the advancing columns of fluffy white clouds parading across the retreating blue sky. What he was looking at was well beyond the sterile confines of the center where he, like the yellow grass outside, was withering away to make way for the next generation. He was fixated on the distant past.

He studied his gnarled hands resting on the handle of a black cane. They were large hands, albeit shriveled and browned by the erosion of time. For a moment, he contemplated the wrinkles in those hands which had decades earlier held the reins of a plow horse. A fly buzzed restlessly overhead. Slowly, the old man looked up to focus his dark eyes on his two nephews.

"We was beating the draft—that was our aim," he began. "You'd think it was done in fear. But when I get done telling you all about it, you'll understand it wasn't fear a'tall."

He stopped talking again as if to let his words sink in, in the event his nephews were a little slow on the uptake. I sighed inwardly, knowing he would be telling us his full story.

"I don't fear most anything," he stressed. "But killing people, that's wrong. That shouldn't be happening. Killing people is murder no matter where it is, in war or anywhere."

The brothers were conscientious objectors in a time and place where the very idea a young man would refuse to serve in the military triggered clinched fists and raised eyebrows. After all, this was rural Oregon where patriotism ran as deep as the wild rivers cutting through the steep canyons. These were proud Americans hailing from sturdy stock. They were largely pioneers or the sons and daughters of pioneers who had settled the Oregon Territory. They were at beckon call to throw aside the miner's pick or farming hoe to fight for their country. They had already fought to build a home and a future in the West. For many, fighting for country was seen as an accepted duty as well as an honor.

In the eyes of the lion's share of Oregonians, there was little time for

anyone who would dare question fighting for their nation. Those few refusing to fight were considered less than men. Scornfully dubbed
slackers, the pacifists were branded with an invisible scarlet letter which
would have shamed Hester Prynne.

Regardless of what one thinks of draft evaders, no one can argue that
WWI was not a bloody conflict. Before the last shot was fired on Nov.
11, 1918, the war would kill some ten million people while wounding an
estimated twenty million. During the twenty months the United States
fought in Earth's first global war, more than 116,500 young Americans
would die in service to their country. While it stirs the patriotic heart to
believe they were all fighting on the frontlines when they perished, that
was not the case. In fact, 63,195 young Americans died of disease and
accidents during the war compared to the 53,513 who perished in battle.
No matter the cause of death, this was a war that kept the Grim Reaper
working around the clock.

Of those who died in the war, some 970 were Oregonians. The 1910
U.S. Census, the last one taken before the conflict, showed there were
672,765 residents in the state. With a population of 25,765 in that
census, Jackson County, where the brothers were summoned to serve in
the military draft, would lose twenty-eight young men in uniform during
the war. Neighboring Josephine County, then with 9,507 residents, had
thirteen war dead. In coastal Curry County, population 2,044 during the
time the brothers hid out in the Madstone country, five young men in the
military died during WWI.

Many others died from war-related illness shortly after shedding their
uniforms, although they were not officially counted as war dead. Consider
Army Corporal Osborne de Varila who enlisted in Grants Pass in April
of 1917, the month we declared war on Germany. The gunner would fire
a three-inch shrapnel shell from a French 75 field piece at 6:10 a.m.,
Oct. 23, 1917, making military history. That artillery shot in France was
the first round fired at the enemy by the American Expeditionary Force,
according to an article in the *San Francisco Examiner* the following
spring. The young soldier was sent back to the states to promote the war
and, with the encouragement of his Uncle Sam, wrote a short book, *The*

First Shot for Liberty, about his experience. Sadly, he would be gassed after he returned to the front. When he came home to Grants Pass in the fall of 1919, he was deathly ill. He was twenty-one when he died in San Francisco on June 4, 1920. We will revisit him and his book in depth a bit later.

There is no question most Americans were initially enthusiastic about going to Europe and mopping up the conflict that had started back in 1914 but was nearly at a stalemate when the Yanks arrived. But that's not to say everyone was gungho about the war. Oregon U.S. Sen. Harry Lane, a Democrat, was one of a handful in Congress who voted against entering the fray. Those opposed to joining the fight felt it was better to stay out of what they perceived as never-ending European infighting. When our boots hit the ground, we helped move the football forward on the French soil, ending the deadlock. Whether the first world war set the stage for the second global war as well as the on-going upheaval in the Middle East we'll leave for others to sort out, although there is an argument to be made that staying out of the conflict while pressing the opponents into a negotiated peace could have avoided a lot of unnecessary death and destruction that continues today.

Uncle Alfred's exploits were on my mind as a youngster in high school in southern Oregon, a time when draft evaders heading north to Canada during the Vietnam War were spoken of with disgust by local residents. I would be remiss if I didn't mention that my brother Jim served a tour in Vietnam after being drafted into the Army. As it happens, Oregon U.S. Senator Wayne Morse, a Democrat like Lane before him, was one of two lone senators to vote against the Gulf of Tonkin resolution which got us into that war. But most folks in our rural region of the state didn't much appreciate his vote. I don't recall ever bragging to classmates that my dad had been an admirer of Morse or that I had two uncles who were WWI draft dodgers. It certainly wouldn't have impressed my gungho childhood chums who would be joining the military upon graduating or, at least in my hormone addled teenage brain, the girls I very much wanted to impress during the few times I muster up enough courage to talk to them. Unlike the Vietnam War which never really caught fire with most Americans, WWI, particularly when the Yanks entered the fray in the spring of 1917, was popular when we marched into it. It wasn't until the bodies started piling up like cord wood that enthusiasm beat a hasty retreat.

It could not have been easy for Alfred to relive those distant days when he was a wanted man on the run. While they shared the bond of two men on the run who had each other's back, Alfred and Charlie were diametrical opposites when it came to many things, including religion. Charlie was a staunch atheist while Alfred was devoutly religious, something he brought up shortly after meeting his two nephews from Oregon.

"He was an infidel, a hard-headed infidel," Alfred said of his older sibling. "I didn't much like him, the way he was."

With that, he turned his attention to his nephews and stared for a moment before demanding our religious credentials.

"Are you infidels?" he challenged us.

We both assured him that we were not. A practicing Christian, Jim was on the right side of truth but I was skating on the thin ice of heresy. In the interest of full candor, I should have fessed up that I have no faith in religion, having lost whatever belief I was nurturing at roughly 3:30 p.m. Feb. 16, 1961. That was the moment the school bus dropped us off in front of our house while a long black hearse was backed up to the front door. They had just carried out the body of our father who had succumbed to cancer shortly before the bus arrived. Although only nine, I had been praying that God would intervene and save him. When he didn't, I felt let down by both my father and whatever supreme being had permitted all the hurt I had experienced on earth. That childhood disillusionment has never fully left, although I am still searching for the elusive answers to questions regarding what happens after we spring this mortal coil. Given how we humanoids continue to botch things up down on the terra firma, I fervently hope there is a supernatural entity on high who can one day alight and straighten us out. The mere fact we use wars as historic milestones is cause for concern.

As a journalist, I learned early on that getting into a philosophical debate with a source is not only unprofessional but decidedly stupid. So you sit there and nod, no matter how zany the comments. I once was interviewing a couple in far northern California who were waxing eloquently about their firm belief alien beings dwelled inside Mount Shasta, a beautiful volcanic peak in the southern Cascade mountain range. I just kept nodding, biting my lip and looking at my feet. I knew I would start laughing so hard I would be blowing snot bubbles if I glanced up at the photographer who was also fighting hard to maintain any semblance of professional decorum. We managed to stifle the guffaws until we were back in the car and headed back to the relative sanity of Oregon.

In this case, the source was family; the subject no laughing matter. Moreover, Alfred was not zany. It was his strong religious faith that led him to make the decision not to kill other humans. I was not there to judge him. Besides, there was no doubt in my mind that he would have booted us out had I answered in the affirmative. So I joined the Greek chorus when Jim assured him he was a believer. I hope Uncle Alfred has forgiven me that transgression.

Despite his vernacular which reflected his lack of a formal education, he was bright and witty, the kind of elderly person I've always enjoyed chatting with. Fascinating is his tale of retreating from the military draft during World War I to the mountains of southwest Oregon, of rural America's initially unflagging patriotism and support of war, of being imprisoned for his strong objections to the conflict. The dust of time had settled over many memories, clouding his mind. But, like a farmer brushing off an old hat, he carefully began dusting off long forgotten names and places.

"My memory, it ain't too good anymore," he cautioned. "I can't remember all of it. Too many years slipped by. Some things, I got to study about. You know, a hundred years is a long time for a man to live. I'll surely make the rest of it. But I guess I forgot most I ever knowed."

The old man, who did not quite reach the century mark, paused again as he pondered the past. He was marching mentally over the years to the turn of the 19th Century, from the flatlands of northeast Texas to the rugged mountains in Oregon's upper Chetco River drainage. Like the fleecy clouds forming outside his window, images of the past began to appear in his mind.

"I'm not going to tell you no lies," he stressed. "If I can remember it, why, I'll tell it like it is, you can depend on that."

FIVE

The Wonder Years

B EFORE MARCHING ANY FURTHER into the war years and farther along the Madstone trail, the intrepid reader needs to be become familiar with the Fattig family and its eccentricities. In point of fact, our familial way of life and oddities contributed to the brothers' decision to head into the hills in defiance of Uncle Sam. The lifestyle chosen by our father no doubt reflected that of his parents, a rustic way of life Alfred knew well. Gaining an insight into the lifestyle will help you understand our quirky past. You may want to don combat boots and a Kevlar vest. A helmet? Sure, why not. After all, there are projectiles ahead, one of which stuck in my head. Literally.

While they may be fighting words to some family members still standing, to say our family has a few quirks is like saying Crater Lake in Southern Oregon, at some 2,000 feet the deepest lake in the United States, is a puddle. If you consult Mr. Webster, you would find our surname under the word "contrary." As you shall discover in the next couple of chapters, those family idiosyncrasies make for anecdotes which cause both cringing and chortling, sometimes simultaneously.

We were hillbillies of the first rank so brace yourself for a little shuddering at our rough-as-cob lifestyle, particularly when we get into rat hairs in our drinking water and the arrow-in-the-head incident. For the squeamish, the following pages are a little wince worthy.

However, to get the full Monty, we need to leapfrog ahead to spend a little quality time with the Fattigs in the late 1940s and the 1950s before retreating back to the comparative sanity of war and the brotherly draft evaders. Although Uncle Alfred had left the family and the region in 1927, his legacy still hovered in the air like the scent of an Oregon wildfire threatening in the distance. He may have been gone but his presence lingered.

Incidentally, my desire to write this book is not out of nostalgia, at least not in the modern sense of the word rooted in Greek. *Nostos* means to return home; *algos* signifies pain. I feel an emotional pang when I walk down memory lane to my childhood home. Acute homesickness I have not. What I do have is an insatiable curiosity to find out what causes folks to do what they do.

In due diligence, I also need to throw out this caveat: memories can be faulty. They are often unruly creatures given to wandering off like wayward children. Just when you are sure you can depend on a memory, evidence to the contrary is presented to the jury of your peers, proving you are full of horse hooey. As for those claiming to have total recall, I don't recall ever having met one. Perhaps we all ought to give some thought to replacing those pet memories with gerbils.

Yet our recollections are largely what we are left with when we reflect upon our childhoods and its formulating moments. Those old photographs your parents took are helpful but they are merely mileposts along yesteryear's misty road. Even old items from childhood, like the inkwell and fountain pen from my dad's roll top oak desk that now sits next to my computer, are themselves nothing more than pleasant props for reminiscences of a bygone world. As far as I can remember, he seldom used the fountain pen or the desk, although they are certainly indicators he toyed with the idea of writing. Had he followed his Muse, I suspect he would have been an extraordinary teller of tales. He kept a small photograph of mountain man Jim Bridger on that old desk. Perhaps he was contemplating writing his version of *The Revenant*, the 2002 historic novel by Michael Punke about mountain man Hugh Glass who was ravaged by a grizzly and abandoned, albeit reluctantly, by fellow frontiersman Jim Bridger in real life. Bridger was just a teenager at the time so he could be forgiven.

While I shall endeavor to avoid venturing too far into the weeds, you will encounter a few dates and anecdotes in the next few pages. Again, this is not being presented to cause your eyes to glaze over but to put into context the events that led to the strange story of draft dodgers and mountain men. After all, the lifestyle we led was something Alfred would have recognized in his younger years. In comparison, life in Texas must have seemed mighty tame. Meeting the family will give you the perspective necessary to make sense of it all. Scout's honor.

My parents—Paul R. Fattig Sr. and Gladys Clara Cooke Fattig—celebrated their nuptials in Grants Pass on Oct. 23, 1945. The wedding day happened to be mom's thirty-second birthday; our dad had turned thirty-nine the previous June. I don't believe dear old Dad was such a romantic he insisted they get married on the anniversary of her birth. More likely he figured life would be less complicated if he could halve the anniversary dates he needed to remember to maintain marital bliss. This wasn't their first rodeo: both had been married before. Dad's first wife, Lorena, died in 1935 during a miscarriage; his second wife, apparently acquired on the rebound, became more than a little chummy with his best friend while Dad was on a gold mining adventure in Alaska. Mom's first husband was a semi-professional boxer and a professional drunk. As a result, they were a little gun shy about entering into another marriage. But their reluctance was overcome by a mutual magnetism.

The infatuated couple made up for a late start by having five children in less than four years. At a time when most of their peers were beginning to look forward to their first grandchildren, our middle-aged parents were producing offspring like Henry Ford was spewing out automobiles. First to arrive was James Bridger, born on Oct. 5, 1947. Being an avid hunter like his older brother Alfred, Dad was apparently enthusiastic about naming his first born son after the famous mountain man. It is a cool name but Dad should have stopped with the creative names while he was ahead. When twins Charles and Delores were born on May 13, 1950, he originally wanted to name them Hiawatha and

Minnehaha, the characters in the epic poem "The Song of Hiawatha," written by Henry Wadsworth Longfellow in 1855. Dad was obviously a great admirer of the poet and Native Americans. Our mom also loved the poem but she and the alarmed nurses in the small Grants Pass hospital talked him out of naming the first set of twins after an Ojibwe warrior and the maiden who was the tragic love of his life. My brother Charles, the one who told me about our father's desire to name him after Hiawatha, figured he dodged the arrow on that one. Can you imagine the razzing he would have received? It would have been brutal. They were wonderful names for the poem but not monikers two little kids would want to wear to school in the mid-20th Century. Fortunately, when my twin George and I tumbled into the world on July 15, 1951, Dad had already thrown up his hands when it came to coming up with unique names for his offspring. I would like to say I was named after our father because it was obvious at the outset that I had his impressive intellect. Unfortunately, that was not the case. My junior status simply derived from the fact I emerged with dark hair and somewhat swarthy skin like him, according to our mother. When it came to smarts, he was a naturally gifted quick thinker while I tend to ponder problems until they retire and go on Medicare.

As one who appreciated peace and quiet contemplation, Dad's constitution was sorely tested by our presence. Our largely deaf mother was equally overwhelmed in spite of not being able to hear our constant din. Despite their advanced age for starting a family, or perhaps because of it, they were slightly dumbfounded as to what to do next. It was as though they suddenly had five puppies and didn't have the foggiest how to care for them beyond regular feeding and letting the pack out periodically to prey on innocent passersby. While no more than a tyke, I recall standing by what was then a dirt road running past our home and waiting for a passing vehicle, small rocks clutched in my grubby little hands. One of my favorite targets was an old yellow panel truck driven by upstream neighbor Vic Lunt. Fortunately, he was an easy-going fellow with an easy laugh who was a good family friend. He also knew his tank-like truck with cracked windows was invincible to rock-throwing toddlers, although I like to think I contributed to the spider web design in his side windows.

Whether a conscious decision or the result of throwing up their hands in despair, our parents adopted the "White Fang" approach to raising offspring. If you are a Jack London fan, you know the story about the hybrid wolf who becomes the alpha male among his canine brethren in the Far North. Our parents allowed our big brother Jim to become the alpha wolf; we younger siblings were submissive members of the pack he kept in submission through brute strength. But I'm happy to report he only shot me once in the head with an arrow. We'll get to that painful thunk in a bit.

Dad most definitely did not plan on having five kids, let alone at a randy rabbit's reproductive pace, although he was obviously instrumental in their creation. He was a brilliant fellow who could talk with confidence about subjects ranging from botany to the body politic. He just wasn't big on planning. He lived his life without a lot of preparation, taking things as they came. As it happened, a chain of seemingly unrelated ill-fated events formed a thread through his adult existence. Dangling at the end of that chain were his children, hanging on for dear life.

But don't get me wrong. Our parents were good people, of that there is no doubt. They never fought, never yelled at each other. They were neither mean nor cruel. Corporal punishment was never administered. They were merely parentally challenged. Our dad was the strong and silent type who seldom showed his emotions around his children, although he could tell a good tale once he got started. I don't ever recall having seen him cry, even as he faced death. He was the epitome of stoic.

My earliest memories of our father are of a tall man with a pencil thin mustache, creating a passing resemblance to Hollywood movie legend Errol Flynn when he was young man. I'm not in the habit of describing men as handsome—not that there is anything wrong with it, per Seinfeld—but I would describe our dad as a fine looking fellow. He had a pencil-thin mustache, dark penetrating eyes glinting with a hint of humor and dark hair combed straight back. Like the Australian-born actor, he may have also been a bit of a philanderer but we aren't going there. Some things are best left to the ages. Like most of us, he didn't always live up to his high ideals.

While I will always remember Dad as a big fellow, truth be told he was only 5' 10" and somewhat lanky, making him of average build. No doubt he loomed larger with his fedora hat that was not unlike the one Indiana Jones sported in his adventure movies. In our little world, the Fattig kids did not question their father. His word was sacrosanct. In our view, there wasn't much separation between God and our dad. You dared not question. With one being present and the other only supposition, you obeyed the earthly one and let the celestial one fend for itself. There was never any physical punishment. Add a deep voice that would make James Earl Jones sound like a soprano and here was a towering presence, particularly if you were a bewildered tyke looking up at the world. His voice was like a command from the burning bush. There was no need for a switch, even if he had subscribed to corporal punishment.

Our mom was the consummate hugger, at least when we were little. Like our father, she was an interesting humanoid with her own unique characteristics. In keeping with the Hollywood analogy, picture a homespun Kate Winslet with dark hair, large, dark eyes and a wide smile with just a hint of sadness. As a child, I remember thinking Mom looked like a movie star in the beautiful red coat Dad bought her one Christmas. Of course, Mom didn't have a British accent like Kate and was born in 1913, a year after the Titanic hit the iceberg. According to family lore, she weighed barely three pounds when she was born on the family ranch high in Washington's Columbia River drainage. The newborn fit into a shoe box with room to spare, according to our maternal grandmother. Stricken by scarlet fever as a young child, she was left largely deaf, contributing to her routinely mangling the King's English. Since our father didn't spend a lot of time with his youngest children, we learned to speak mainly from our mother. Hence simple words like "battery" became "batrey." That siren you hear when police or firefighters are responding to an emergency? We learned to refer to it as a "si-reen." As you can imagine, our peculiar vernacular was not welcomed when we started elementary school. Undoubtedly, the ensuing teasing prompted us to retreat back into our little world from whence we came. I was hoping speaking that special homespun dialect would be an asset when I took French in college but it didn't have any correlation with the romance languages. Still, I managed to get passing grades, merci beaucoup.

In 1946, our future parents moved onto a twelve-acre parcel in Wonder, a hamlet about eight miles south of Grants Pass. The non-incorporated community included rustic dwellings hidden among the picturesque rolling hills and vales. Public gathering places were limited to Jacks Tavern, the Wonder General Store and the Wonder Bible Chapel, often in that order of attendance. The tavern has changed hands and names over the years, even had its tap turned off periodically, but the store and chapel have endured the years. In this tiny community, food and faith trumped the fermented.

Our extremely humble abode was on the north bank of a stream known as Waters Creek, an appealing little stream which chuckles along the bottom of the narrow drainage. The name of the stream was likely derived from the name of someone who originally settled there, although it may be simply the result of a lack of creativity by the person who came up with the moniker. After all, water flows in the stream so the appellation was an obvious no-brainer for the creative challenged. There are countless Waters creeks across this land, indicating a troublesome national pattern, by the way. As it happens, the community's name originated when someone allegedly observed that wonders never cease with respect to the fact a little general store could survive in the area. Wonder is an innovative name in my book. A post office established in the tiny burg in 1904 inside the grocery store with business owner J.F. Robertson named as post master.

If you were to drive a quarter of a mile up Waters Creek Road now, you will see a picturesque flat spot on the south side of the road where a stone fireplace sits forlornly near an aging broadleaf maple tree. When I drive by the site, I always feel a pang of melancholy. It was in front of that fireplace where my family huddled on winter nights in the 1950s, where we baked apples on the edge of the fire and listened to Dad's hunting and fishing tales. But standing in front of the fireplace was like being in front of a campfire on a cold night: your front was baking while your back was chilled. As a heat source, the fireplace was sorely inefficient, a serious problem since our ramshackle house had no insulation.

Our father, with the help of Uncle Charlie who also lived on the property, built the fireplace in the late 1940s out of stones gathered from the stream flowing less than twenty feet away. For fireplace ingenuity, it was rather artsy in its time. Both avid rock hounds interested in all things lapidary, the brothers fashioned a remarkable mantel in which they embedded polished agates, crystals and even thunder eggs, the state rock. We spent a lot of time gathered around the fireplace since it was the only heat source in the drafty house. Roasting apples in the fireplace was a pleasant family pastime on cold winter nights. As a child, I thought the mantel was incredibly beautiful. I wasn't the only one who found it attractive. Long after we moved away and the house literally fell down around the fireplace, the unique mantel was purloined by someone who also liked the looks of it.

Despite the fine start with the fireplace, the dwelling was not a thing of beauty. After completing the fireplace, the brothers began wrapping boards around it. They no doubt had a plan in mind but it looked like they made it up as they sawed and nailed away. They neglected to build a foundation for the house, something competent home builders deem essential. Basically, they built what would euphemistically be called a shanty, although it was a bit larger than the Madstone cabin. I would call the place a shack but that would offend shack dwellers across the land, most of whom enthusiastically exercise the right to bear arms. Once riled, they can be a trigger happy bunch.

The place had an open living room with the fire place at one end and a kitchen at the other. Our parent's small bedroom was off the living room. On the opposite side of the living room was an alcove in which there were five bunks built into the walls. The closet-like bedroom was far too small for five rambunctious kids. But that was our sleeping quarters. "You kids be quiet and go to sleep," was a constant nightly refrain from the house's sole bedroom.

About now you are thinking there was something missing in our rustic home. Actually, the lavatory, such as it was, was there, just not convenient. If you had dropped by for a visit and requested to use the facilities, you would have been told to take a hike. But the instructions would be given with an apologetic smile. You would be directed to step out on the back porch which overhung the edge of the stream, walk upstream about twenty feet and cross the log footbridge spanning the creek. Apparently not anticipating a family, our dad fell two narrow trees side by side across the creek, nailed some slats of various sizes over the logs for a rudimentary walkway and called it good. During the summer, the drop from the footbridge to the rocky streambed was about four feet. After studying his chancy creation, he cut a long pole cut from a willow and nailed each end to trees standing on both sides of the creek, fashioning a crude handrail to slightly reduce the possibility you would fall four feet into the water below. The good news was you didn't much have to worry about getting wet in the summer. The bad news? The rocks would break your fall. The water wasn't much more than a trickle by late August but could turn into a swollen torrent during the heavy rains of winter. If you made it across the log bridge, you would then walk about twenty-five feet up the hill to the outhouse. We dubbed it Bears Hill, a tip of the hat to bruins in the neighborhood. At that point, it was best to conduct your business as quickly as possible in the event one of the local fierce creatures come nosing around. As a child, I was afraid to cross it in any season, resulting in delaying necessary trips to the privy until bad things happened. If poor potty training truly accounts for maladjusted children, I was a poster child.

You are thinking one word right now: gross. No argument there. The outhouse was hot and stinky in summer and cold and stinky in winter. But bear in mind that some twenty-five percent of Americans did not have access to a flush toilet in the comfortable confines of a home in 1950, according to the Outhouse Benevolent Society of America. OK, there is no such organization but that is one of the official census statistics that pops up for that era. The bottom line is our father was not one to hurry the future along. Suffice it to say no guest used the facilities unless they really, really had to go. The same can be said of our parents' two sets of twins.

That lack of interest in earning the Good Housekeeping seal of approval was readily apparent inside our house. There was no telephone, although Dad did consent, at our mother's insistence, to plug our home into the grid. A light bulb dangled from the ceiling near the fire place and another hung over the kitchen. He also agreed to buy an electric stove, albeit a small one with two burners. What's more, we even had a small refrigerator. But he didn't get too carried away, mind you. While he did install an electric pump in the hand-dug shallow well near the creek and ran a water pipe to the house, hooking it to the kitchen sink, he balked at getting a hot water heater. After all, he had his limits beyond which he refused to budge. As I said, contrary.

Sunday evening at the Fattig domicile was bath time for the kiddies, whether you needed one or not. A round tub was placed on the kitchen floor and filled three-quarters full with water heated on the new-fangled electric stove. One by one, each child would sit down in the tin tub and scrub away. One lesson I learned early on was not to be the last child into the tub, particularly if you are not too keen on bathing in murky water containing mystery floaters.

Even before the last dirty urchin climbed into the opaque bath water, there was the potential for the well water to be a little iffy. Accustomed to life being a little rough shod, our dad laid two loose planks over the well as a partial cover and stood back to admire his handiwork. He neglected to notice he left a slot for things to fall into the well, including nasty critters one does not want floating around in water going into your mouth. A fir needle popping out of the faucet into your water glass was not too disconcerting. You just picked it out with your grimy pinkies and drank the cool water. No major worries.

But the day black hairs were discovered in the water by our mother was more than a little worrisome. She was not the persnickety type, having been reared on a ranch in Washington state. But she had a tolerance level, and the black animal hair exceeded her acceptability threshold. She did not panic. In one of those rare moments when she took over the family reins, she informed her hubby in no uncertain terms that hairy water would not be tolerated. He obligingly strode out to the pump house and fished what turned out to be a drowned rat from the well. While he didn't seem overly concerned, he nonetheless fashioned a cover over the well which sealed it off from vermin and other creatures wanting to do a one and a half gainer into our drinking water. I'm not sure what horrible illnesses can be contracted by drinking rat water but bubonic plague and cholera come to mind. It's a wonder we didn't all keel over in Wonder.

Suddenly, I feel the need to take something for an upset stomach, followed by a hot shower. I'll be right back. There, that's better.

You get the gist: here was a place that would have given the biggest, baddest hillbilly the willies. Even the most fearless mountain man would have slept with one eye open in our Waters Creek encampment.

It was in that challenging environment I first heard of Alfred Fattig and the Madstone cabin. When we gathered around the fireplace, Dad sometimes talked about the cabin in a way that suggested he was proud of his brothers and their adventure. But he also hinted there was a danger connected to Alfred but always stopped short of an explanation.

In my wildly imaginative young mind, Uncle Alfred was out there and he was coming back to seek revenge on some past wrong. I was waiting for the front door to burst open on some dark and stormy night. Standing there would be an angry uncle, dripping rainwater and glaring at us as lightning lit up the dark background. For some reason, I always expected him to be holding the reins of a horse. Perhaps that was because our mom had mentioned he lived somewhere in Texas, and I figured all Texans rode horses. I also assumed he would have a six gun, and that Dad and Uncle Charlie, who lived in a nearby cabin on the property, would grab their pistols. The images in my mind scared me and I always pulled the covers over my head at night to ward them off. The covers also protected me from the bears, monsters and other assorted hellish beings our big brother warned us were out there, lurking in the dark.

Of course, the sinister Uncle Alfred in my productive little mind, like the main character in Samuel Beckett's head-scratching play, *Waiting For*

Godot, never arrived. However, unlike Vladimir and Estragon in the play, I would eventually meet our Godot, albeit some four decades later.

Incidentally, the area is a little less wild than when we were children. There is now the 3.2-mile Waters Creek Interpretive Trail just upstream from where we once called home; illustrating the area may be a bit tamer than in our day. Local residents probably even have telephones and television. And outdoor toilets are no longer the norm.

The real danger on Waters Creek in the early 1950s was neither the mysterious uncle nor the rat hair in the water and the scary trips to the privy. That threat came from the alpha wolf in charge of our little pack of adolescents. To elucidate an important point, Jim was no future serial killer training for a career in murderous mayhem. Clearly, he was not an angel, either. He was simply a kid with no instruction on the care and feeding of his younger siblings. So he winged it, backing his ill-conceived choices with his superior size and strength. I would be remiss if I didn't note that he became a decent humanoid in adulthood, although one could quibble with his politics. But we'll let buyer's remorse right those political wrongs.

As it happens, William Golding's *Lord of the Flies* was published in 1954, about the time Jim became the leader of our childish pack through parental default. You may remember the book tells of the boy's school students' descent into savagery after they survive a plane crash on an isolated island. Since Jim was the only "bigun" among the urchins marooned on our Waters Creek isle, he naturally stepped forward to fill the void. If any of the twins questioned his leadership style, they were immediately cuffed into whimpering submission. One day when Jim was around nine and I was about five, big brother received a bow and a set of arrows, a gift from our uncle across the road who had painstakingly fashioned them by hand. The Madstone veteran apparently figured it wouldn't hurt for his nephew Jim Bridger to get in a little target practice while still a pup.

However, as parents not spending an over abundance of time in raising their bairns, Mom and Dad let Jim develop his archery skills on his own. Now consider this scenario for a moment: your grinning nine-year-old son, clutching his brand new bow and arrows, is leading your two sets of young twins out the door, heading to a bend in the creek we called "The Jungle" because of wild grape vines climbing high into a grove of cedar trees. As a responsible parent, would you not be just a tad concerned? Granted, Uncle Charlie had provided arrows with round and somewhat blunted heads for target shooting, not razor sharp tips for hunting. Still, the sight should have raised a parental eyebrow or caused a nervous twitch or two at the very least.

When we got to our version of a jungle, Jim lined us up in front of him. Big Brother had just read the inspiring tale about William Tell, the expert with a crossbow back in the early 1300s in old Switzerland. When Mr. Tell refuses to bow to the hat of a dictator, he faces execution unless he can shoot an apple off the top of his son's head. He successfully hit the apple and not the head, becoming a hero for the ages. Apparently Jim was itching to prove his skills with his newly acquired weapon. Never mind he had precious little practice, that his rustic weapon was not a crossbow and that we were lacking an apple. I don't recall the selection process but I do remember being the one picked to be the target of the archery test. I also recall blubbering but was convinced, after a bit of cuffing about the head and shoulders that serving as a target may be the least painful path. Turns out I was wrong.

Standing there, whimpering like a puppy, I tried not to look at the arrow aimed at the top of my head. I scrunched down a bit. The archer, standing perhaps twenty-five feet away, adjusted his aim accordingly, lowering the arrow just a hair. Now, you should know that Jim is a great shot. With wild game, his aim was almost always true. But he hadn't quite reached the perfection he achieved later in life. Perhaps he was feeling poorly that day. Or he was having misgivings and closed his eyes at the moment he let fly.

Thunk.

It felt like the top of my head had been struck by, well, an arrow. Looking up, I could see the shaft dangling from the top of my head. But my sight wasn't all the good, what with the blood cascading down my forehead into my eyes. There was also a very loud noise which I came to realize was a constant scream emitted from my mouth. Not only did it hurt but I just knew bits of brain were about to start oozing out of the arrow hole.

Thanks to my noggin being as hard as a block of oak, it turns out it wasn't punctured. Gray matter was not leaking out. The arrow hit just above my hair line, skidded along the top of the skull and burrowed under my scalp an inch or two. When I leaned my head forward to wipe the blood out of my eyes, the arrow fell out.

"You better tell them you fell down and hit a rock," Jim yelled at me as I ran, still screaming, for the house. I spilled the beans once I was in the relative safety of the house, of course. While our alarmed mom cleaned the wound and bandaged my head, an equally concerned dad lectured James Bridger on the finer points of shooting at human targets, reminding him to adjust for the pull of gravity when aiming to graze the top of a little brother's head. Just kidding. Jim received a very stern lecture and had his archery privileges revoked for a time. Big brother did cuff me later for squealing.

When I later went up the hill to show Uncle Charlie my war wound, his response was a gruff, "Damn fool kids."

Although I still quiver (pun intended) when I see an archer about to unleash an arrow, I understand how such an unfortunate event can occur. Obviously, when a rowdy young boy is given free rein over his younger siblings and provided with a bow and arrows, things will go awry. Clearly, our dad and mom needed a remedial lesson in Parenting 101. I don't bear a grudge, just a small scar where I was once stuck by an arrow. Besides, I like to think the practice did improve his aim. When he was ten, he went hunting by himself up the Waters Creek drainage and bagged a bear in a little tributary appropriately called Bear Creek. The young hunter was armed with a Winchester model 1894 .25-35 rifle, apparently figuring he needed more firepower for a bruin than when winging a younger brother. When it came to hunting, he was a child prodigy. The skinned carcass hanging from the maple tree in our yard must have brought back memories of the Madstone days to Uncle Charlie since bear meat was sometimes on the mountain menu. Meanwhile, bear and deer throughout southwest Oregon became incontinent at the mention of the young Jim Bridger's name.

In reflection, I spent much of my six years at Waters Creek doing what I believe was a very fine rendition of "The Scream," the disquieting painting created by expressionist artist Edvard Munch back in 1893. While the arrow in the head created an impressive high-pitch example, the hatchet episode nearly eclipsed it in volume. Kept near the fireplace to cut kindling, the small hatchet would not be a weapon of choice for most folks. But, when unsupervised little kids start playing with one, bad things happen. Delores, age five or so, had taken up the small ax and was working on a small block of wood when I decided I wanted the block. I tried to grab it and she fended me off, feigning a hatchet blow. I persisted, grabbing the block just as she chopped at it. Bad move on my part. The hatchet bit into my right forefinger, cutting into the bone. Encouraged by pain and spurting blood, the Scream emerged at full volume. However, as a novice with an ax, Delores did not deliver a severing blow. A fussy veteran ax murderer would note she needed to swing a little harder and cut straight across rather than try to cut at an angle like she did. Having grown fond of it, I was happy not to be separated from the digit. With a fairly straight face, she said she was sorry, burying the hatchet, so to speak. Mom bandaged the finger which still sports a scar from the first knuckle down to the second knuckle.

Yet the arrow and the ax incidents turned out to be minor events in the grander scheme that fate had in store for us.

Our dad, who had previously worked in the logging woods, was working as a log scaler at the SH&W Lumber Co. sawmill in Grants Pass. Tallying the amount of wood on a logging truck was a safe job compared to firing up a chainsaw to bring down a big tree or setting chokers in the woods. A timber faller, a job our big brother the shootist did before retiring, is arguably the most dangerous logging job. I set enough chokers, lassoing logs with a steel choker cable so they can be dragged to a landing, to know I preferred wrangling words, although the pesky little things can also be dangerous. But a log scaler was a job that took smarts. The scaler measures the logs to determine the scale—volume—of wood. This was before computers so the scaler had to have a sound grasp of mathematics. In a dangerous profession, it was one of the safest jobs.

But we knew the moment Keith Owen, Dad's boss and longtime friend, pulled into our yard late in the spring of 1956, that something had gone terribly wrong at the mill. He came to the door, told our mom there had been an accident and that Dad had been injured. When she rushed into the bedroom to change her clothes to accompany him to the hospital, he returned to his vehicle and came back, carrying a large cardboard box. Sticking out of the top of the box was a pair of bloody work boots, the ones our dad had strapped on that morning. Inside the box were his pants and shirt, torn and bloody. Upon seeing the box, our mother let out a cry of anguish, sounding like a wounded animal. The sound haunts me still.

Interviewed in the fall of 2005 when she was ninety-two, our mom recalled that terrible afternoon.

"Keith came to the door and said Paul had got a log on him," she said. "The truck driver who brought in the load thought your dad was done scaling the logs. He released the binders. One big log came down on your dad, smashed him right up against the back wheel in a sitting up position."

The shocked truck driver promptly upchucked at the grisly sight of what he likely thought was a dying man, she said. The trucker wasn't far from wrong.

"The doctor told me if that log had busted his bladder it would have killed him," Mom said. "As it was, it broke some of his ribs and his right arm just horribly. It broke his right leg so bad they had to cut it off. He wasn't the same after that."

We learned later that while Dad was standing with his back to the full log truck, busy calculating the volume of wood in the load, the driver, apparently believing all was clear, released the log binders. The logs thundered down, crushing Dad, peeling the flesh off his right arm, breaking ribs and shattering his right leg. Surgeons were able to save his right arm but amputated his right leg high on his hip. Life would never be the same for him or his family.

In short, for our family, the good old days never were and they were about to get dramatically worse. After more than two months in the hospital, Dad returned home on crutches, his right leg now a stump. It wasn't just his leg that was gone: he had lost his former quiet confidence. I remember wondering if, like the tail of a western fence lizard, his leg would grow back. But it turned out Dad did not have the requisite reptilian genes.

Yet he didn't give up. He exchanged his old pickup truck with its standard stick shift for a 1954 Plymouth station wagon equipped with an automatic transmission and a gas pedal installed on the left side so he could access it with his good leg. With its pea green paint, it was one butt-ugly car.

But it gave him legs, so to speak. Consider this blurb in the *Mail Tribune* on Sept. 22, 1957, page twenty-seven, under a column titled "Illinois Valley News." Keep in mind newspaper correspondents back in the day posted anything they could dig up, much like internet bloggers do today.

"Paul Fattig, who lost his leg in a mill accident about a year ago, is learning to operate his new Plymouth station wagon," the article noted. "He drove out to Kerby Sunday from his home in Wonder, and celebrated his prowess with a dinner at the Arthur Cribb home."

In the interest of full disclosure, it should be mentioned the writer was Letha Cooke who was married to one of our mom's brothers. She was a correspondent for both the *Tribune* and *Daily Courier* in the late 1950s and early '60s. Art Cribb was a longtime friend of our father's who had worked with him as a fellow U.S. Forest Service employee in their younger years.

While Dad was learning to drive with one leg, our mom, who was raised Christian but was no longer a faithful practitioner, decided we urchins needed to attend the local church near the mouth of Waters Creek, a little church perched on a rise above where the stream flows into Slate Creek, a tributary to the Applegate River. No doubt she figured it may help avoid further arrow thunks or hatchet hackings.

While Dad balked at attending religious services, he consented to his children going to Sunday school. He leaned toward atheism, apparently the result of being force fed religion by his parents when he was a child. He invariably threw out the noun "hypocrite" when referring to church goers. Before the accident, he periodically attended services about a quarter mile south of the church at a place then known as Jack's Tavern. He would stop for a beer after work and chat with owner Jack Wilson. In my mind, I see him sitting on a stool with a cold glass of beer in front of him, his hat pushed back on his head as the bar flies hashed out world events, discussing issues like the Cold War that was emerging in the early 1950s. After one beer, he would stand up, pull his hat brim down and bid Jack farewell before he climbed into his old pickup truck and went home to face five energetic children. The accident obviously changed that faithful little diversion.

Jim was able to weasel out of the religious punishment but the twins had no choice in the matter. As was often the case with most things in my childhood, I was a little puzzled by the whole church thing, an affliction which continues today. The Sunday school teacher was a young woman who seemed caught up in the spirit but was a little short on details when it came to enlightening her young charges. There was a large poster on the wall which showed a path that forked. One fork led to heaven, the other to hell.

"You must choose the right path," she admonished us. What she failed to tell us—or I failed to ascertain—was that it wasn't, according to the "good book," a choice to be made by a mere flip of the coin. I was hoping that when I came to the fork in the trail that I could peek up ahead and see which fork led to the flames of hell. It worried me for several years. Still does a mite, for that matter.

My other main memory was that a large poster of Jesus showed him to be light skinned with blue eyes and light brown hair worn long. He looked like one of the counter culture folks who would inhabit the Illinois Valley in the late 1960s. Much later, when I traveled to the Sinai as a journalist, I never saw any folks, save for fat tourists, who matched his complexion on the poster. In retrospect it seemed fraudulent at the very least, not depicting this wonderful individual as swarthy. As you can see, it helped send me down a path which led to questions and precious few answers.

But Sunday school was a welcome break from the bleak world we faced back home. What's more, we were each given a little bag of hard candy at the end of each lesson, no small thing in those lean days. Never mind the candy was old and fused together like plastic melted by flames. For the Fattig twins, the little church was a warm respite from a cold reality.

In the interest of journalistic research and out of curiosity, I wanted to attend the church as an adult to see if it would shake loose a few memories. A call to the nondenominational church beforehand was rewarded by a friendly recording indicating that all comers were welcome.

My wife Maureen agreed to go, providing I behaved myself. Joining us was my sister Delores, who also wanted to see the interior of the old church again, and a longtime family friend, Pat. As you have correctly gathered, I am not a church goer. By the by, my wife is a Christian who chose that path long ago. Her life's work is to show me the way. She allows it would be easier to herd our ten cats into a dog kennel.

So it came to pass that we attended the church the Sunday before Memorial Day weekend in 2016.

"God is about to test your little heathen soul, sweetie," Maureen cautioned me when we pulled into the church parking lot. "Just keep your mind open and your mouth closed."

"Scout's honor, dear," I promised, feeling very much like the five-year-old youngster who had entered the Wonder church sixty years earlier. Admittedly, my church-going days of yore were about as limited as my short-lived cub scout days.

As it was back in the 1950s, it is still called the Wonder Bible Chapel. The church is also on the same spot but was rebuilt after a transient broke in one night in 2006 and torched it, burning the chapel. Fortunately, the concrete walls withstood the flames and the church was rebuilt. The arsonist claimed God told him to do it, although there are those who would argue that Beelzebub was more likely the culprit. I would submit it was either mental challenges or too much bad brew for too many years. Or both. In any case, it's sad that we humans feel the need to destroy things that bring others so much joy. No other animal on earth trashes things out of sheer spite.

I was a little apprehensive when I stepped over the threshold, concerned about how we would be received and whether I could keep my emotions in check. I always liked that little church which my maternal Scottish ancestors would have referred to as a *kirk.*

My trepidation was without merit. They received us strangers into their midst with open arms. It was as though we were long lost family members being welcomed home. It was quite touching, actually.

The service began with the singing of hymns which filled me with emotion. It was as though we had just dropped in at the church when it and I were both young sixty years ago. The first was "When the roll is called up yonder," a song written in 1893 by James M. Black, a Methodist Sunday school teacher in Williamsport, Pa Among the other hymns sung with gusto were "Go Tell it on the Mountain," "Lily of the Valley," and "Amazing Grace." I managed to hold it together but the latter, written by a reformed slave trader, got to me. I could feel my eyes glistening. Maureen reached over and held my hand.

As the congregation sang in perfect harmony, apart from my voice which my wife controlled with an elbow when it wandered to far afield, a lady enthusiastically played the piano. Her skill easily overcame the fact one key was out of tune, my wife observed. Each time a song ended, the gentleman leading the session called on those raising their hands to suggest another hymn. Even the children were eagerly raising their hands to be called on.

After the singing, a white-haired gentleman named Ken Gavlik walked up to the pulpit and read from the *1st Chronicles,* focusing on the tale about the Philistines battling the Israelites, ending with Saul taking his life. A gifted speaker, the minister didn't berate it to the point his listeners became envious of Saul's ability to put an end to it all. A retired cabinet maker who is not an ordained minister, he had stepped in after the longtime minister retired, Ken told me later. He did his duties well, not wandering off topic into an opinionated quagmire.

It turned out to be a wonderful day which left us all feeling good about the world. There had been no judgmental hyperbole, no digression into politics, no reaching for your wallet. When I asked a parishioner how we could tithe, he scratched his head for a moment before asking others. Someone eventually pointed out a small basket on a nearby table. We left knowing the little church is in good hands.

Somewhere, the parishioners of old are smiling. There was no hard candy among the refreshments offered afterwards but I forgave them that little oversight.

MADSTONE

SIX

A Misanthropic
Draft Dodger

WHILE OUR CRUDE ABODE WOULD HAVE made the poorest church mouse feel destitute and condemned, it was palatial compared to the austere little cabin where our draft-evading uncle holed up. Uncle Charlie lived in a wood-frame hut on the north flank of the little valley about 200 feet from our house. Waters Creek Road, then a dirt track, ran dead center across the property and between the two shacks, providing him with a small buffer from the urchin rabble across the way. His cabin was perched on the side of a little hill in the fashion that would have made Li'l Abner feel right at home. It had electricity but no running water, although there was a seasonal spring above his cabin. He built his outhouse downhill from the water source, demonstrating that even a former Madstone cabin inhabitant could be fussy when it came to drinking water filtered by you know what.

Incidentally, when I think about those outhouses of my early childhood and the two modern bathrooms in our home today, I can't help but feel an embarrassment of riches. I still feel slightly thrilled every time I step into one. Of course, that could be related to being easily amused as I approach the doddering years.

Back on Uncle Charlie's cabin on the hill, his rustic domicile certainly reflected his chosen lifestyle. After all, he was no social animal who would be having guests over for a five-course dinner. While it may not be fair to say he detested people, he certainly found most highly offensive and more than a little stupid. The only people Uncle Charles disliked more than adults were adolescents. He did not tolerate them for long, especially when they came in the form of twins. To call him a curmudgeon would be diplomatic. As a youngster, I wasn't quite sure what constituted a bachelor but I figured it must be synonymous with bastard—whatever that was—since I had heard him described as both.

Yet there were times when the dark clouds of loathing toward all humankind parted and the somewhat sunny disposition of a friendly fellow emerged, albeit about as often as a warm December afternoon high in the Siskiyou Mountains. Maybe his abode made him stir crazy and cranky. But keep in mind he was in his sixties when I knew him. Perhaps he had a happy outlook in his early years but lost it when the horde of urchins arrived at his doorstep. Or it could be the rough road he had chosen bounced all the joy and optimism out of him.

The cabin was a one-room affair with a glass show case for his agates at the east end and a bunk, small woodstove and what passed for a kitchen at the other end. His little home could not have been much more than twenty feet long and perhaps a dozen feet wide. In comparison, the Chetco River hideaway would have seemed spacious, even grandiose.

Yet inside his tiny cabin was his world, at least his abridged version of it. Overhead dangled a lone light bulb, doubtlessly the handiwork of the same interior decorator whose arrested creativity inspired the rustic charm of our Spartan abode down by the creek. An old upright radio, the kind with a circular dial and crystal tubes, stood against the east wall. It looked like a big wooden tombstone. Back then, he was able to pick up a few radio stations, but listened mainly to an AM station out of Grants Pass which filled the cabin with elevator music and local weather reports. Too bad this was before frothing talk radio filled the air waves. It would have been a memorable sight to see him throwing the radio out the door after an announcer said something our grouchy uncle found objectionable.

One day when a singing group known as the Chipmunks was broadcast on the radio, Uncle Charlie grew more and more incensed at the sophomoric sound of the fictitious crooning rodents led by the mischievous Alvin. Jim tried to explain the singing sensation popular in the 1950s but that only fired up our uncle's ire.

"Those damn varmints," he snorted. "I don't know what the hell this world is coming to."

On the north wall of his cabin were shelves which housed his hardback books along with a collection of *National Geographic* and *Readers Digest* magazines going back to the turn of the 20th Century. The books were largely scientific tomes covering everything from botany to zoology. As children we had no television to watch and precious few toys. Throwing rocks at passing vehicles grew old after a while so we would scurry up to see Uncle Charlie and his library. He would dutifully hand down the volumes we would request. We weren't much interested in *Readers Digest* since there were no photographs. But the *National Geographics* were chock full of photographs of polar bears, storks, orchids and an array of other things which captured our attention. At the time, Jim was the only one who could read but we younger siblings could average it out by looking at the photographs. There were always the shots of topless African women which caused us boys to giggle and our uncle to growl at us to quit acting like children. When we weren't giggling, we constantly peppered the grumpy Waters Creek librarian with questions.

However, his tolerance level was even lower than his appreciation of children. After we bugged him for about an hour, repeatedly asking for more magazines or books while continuing the barrage of questions, his patience ran out.

"Get the hell out of here!" he would yell. "Go play on the road. Goddamn varmints." I had no idea what a varmint was, although I assumed it was a vile creature, one likely comparable to a bastard.

As a gray-haired varmint now, although whether I'm damned remains to be seen, I have my own book collection at home which includes two volumes which once sat on Uncle Charlie's shelves alongside the rest of his hardbacks. *The Prospector's Handbook* by J.W. Anderson, published in London in 1916, is well written from the perspective of an accomplished geologist who takes a scientific approach to gold mining. That book is in keeping with the self-educated uncle I knew, at least when it came to exploring the scientific world. But the other book from his library, *Give Me Liberty*, is a real head scratcher. Written by World War I veteran Ed "Vagabond" Bodin and published in 1946 in the Big Apple, the book is dedicated to what the author refers to as mental vagabonds. It sounds like daydreaming drifters but Bodin defined such a person as "a wanderer who seeks truth, peace of mind and human kindness." It takes the reader on a strange journey via poetry, connected by bits of prose, into hobo jungles and deep into Christian theology. A former mystery writer whose books would cover everything from flying saucers to zombies, Bodin seemed to conclude that hoboes were the real Christians. Since Jesus was a bit of a wanderer, perhaps he was on to something. But the fact Bodin was a mentor for L. Ron Hubbard may give you pause. What's more, Bodin founded the "Spiritual Party" and ran for president of the United States in 1952, providing manna for my theory that all writers, including yours truly, aren't typing with all the letters of the alphabet.

Considering his diverse reading habits, Uncle Charlie did not fit nicely into a neat little box. Very strange juxtaposition, an atheist reading a book that was fundamentally about Christianity. Although he had virtually no formal education, he was certainly bright and fairly well read, at least when it came to the natural sciences. Yet there is no question he was eccentric. It would not be insensitive to call him an odd duck.

Seldom did our skinny uncle leave his little enclave. When he ambled down to our place for a rare visit, he invariably clasped his hands behind his back and leaned slightly forward as he walked, his head slowly bobbing at each step. His gait brought to mind one of those storks in his old National Geographic magazines.

He didn't smoke but always seemed to have what sounded like a smoker's cough, leaving gobs of phlegm in his wake that looked like raw oysters. He was a world-class hacker, creating a gasping sound reminiscent of an old Studebaker whose engine continued to wheeze long after the ignition had been turned off. Healthy he was not. That pile of empty wine bottles outside of his cabin? Medicinal, he would growl. When I asked our dad what he meant, he replied with a hearty laugh. Based on that response, I gathered that our uncle simply liked to drink wine. These were wine bottles with screw-on caps, not corks. No wine connoisseur, our uncle. However, he was not an alcoholic. He was never drunk, and never drank hard stuff.

Even if he ever got tipsy, there was never a concern about his driving drunk. He did not have a car and, as far as it can be ascertained, never learned to drive. What is ascertainable is that he hated riding in a car, insisting the speed of a car was unnatural and unhealthy for humans. Dad would periodically take him down to the Wonder store for groceries. When they returned, Uncle Charlie always looked pale and shaken but thankful he had once more escaped death on the highway. Never mind our father was not a fast driver and the store was no more than a mile away with only half the distance being on asphalt. If they exceeded forty miles an hour it would have been tantamount to a local speed record.

Then there was our uncle's attire. Those who study society's subculture will tell you the Goth anti-culture movement began in jolly old England in the early 1980s when punk rockers began looking for a fresh genre to tick off their parents. Don't you believe it. Uncle Charlie didn't wear the walking-dead makeup but he was sporting Goth clothes in the early '50s on Waters Creek. His couture was always dark and never, ever did he wear a short-sleeved shirt. Even in summer when the mercury rose into the triple digits, his clothes were dark and his sleeves long. His dark clothes reflected his disposition. It was like a religion to him.

Our gothic uncle had no religion, of course. In fact, the best entertainment on our Waters Creek spread in the 1950s were those wonderful days when religious missionaries would pay a call on the old bachelor. Missionary schools apparently sent their bravest and most devout to test them on Uncle Charlie before rewarding them with an easier assignment such as the mountains of Afghanistan or the jungles of the Congo.

Always arriving in pairs, the missionaries first stopped at our house. Our mom would invite them in and politely listen to their spiel. She invariably cautioned them not to visit her brother-in-law in the little cabin just across the road. They would leave their literary tracts, get into their small sedan as though they were driving away but always pulled up at the end of the short path leading to Uncle Charlie's cabin. But the religious fellow behind the wheel would cleverly park for a quick exodus. This was important strategic positioning which would have impressed a veteran getaway driver in a bank heist. They would sit there for a few minutes, probably in prayer. Then, like two Daniels heading into the lions' den, the missionaries, each dressed in a white shirt and black slacks, walked slowly up to his cabin. Grim faced, each carried a black bible which would be a handy shield when they beat feet. Taking a deep breath, one would rap gently on the door.

The door slowly opened. The conversation would start out friendly enough with comments about the weather. Sometimes the old man would even invite them in. But they were in for a rude awakening if they thought he was being polite. Like the driver, he was merely positioning himself to be ready when they took flight.

Forever etched in my mind is the scene of two young missionaries sprinting toward the getaway car while holding their bibles behind their heads as Uncle Charlie hurled rocks, jars and other missiles at the retreating targets.

"Get the hell out of here!" he yelled. "Goddamn vermin."

For an old geezer, he had a fairly good arm and sometimes hit his fleet-footed quarry square in the back. Afterwards, he would gather up his ammunition and place it in handy piles near the door. One of his favorite missiles was an oil can, the kind with a spout to oil door hinges and other squeaky things, including fleeing missionaries who squeaked when smacked soundly in the middle of the back. It wasn't large but it had just about the right heft when filled with oil. When he retrieved it, he always checked to make sure there was no damage to his beloved weapon. Satisfied the projectile was still in good shape, he would sit down in a wooden chair in front of his cabin, full of faith that the religionists would one day return and that he would be ready for them. All was right in his world.

About now you are thinking that Charles Savannah Fattig was evil personified, a mean and vicious rascal who hated everybody and everything. He was not. Sure, he could certainly be a *scheisskopf* at times. Our grumpy uncle definitely fit the definition of an outlier who preferred to view society from a distance and with more than a little scorn. He definitely disliked people, particularly if they were little urchins, communists or religious fanatics. Was he bitter because of the rejection he received by society after avoiding military service? No doubt that influenced him but I suspect he was antisocial by nature. He preferred a life of quiet contemplation. Yet he did have a few friends who stopped by periodically. These were all old men who sat outside with him in fair weather to talk about the weather and politics.*

Naturally, anyone who disagreed with Uncle Charlie was an ignorant fool or a damned communist in his mind. While he treated our mother congenially enough, he kept his distance from the opposite sex. Perhaps he was afraid of them or it could be he was of a persuasion that dared not speak its name back in the early 1950s, a time when social sexual mores were a mite more unforgiving than they are now. The atheist already had a heavy cross to bear in having been a draft dodger; another cross might have been too much. Besides, as he would have rightfully barked, his sexuality was none of our Goddamn business.

In addition to being an avid reader, he was a rock hound who periodically fired up his old rock tumbler to polish his agates that he had collected around the property during his stork walks or that other people had dropped off. Powered by a little electric motor, the machine had a belt-driven metal barrel turned by a small engine. Along with the rocks,

---

* Interestingly, James and Rosa Deveny, friends of our parents who lived farther up Waters Creek with their young son, sometimes dropped by to chat with our uncle when they visited us. Just two years younger than our father, Jim Deveny had joined the Army during World War II and served in the Philippines where he was among those captured by Japanese forces in 1941 and forced on the Bataan Death March. He was brutally tortured and starved while a POW through the end of the war in 1945. A friendly fellow, he apparently held no resentment towards the man who refused to fight in the first world war. But it certainly would have been interesting to have sat in on one of their conversations regarding the politics of war.

he placed grit and water inside the barrel to mimic Mother Nature's eons-long method of polishing stones in a stream. The grumbling, rumbling noise filled our world, continuing for hours and hours. I hated the sound but always ran over when he started pulling out the glistening agates that sparkled in the sun. It was as though he was pulling pirates' treasures out of his tumbler. Inside his cabin he had a little electric polisher which added the finishing touches. He also had a saw which would cut the polished stones into agate jewelry, making settings for rings, brooches and necklaces. He was talented, of that there could be no doubt.

Some of the rocks he put into the tumbler were ones he gathered along Waters Creek. Others were dropped off by acquaintances and friends who knew of his hobby. Until he could tumble them, he stacked the rocks along the south side of his cabin where, when it rained, they formed a colorful pile. In a way, his multi-layered personality reflected his rock pile: he had rocks that floated in the form of pumice and iron wood that sank in water. Like his rocks, he was difficult to pigeon hole.

Of course, all of his stones were too valuable to him to use as ammo to wing fleeing missionaries but he may have grabbed one periodically when the oil can wasn't handy.

Yet, to reiterate, it would be wrong to paint him as an irredeemably malevolent person. His bark was worse than his bite. True, he had a mighty short fuse when it came to bipeds, particularly the missionaries he figured were on earth to make his life a living hell. Yet he was not the ogre the aforementioned actions and words professed him to be.

For instance, although he clearly was not a fan of little people, he invariably tossed a bag of sugar cookies into his groceries for his nephews and niece. It's likely he bought us kids some cookies once in a moment of weakness, and figured it would be dangerous to return without them in the same way you try to placate frothing dogs with raw meat. However, to give him his due, he also fashioned tin boats out of coffee and fruit cans for us, using a pair of tin snips and his impressive creative skills. Shaped like canoes, his toy boats were treasured by us. We immediately ran down to the creek and launched them. Of course, they quickly sailed away, prompting us to race back up to his cabin for another flotilla. For a while, he would continue his thankless job of manufacturing tin boats out of old cans. But after a tin fleet was lost to the creek, he had enough.

"Get the hell out of here!" he would yell as he threw down his tin snips. "Goddamn varmints."

In retrospect, I find it interesting that he was a staunch atheist yet would call up to the all-powerful creator to damn the pesky children who harassed him. If he had been a believer, it would be a more than a little harsh. However, as a non-believer, an infidel in the words of Alfred, it was likely he was just uttering his frustration. In my mind, he was not a jerk, albeit he had his moments.

As young kids, we often tripped and fell headlong as we ran across the uneven ground of our first home. But Uncle Charlie was always there for us."Come here and I'll pick you up," he would yell from his chair beside his cabin. Then he would chuckle. No, he did not like the wee human vermin. However, since he didn't care much for adult humanoids either, we took little offense.

Such was the unusual fellow who shared the Madstone cabin with Alfred Fattig. In defense of Uncle Charlie, living with anyone in close quarters in such conditions would be taxing for all involved. After all, a logged fortress can also be a prison. Add the fact the brothers were not compatible and you have the potential for conflict. They had no way to vent their frustrations other than on each other. They may have had a couple of books but there were few other pursuits to pass the time. According to Alfred, there were days when they were on the lam that his brother uttered not a word, something that bothered the gregarious younger brother to no end. To have been a fly on that cabin wall would have been fascinating, providing you didn't get flattened by a thrown rock or splattered by a bullet fire in anger.

MADSTONE

SEVEN

Moving Uptown

H AD IT NOT BEEN FOR THE LOGGING accident that nearly killed our father, we would have never lived at the gateway to the Madstone country. I would probably not have explored the region where our uncles once hid from the long reach of the law. Other avenues would have opened up but life would have likely been far different and likely less interesting. All things considered, we would have preferred to have had a two-legged father who lived longer, of course.

However, if we stayed at Waters Creek, living without the trappings of civilization in our rustic retreat, we likely would have gravitated toward the metropolis of Grants Pass and its comparatively cultured society. It was our version of the Big Apple. True, some wisenheimers would snidely observe that fair town had denizens known as the Grants Pass Cavemen Club and that athletes from Grants Pass High School are known as the Cavemen, monikers which can't help but conjure up mental images of Neanderthals, squinting at the world under a sloping forehead adorned with one long furry eyebrow. Yet GPHS honor students, some of whom are also gifted athletes, are Cavemen and many end up at ivy-league colleges. As for the town's notorious Cavemen Club, its fur-clad members grunted and growled at public events, including initiating Republican vice-presidential candidate Richard Nixon when he was campaigning in 1952. We know this because *Daily Courier* reporter Russell Working, an extremely gifted journalist who would later write for the *Chicago Tribune* and the *New York Times*, received a letter from Nixon early in 1994 in reply to Working's inquiry about the candidate's memories of meeting the Cavemen in the 1952 campaign. Nixon, then eighty-one, died of a stroke not long afterwards, hopefully not one triggered by memories of his Caveman initiation. A 1957 edition of the *Illinois Valley News*, a weekly newspaper published in Cave Junction, carried a photograph of Oregon Gov. Robert D. Holmes surrounded by hairy members of the Grants Pass Cavemen Club under what was known as the hangman's tree in Kerby. The massive oak, which fell in 1964, stood in front of what is now the Kerbyville Museum. Local youngsters walking past it on a dark and stormy night invariably picked up their pace. Word had it the ghosts of outlaws, having met their end on the tree, lurked about. I believe I'm on partially solid ground here when I say none of those hung were kinfolk.

The club formed in 1922, shortly after the brothers built the Madstone cabin. You see where I'm going here, right? If a region can produce such a club nearly a century ago, then retreating into the mountains to avoid the military draft during that era would not have been too far off the beaten path.

Point of fact, the club and school mascot came about, not for having dimwitted inhabitants, but because the town was known as the gateway to the Oregon Caves located in the mountains east of the Illinois Valley before the little burg of Cave Junction popped up in that beautiful river vale. In passing, my wife is an alumna of that fine school and doesn't sport eyebrows resembling hairy caterpillars. When it comes to smarts, she often leaves me furrowing my heavy forehead as I try to comprehend her latest brainstorm. A Cro-Magnon she is not.

Regardless, our parents chose to move south when it became clear we could not continue to eke out an existence on Waters Creek. Obviously, a one-legged man with crutches trying to hurry across the narrow footbridge to the outhouse was a real problem. Add the other challenges—no phone, no hot water, no heat to speak of since the fireplace produced little warmth—and it was clearly time to leave.

The community our parents chose was Kerby, an unincorporated hamlet in the Illinois Valley some two dozen miles south of the cavemen's lair. Both of our parents had connections to the area; our dad was a teenager when his parents moved to the valley in the early 1920s and mom's parents had adopted the area after losing their ranch in Washington state during the Great Depression. Our paternal grandparents' decision to move was inspired by the notoriety brought to the Applegate Valley family by the jailbird brothers. Remember, this was back in the day when moving over the next mountain range was tantamount to starting afresh.

For the Oregon challenged, Kerby is some 250 miles south of Portland. It's roughly a dozen miles shy of the California state line. To put it in proper perspective, look at a map of the West Coast. Starting at the north and heading south, you will find Seattle, Portland, Kerby, San Francisco and Los Angeles, all strategically spaced apart roughly the same distance apart so their basketball teams would each have a large enough fan base. OK, you won't actually see the tiny town of Kerby on a map of the western US but it is there, halfway between Portland and San Francisco. It looks a bit like a smudge on the state map. As for a basketball team, the Kerby Vikings did have a team when I was in the now defunct Kerby Elementary School. If it weren't for the inability to dribble a ball and make a basket, I could have made the team.

In its heyday, Kerby was not a place to be trifled with. Humor aside, it was the Josephine County seat from 1856 to 1883. It was founded before the upstart Grants Pass popped up along the Rogue River and stole that distinction from us. However, since Oregon's version of River City is the place of my birth and a pleasant little burg, complete with pool tables, we'll forgive the Cavemen—and Cavewomen—their trespasses.

Parenthetically, Kerby was initially known as Kerbyville, named after James Kerby, a community founder who served as postmaster for two years beginning in September of 1856. In the weird history department, a political gadfly led a successful effort not long after the community was founded to change the community's name to Napoleon. His unique campaign argument was that every Josephine needs a Napoleon. Get it? Most of the residents didn't either. After little more than a year, the name was changed by the then territorial legislature to Kerby on the eve of Oregon becoming a state on Feb. 14, 1859. The third moniker stuck, leaving then 33rd state without a Napoleon. Our Josephine did not pine, although the few resident Francophiles may have sniffed a little. They saw it as the second Waterloo for Monsieur Bonaparte, albeit in absentia.

Back when the brothers were hiding in the mountains, Kerby was still a bustling little town. Consider the 320-page *Oregon Almanac* published in 1915 by the long departed Oregon State Immigration Commission. The book was promoted as a guide to potential "homeseekers, settlers and investors."

Under Kerby's listing, the almanac noted the following: "Stage to Grants Pass and Crescent City, California, daily. General farming, dairying, livestock raising and lumbering. Two sawmills. Creamery. High and graded public schools. Methodist Episcopal church."

But things were already starting to slow down, judging from an entry in Sept. 23, 1910, *Rogue River Courier*, the Grants Pass paper's name before morphing into the *Daily Courier*. It seems the saloon in Kerby had closed.

"This will make the heart of many a wife and mother feel glad, for if there ever was an unnecessary evil, it surely is the saloon," the correspondent wrote. You just know there were others who held a lively wake for the old saloon.

A clipping from the *Oregon Observer* newspaper on March 7, 1896 also provided an interesting insight into the lifestyle differences between our internet world of today and those years of yore. Back then, entertainment was homemade and mostly out in the elements.

"The latest advices from Kerby are that the snow is 32 inches deep in that town," the article noted. "The young folks in and around Kerby are having lots of fun by taking large dry beef hides, hitching horses to them by the horns of the hides and going sleigh riding."

There would have been a picture truly worth a thousand words. Perhaps it is the Kerby kid in me but I would have loved to have taken a spin on a beef hide, hanging onto the horns. Of course, that was when the place still had a saloon so they knew how to party. It was also before our weather went south, so to speak.

By the time our family arrived in 1958, a tavern known as the Stony Front, so named because of the round river rocks gathered from the nearby Illinois River and used to decorate the outside walls, was serving as the local watering hole. In keeping with descriptions of other Oregon towns included in the 1915 *Oregon Almanac*, it didn't note whether there was a drinking establishment in the community. Having known the descendants of those folks living in Kerby a century ago, I can assure you alcoholic beverages were available in abundance.

When we arrived in Kerby, there were a still a couple of fine old homes from the 1800s, including the 1871 two-story Naucke family home which is now well preserved as part of the wonderful Kerbyville Museum & History Center. By the by, if you ever find yourself in downtown Kerby with nothing pressing to do, stop in at the center. You will be impressed. As a museum aficionado who has visited museums from villages in Ireland to the Smithsonian in the village that is our national capital, I can attest the Kerby facility is a remarkable place. It reflects the life and times of a lively small town going back to pre-statehood days. I may be a mite biased, of course.

The Nauckes who built the stately old house at the site were the first owners of the Kerby general store. Before it became part of the museum, their house was owned by Lela Ingersoll Cooke, my maternal grandmother who bought it during World War II. Like the grand house, grandma was a wonderful character in her own right with a can-do attitude that was the quintessence of Yankee ingenuity.

Unfortunately, the small house our parents bought was not stately, not even remotely. It was a butt-ugly hovel with a tar paper roof and sided with gray shingles, the cheap kind intended to mimic cinder blocks. Unfortunately, many of the shingles hung loosely like drunken sailors hanging over the gunwales. It also squatted by Highway 199 for the passing world to see. Remember the place your respectable parents shuddered at when they drove past, all the while warning you and your equally appalled siblings in the back seat you would end up in something like that if you didn't get good grades? We moved into that heap.

And I was thrilled.

For I knew that inside the house was a throne: an honest-to-goodness flush toilet. I was beyond ecstatic. Upon our arrival, even before the unpacking began, I dashed into the bathroom and flushed the toilet several times until Dad told me to stop. Hey, it was exhilarating, watching the water swirl away. Only humans who have endured an expedition to the outhouse perched on the side of Bears Hill could appreciate the luxury. Actually, bears, who most certainly do defecate in the woods, would have also revered the indoor commode, although the potting training would have been a bit hazardous and more than a little messy. Not only was there a flush toilet, there was a shower stall adjacent to it. No more taking a bath in a washtub in water containing flotsam left by previous occupants. There was even a hot water tank. Hot water actually poured out of the faucet.

What's more, shortly after our arrival we had a telephone installed in the form of a landline. Our telephone number was 14202. No, I don't have total recall but the Kerbyville Museum does. You will find the number in its 1963 edition of the Redwood Telephone Co. directory under Gladys Fattig, page 6. It was a party line, meaning that you had to check if anyone was on the line before dialing. Cell phones were still half a century away, of course.

Finally, the house had air conditioning in the form of a swamp cooler for the hot summers and a wood stove for the winters. Would wonders ever cease? I was giddy with the extravagance of the avant-garde digs.We had finally arrived in the modern age. Actually, that is piling the happy horse hockey on a smidge. We still weren't quite into the late 1950s but we were certainly well into the 1940s, at least the early part of the decade. Yessirree Bob, the Fattigs were definitely moving up in the world.

But once I sobered from the elation of having a flush toilet, it slowly became apparent to me the house was a calamity, a place no self-respecting termite would call home. It turned out there were serious limitations in the septic system for a family of seven, a problem whose solution periodically required a walk in the nearby woods to do what bears do in the Madstone country. There were also vines growing up through the holes in the bathroom floor along the outside wall, forming a rather nice floral arrangement for the bugs that made their home there. No snakes, though. They had their standards, after all.

Unlike our previous abode, the house did have two bedrooms but they weren't much bigger than walk-in closets. The Fattig urchins were back in bunks but at least these were store-bought beds with real mattresses from Sears & Roebucks, not bunks built into the wall like the ones on Waters Creek. Our parents did have a regular bed, although a small one to fit their small bedroom. As for our furniture, we had shabby chic décor decades before it became popular. Television? Surely, you jest. One wouldn't come along for years and it was in the form of a black and white one handed down by our maternal grandmother. For our meals, we ate at a little table crammed into our tiny kitchen.

Like a longtime two-pack-a-day smoker, the wood stove coughed up smoke periodically through holes in the stove pipe near where it went through the roof. Dad spent an exorbitant amount of time daubing plaster of Paris between the pipe and the ceiling. Even when the pipe wasn't smoking, the stove provided little heat. "It doesn't draft very well," Dad observed by way of explanation. I had no idea what he was talking about, although I rightfully figured it had nothing to do with the military. Oh, and the air conditioning? Turns out it was basically an electric fan built into a wooden box placed in the wall where a window had been. The fan blew air cooled by water delivered by a garden hose. You don't need to be an electrician to know that water and electricity ought not to mix, particularly when there are old wires with cracked insulation involved. I discovered that the first time I turned it on one hot summer day. Happily reaching up to turn the dial to engage the fan as water dripped onto the cooler, I couldn't wait to feel the cool air on my face. The next thing I remember I was sitting on the floor, having been knocked backward from the electric shock. I was afraid of the swamp cooler from that day forth. For me, it could have been the creature from the Black Lagoon.

While we didn't have much in the way of decorations in the house, we did have an old mantle clock that chimed. That clock is now in the aforementioned Kerbyville Museum. Hanging on the wall was a pine slab that spoke volumes when it came to Dad's philosophy. "Life is a struggle, but not a warfare," read the quote by John Burroughs, which came from his 1913 book of essays, *The Summit of the Years*. Born April 3, 1837, on the family farm on Old Clump Mountain near Roxbury in upstate New York, Burroughs was not acquainted with the Oregon mountains, let alone the Madstone country. Yet his childhood ramblings in the Catskill Mountains schooled him in the ways of Mother Nature as much as Alfred's wandering the mountains of southwest Oregon in his youth. Burroughs became a teacher, journalist and conservationist as well as a good friend of Henry David Thoreau and Walt Whitman. Like Alfred Fattig, Burroughs had both deep religious and naturalist beliefs. He was definitely not a proponent of war as a way to solve human conflict. It is also clear that our father subscribed to Burroughs' beliefs when it came to turning to war to solve international conflict. However, whatever our father's views were on our uncles' decision to evade the draft was never mentioned, at least to me. He no doubt told others but children were not in that conversational loop. The fact he joined the merchant marines may reflect the fact he wanted to serve his country in some fashion during World War II, although it may very well be that he simply wanted to travel a bit.

To his credit, Dad tried to spruce things up a bit in our Kerby home. One of his first projects was to build a cellar onto the back of the house, just outside the back door. As his father did before him when creating a cool place to store food, he built two-by-four frames, sided with one-by-six boards, and filled in the space with sawdust to create insulated walls. These were walls built since logs were first made into lumber. It is remarkable how cool it was in the cellar where the wonderful canned peaches our mother made were kept.

Keeping a promise made to our mom, he added a little back porch which would house a washing machine and—hold onto your hat!—an electric clothing dryer. Back on Waters Creek, we had a washing machine but a clothes line out back dried the clothes.

In keeping with a long Fattig tradition, we planted a vegetable garden out back. Despite having only one leg, Dad tilled the garden and instructed his children how to sow seeds and plant seedlings. While it wasn't exactly slave labor, our father didn't make gardening fun for kids. Many of the local urchins were heading down to the river for a long afternoon of frolicking in the cool water while we tugged on stubborn weeds that didn't much like being tugged. The weeds balked while we sulked in the sun. By the time the vegetables were ready to harvest, I resented them all. They represented hours of drudgery on a broiling summer day. In college, I recall my initial disbelief upon discovering the great American novelist Henry James believed the words "summer afternoon" were the loveliest two words in the English language. He obviously never sweated out a sweltering summer afternoon on his knees in a vegetable garden, both hands tugging on a stubborn weed whose top invariably broke off just above the ground. But it eventually dawned on me he was referring in part to lazy days spent reading a good book, a sentiment I share. Even on a late winter day, merely poring over a garden book while you are waiting for the last frost always warms you with sunny thoughts of summer.

Dad's next project was to build a small greenhouse, the kind with a lumber skeleton covered with see-through plastic. The greenhouse was heated with a small wood stove during winter. The goal was to maintain a temperature well above freezing but not over ninety degrees Fahrenheit in winter and a humidity of about fifty percent. Fans were employed during the summer to keep the plants from overheating.

With the help of his children handing him tools and lumber, he did all the work himself, using a table saw to cut the lumber. Watching the one-legged man stand on a short ladder, I figured he was invincible. I was wrong, of course. One day while cutting a board on the saw, he bumped his wooden leg on something and glanced down for a second. Bad move. He instinctively moved his left hand and sliced off the end of his left thumb, nail and all. The former logger calmly asked for a towel to wrap his blood-spurting stump, then drove to Cave Junction a few miles away to have it sewn up by the town doctor. Brother Jim, who accompanied him, said our father didn't flinch when the doctor drove a needle down into the stump to kill the pain. Although always a stout fellow, Jim admitted his knees grew a little weak at the sight. As for the end of the thumb, the saw had thrown it into the nearby tall grass where our sister Delores found it. Dad's body part looked like the end of a pale hot dog with a thumb nail attached. We kids buried it out back by some willows, conducting our version of a little funeral ceremony.

Sans the end of his left thumb as well as his right leg, Dad dutifully went back to the work at hand. Thanks to the carpentry skills he leaned in the Civil Conservation Corps in the 1930s, he built a solid framework for the green house. I can still see him hopping up a ladder to work on the rafters. The only aid he had was his children handing him tools or carrying boards for him. When it was done, it looked like a professional job.

When you stepped inside, you were enveloped by a humid, earthy air which I found comforting. Even now, I tend to linger when I go to a nursery for garden plants, breathing in memories of that Kerby greenhouse of long ago.

Inside Dad's green heaven were remarkable plants which were surely the first ever grown in Kerby, including pansy orchids (*Miltoniopsis*) and birds of paradise (*Paradisaeidae*). Although both the orchids with their waxy blossoms and the birds of paradise whose blossom resembled Donald Trump's orange-yellow coiffure drew attention, my favorite was the touch-me-not plant (*Mimosa pudica*). Originally hailing from Central and South America, its leaves fold inward upon being touched. I always reached up and touched it when entering the greenhouse. I couldn't help myself. After all, its very name told me not to touch it.

Another plant was called the wandering Jew (*Tradescantia pallid*), although it did not wander at all. But it had beautiful purple foliage which stood out in the green plants of Dad's greenhouse. The name came from the story that a Jewish fellow has been wandering out there since Jesus' crucifixion and must continue to wander until Jesus returns, according to our mom.

Perhaps the strangest plant was a Christmas cactus (*Schlumbergera*) that Dad had grafted onto a fish hook barrel cactus *(Ferocactus wislizenii)*. The Christmas cactus would bloom late in the year, covering the barrel cactus with pink-red blossoms. The squat cactus bristling with fish-hook like spikes under a blanket of soft blossoms was a sight to behold.

As an aside, I throw the Latin names out there because Dad would frequently refer to them by their Latin monikers. He may have had only an eighth grade education but he was self-educated in ways that would astound. It was yet another reflection of the contradictory nature of our dad and his siblings. He had a remarkable green thumb that could cause the sickest plant to spring to life. I often tagged along when he went in to greenhouse to putter among his plants. By the time I was seven, I knew the plural of cactus was "cacti." We didn't have much but I was proud of that greenhouse and Dad's botanical knowledge.

I remembered the plant house as a large structure, but it was only twelve feet by twenty-four feet, according to a 1961 clipping from the *Daily Courier*. The short article, accompanied by a photograph of Mom standing by a flowering orchid, told the story of our father's death and his widow and their children's efforts to keep the greenhouse going in his honor. It even included a quote touting his favorite philosophy: "There is more tonic in a flowerpot than in a whole drug store." That may have been botanical hyperbole but stepping into his greenhouse certainly lifted my spirits.

While we always maintained we lived in Kerby, that wasn't literally the case. The house was actually hunkered down along the west side of Highway 199 about a half mile north of Kerby in an area known as Sauers Flat, named for a tough, hard-working family who had farmed the area for much of the 20th Century. How tough were they? Consider this: family patriarch Jack Sauer was eighty-seven when he was crossing the Illinois River horseback on Oct. 23, 2016, heading to the mountains west of the Sauer farm on a deer hunting trip. Never mind he was at an age when most folks can barely climb into a rocking chair. He had crossed at the same spot many times in the past. Unfortunately, on this day his horse was spooked by river debris, throwing its geriatric rider. His grown granddaughter, riding another horse, tried to save the family patriarch but was unable to reach him before he was swept downriver. Although it was a sad ending to a remarkable fellow, you can't help but believe that Jack Sauer, tougher than the saddle leather upon which he rode, preferred to die with his boots on.

The Sauer family patriarch drowned at the same spot his son Nick and I crossed on horses during the winter of 1968 when we were high school juniors. Nick, who would later lose a portion of a lower leg when it was crushed during a log-truck accident, didn't mind when the swift water rose up to the saddle horn but I was mighty relieved when we reached the far bank and climbed onto dry land. It was also near where my brother Charles was bit by a rattlesnake while he and Nick were changing irrigation pipes in the summer of 1965. Charles spent several days in the hospital; the snake didn't require medical attention.

Coincidentally, it was just a quarter mile upstream a few years earlier when I had a close brush with a buzzworm. While fishing in the river late one summer morning, I happily cast into a slight riffle just above what we fondly called our swimming hole. I was standing in the water, barefoot and wearing cutoffs. I was probably daydreaming during what was a pleasant rite of summer.

A stick floating downstream brushed against my leg. It was just a light touch, like a wet feather brushing up against the back of my bare knee. I had just cast across the stream and was reeling in a Colorado spinner so I didn't give the stick drifting by much thought. I was hoping to catch a lunker rainbow lurking under the shade of the willow across the river. But the stick brushing up against my leg persisted.

That's when I glanced down. On the business end of the "stick" was a diamond-shaped head whose flickering tongue seemed intent on discovering just what kind of hairy tree trunk the rattlesnake had floated into that morning. The swimming rattlesnake was as long as my skinny childhood arm but with more meat on it. I didn't walk on water but I did leave that section of the river rather hastily, shouting childhood oaths.

The last I saw of the snake, it was floating lazily downstream, no doubt puzzled by the encounter. It swam slowly with its head and buzzer up out of the water, the latter apparently out of concern it doesn't rattle well when wet. Fangs, on the other hand, are already dripping with venom but I suppose rattlers don't want to get water up their noses. Probably makes them cranky.

You get the gist: the beautiful Illinois River flowing about a quarter mile west of our house offered both danger and an escape from the drab existence in the little gray house. Having worked for the U.S. Forest Service in the region as a young adult, Dad knew the area well, including the old trails used by miners and mountain dwellers. While he could no longer hunt, his first-born child was a man-boy aptly named for James Bridger, the famous mountain man. Whether it was because of his name or the way he was treated from the moment he could walk, our big brother was a gifted hunter.

Consider this article which ran Oct. 27,1960, in the *Illinois Valley News* under the headline, "Youthful Nimrod Bags His Share of Game."

"A young hunter, 12-year-old Jimmy Fattig, brought home the venison last Friday," it began. "Jim has been filling the family larder during hunting season for the last three years. When he was 10 he killed his first bear. At the age of 11 another bear killed by Jim went into the family freezer. This year Jim spent every spare moment hunting, even camping one night alone, at the head of Althouse Creek. At last his determination was rewarded with a five-point buck taken in the Page Mountain area. Jim is an eighth grade student at Kerby school and the son of Mr. and Mrs. Paul Fattig of Kerby."

Our brother had actually turned thirteen on the fourth of the month and the lead was buried, but the gist of the article was accurate. If you are the one East Coast resident reading this book, keep in mind that we Westerners count only one side of the rack for points. Back in Ben Franklin's home state, it would have been a ten-point buck. West of the Mississippi, hunters don't feel the need to embellish their exploits, you see.

Jim came by his hunting prowess through his genes. Before he lost his leg, our dad was also an accomplished hunter and outdoorsman. Our cousin Frank Cooke, now an octogenarian, recalled going hunting as a young man with our father and our mom's brothers—Ed, Ellsworth and Jim, all avid hunters.

"Your father had just married your mother—this was around 1946 or '47—so her brothers, including my dad [Ed], thought they were going to show him how to shoot," said Frank who, like most Cookes, is a great raconteur. "My dad and his brothers all had new rifles with scopes—.270s and .30-06s. Your father had an old muzzleloader with him. We were up there by Biscuit Hill when a buck jumped up and started running up the ridge.

"My dad pulled down on that buck and—boom!—missed him," he continued. "Jim and Unc (Ellsworth) both took a shot. Boom! Boom! They both missed. Well, your father calmly picked up his old muzzleloader and, just as that buck was about to disappear over the ridge, fired. Kaboom! That buck dropped dead."

The muzzleloader he used, now owned by my brother Jim, is a .58 caliber Springfield, circa mid-1860s. The barrel had riflings, meaning the musket ball would have spun like a football thrown in a spiral, making it more accurate than a ball fired through a smoothbore barrel. Riflings or not, it was a mighty good shot. By the way, Biscuit Hill is on the southeast portion of what I consider Madstone country.

Not to blow my own hunter's horn but yours truly shot an eight-point buck—eight on one side, nine on the other—on Page Mountain in the Illinois Valley the last weekend of deer hunting season in 1968. A braggart would smugly observe that is the largest buck—when it came to points—bagged by a Fattig since the family came west. Not being immodest, I wouldn't stress the fact no other hunter in our family has shot one with a rack that big. Ever. After all, mentioning the huge buck would be boasting so I won't bring it up.

Uncle Alfred would have pointed out that I could hardly have missed, what with being armed with what he considered a new-fangled rifle. I was carrying a .303 British, a rifle the English soldiers would have used in WWI. Admittedly, my rifle was modernized with a scope, making it easy to slay the big stag with a shot through the neck. I also happened to be in the right place at the right time. From the buck's perspective, he was at the wrong place at the wrong time.

But there is no question brother Jim was a far better hunter than any of his siblings, following the footsteps of our deer-slaying uncle of Madstone fame. He may not have been very gifted when raising younger siblings but Jim was certainly precocious with a rifle. Daniel Boone could have taken lessons. He went on to bag bull elk and other large creatures but eventually gave up hunting when life got in the way. However, he never relinquished his fishing rod. After retiring, he caught a nine-foot-long marlin in Mexico that weighed 140 pounds. Ernest Hemingway, no slouch when it came to marlin fishing, would have been bragging in his athletic prose about the great fish that was noble and good. Jim caught the whopper in the first decade of the 21st Century, demonstrating that Jim Bridger's namesake could still bag a big one.

Back in Kerby of 1959, big brother's hunting skills led to a memorable Thanksgiving dinner, a meal that could have been served up in the Madstone cabin. The mere memory of it still causes my stomach to churn. In keeping with the family's homespun ways, Dad decided we would forego the traditional stuffed farm turkey and sit down to a Thanksgiving feast featuring wild beasts. In place of the big bird we would be supping on wild critters killed with our own hands. The reasoning was a little vague. Perchance it was celebrating Oregon's centennial birthday that year. Maybe it was paying homage to our family's proud tradition of living off the land. If it was intended to help the former avid hunter relive the gamey taste of yesteryear, it was certainly a roaring success. However, if you prefer your Thanksgiving dinner tame and not gamey, it was a meal most foul.

In those days, it wasn't unusual to see a pickup roaring down Kerby's mean street with the feet of a slain beast sticking out the back. We rural residents were always game for wild game. Still, most Kerby dwellers opted for domesticated turkey on the fourth Thursday in November. Feral critters were normally safe that day.

Naturally, the responsibility for the Thanksgiving beast acquisition that year fell to the eldest son. Little Jimmy Bridger did not disappoint. That fall, he slew a black bear, a four-point buck, some quail and at least one gray squirrel — the guest rodent at the table.

As an eight-year-old, I recall staring at the roasted rodent with its little legs sticking up in the air. With such a sight before you, it's hard to give thanks on Turkey Day and really, truly mean it. Next to what was the skinned gray squirrel was a huge hunk of bear meat, a large slab of venison and a couple of plucked quail. It was not a meal for the squeamish.

Granted, there are wonderful gourmands with a flair for cooking who would have made such a potpourri of creatures into an amazing dinner. Our mom was a wonderful person with a big heart who loved us all with every ounce of her being. She was decency personified. However, as much as it grieves me to acknowledge, she couldn't cook for beans. Actually, she could cook beans exceedingly well. Surprisingly, she also made a terrific pie crust from scratch, something many people find challenging. Memories of her apple pies still causes me to salivate like Pavlov's dog.

It was when she decided to blaze culinary trails few cooks dared follow that were cause for concern. Our mom, who liked to be creative with her dishes, would often say, just before you took a bite, "You'll be surprised by what I put in it." We were always surprised, and never in a good way. Take the memorable cherry pie she once made. Please. For reasons never quite determined, she left the pits in the cherries. Now, there is a reason they are called stone fruit. But it was fun watching an unsuspected sibling eagerly bite down on the golden-crusted pie oozing with that delicious cherry filling. We all cracked a few molars over that innocent-looking dessert. Just thinking about that pie makes my teeth hurt.

The problem with our Thanksgiving dinner that year was she decided to toss everything into one big roasting pan. You had greasy bear meat, stringy squirrel, gamey venison and innocent quail broiling away together along with potatoes, carrots and onions from our garden. We were fortunate Jim never had time to go fishing or there would have been salmon swimming in the bear tallow.

Directly as a result of mom's cooking, I've always been a gutless coward when it comes to consuming strange cuisine. Yet, due to circumstances beyond my control, I have dined on a few stomach-churning delectables over the years. There was the porcupine we siblings roasted on a spit over a fire during a hungry hunting trip in the mountains immediately west of Kerby in the winter of 1962. It would have been far better to bypass the porcupine and nosh on the stick it was roasted on. Nor can I forget the Marine Corps chow back in the late 1960s and early '70s. A fellow jarhead insisted the trick to eating SOS was simple: Just watch it for a while to make sure nothing crawls out of the evil-looking substance, then wolf it down before the tastebuds can launch a counter attack. Later, while working as a journalist in Alaska, I sank my teeth into walrus and *muktuk*—raw whale blubber. Walrus is an acquired taste. Imagine biting into a slab of stringy dark meat laced with globs of white fat. It tastes far worse than it sounds. As for muktuk, it's akin to chomping down on the sole of an old tennis shoe soaked for a year in a vat of dead fish. The aftertaste alone made me blubber. Then there was the thing dished up from the bottom of the stew pot during a journalistic visit to an orphanage in Vietnam in 1999. To this day, I'm not sure whether it was animal or vegetable. I fear it was the former and had something to do with reproductive parts. But the meal that takes the cake was that Thanksgiving dinner of '59 in Kerby.

Bear is not as greasy as walrus, but it comes within a whisker. It is also very strong. Venison, quail, squirrel and veggies broiled for hours in bear tallow ends up tasting suspiciously like bruin. It overpowered everything. The reek filled our small house with a strong smell evoking a sweltering day during wildebeest rutting season on the Serengeti. There was also a hint of musty socks but that may have been my feet. One whiff and the Bigfoot beast would have sprinted shrieking for the deep woods.

The brave souls gathered around the table couldn't taste the difference between carrot and potato; both tasted gamey and greasy. The fowl was beyond foul. And there was that poor roasted rodent with its little legs sticking up in the air. Had the dish been served up in a fine restaurant, a condescending critic would have snidely penned that if ever there was a dish inspired by vomit, he had found it.

While the taste was heinous enough, there was also the problem of periodically chomping down on a bullet. Jim may have been a great hunter but he had yet to perfect the necessary thoroughness required when it came to gutting the animal and butchering the meat so that no lead remained. No doubt our draft-dodging uncles would have happily tucked into the meal during their lean Madstone days. And, like us, they would have been mighty appreciative when Mom brought out her homemade apple pie baked in a faultless golden crust. The perfect pie carried not a hint of bruin.

MADSTONE

EIGHT

Grim Reaper
Pays a Visit

W HEN I MET UNCLE ALFRED, I was pleasantly surprised by his
warm and engaging personality. Although not a native son of
the South, he had adopted a southern charm after living more than half
century in the region. Like his wife, he couldn't have been more wel-
coming. He obviously was glad to see blood relatives after all those
years. True, he may have been putting on a show during the days we
spent with him. Or maybe he had been softened up by his unwavering
religious faith as he approached the century mark, and had been a jerk to
live with during his earlier years. But I think not, judging from the strong
affection shown to him by his wife and a grown stepdaughter during our
visit. We met the genuine article.

And the man we met was diametrically different than his two brothers.
As you have read, Uncle Charlie obviously had a penchant for antisocial behavior. The devout atheist held a deep distrust of all creatures
humanoid, not solely the wee ones who came in sets of twins. Nor did
he much like kittens or puppies, the damned varmints. At his worst, he
made the Grinch seem warm and fuzzy.

Our father was unlike either Alfred or Charlie. For one thing, he
professed to be a non-believer, yet he would hedge his bets by calling

for a minister three days before he died. Alfred the religionist would have likely called his kid brother an infidel since Dad was not a church goer. However, like Alfred, our dad could be warm and charming, especially when friends would stop by on summer evenings. They were often oldtimers like Swedish-born John Valen, a former Josephine County commissioner, and A. Donley Barnes, county sheriff during World War II who was later elected county clerk. These were good folks who had known our dad since his youth and were around during the older brothers' draft-dodging days. When they came over on a summer's evening, our kitchen table chairs would be taken out under the pine trees behind the house where the adults would gather. I always looked forward to the story-telling sessions, which began just as dusk settled on the beautiful river valley. They would be sipping a cup of coffee or nursing a beer, stopping periodically to slap a mosquito.

After discussing their ailments and the sorry state of the body politic, they would eventually start swapping stories about the old days. That was when Dad talked about the Madstone cabin, bragging about Alfred's hunting skills and telling other stories about the mysterious mountains just west of the Illinois River. As a kid quietly sitting nearby in the grass with my siblings, I figured this was better than any television show could ever be. I dearly wanted to see what to me was a famous site known as the Madstone cabin. As I listened to the tall tales of daring-do and periodically punctuated by guffaws and chortles on those entertaining evenings, I told myself I would get there one day. Our world seemed warm and wonderful, despite the pesky mosquitoes. As for seeing the Madstone cabin site, it was an itch I would not scratch for some three decades.

Sadly, our father was not as social with his children as he was with his peers, although he made an exception with his eldest, at least when it came to hunting and fishing. But he never spent much time with his two sets of twins. He was probably waiting for us to become interesting. However, I liked to shadow him when he went out to his greenhouse or on his botanizing forays around the valley.

Dad's aloof ways came naturally. The family Fattig was never touchy-feely. Sure, our mom and our maternal grandmother gave us hugs but they were not cursed with the standoffish Fattig gene which swam away like Olympian gold medalist Michael Phelps from all the other genes in the pool. Not only did we not hug during our childhood but we never, ever told other siblings we loved them. Even as adults, during those rare times when we siblings hug, it is an uncomfortable grip and quick pat on the back before hurriedly pushing away. And that trait came directly from dear old dad. Nor was our father the kind of warm parent who regularly gave verbal pats on the head to his children. He apparently felt it was coddling. Consider the day when he came to our second grade class at Kerby U—a fond nickname for the elementary school—to show his slides of Alaska taken back in the late 1930s and early 1940s when it was still a U.S. territory. The teacher wanted Dad to make the presentation because Alaska was about to become the 49th state. I was asked to introduce my parents to the class. Although a bit nervous, I stepped up and somehow did the job without any major gaffes. That night our mom gave me a hug and said Dad was very proud of me. Yet he never told me what I very much wanted to hear.

A longtime smoker who puffed non-filter cigarettes when he didn't have pipe tobacco, Dad was diagnosed with cancer in 1960. The disease would spread like a wildfire throughout his body. Although no medical specialist ever made any such connection at the time, his love of tobacco was likely the culprit, if later medical research on smoking is any guide. Dad freely acknowledged that smoking was bad for your health. He would not have blamed the consequences of his bad habit on private enterprise, no matter how much a successful legal claim could bring in court. To him, that would have been the height of hypocrisy.

As it happens, an image of the man and his pipe can be seen in the 190-page book of photographs the Kerbyville Museum published in 2015. On page 133 of the *Historic Images of the Illinois Valley—1870's to Present* is a photograph that includes my father standing by several long-time friends, including former sheriff A. Donley Barnes. The shot was taken in June of 1960. With his pipe held firmly in his left hand, the one missing the thumbnail, Dad seems to be pondering the scene before him. Or he may have been thinking about the cancer already attacking him, a disease which had not yet been diagnosed but would take his life some eight months later.

While he smoked constantly, he took care never to abuse alcohol. Periodically, he had a glass of beer with dinner or occasionally had a beer when his old story-telling friends would drop by. But he didn't consume more than one bottle at a sitting. The only time he deviated from that ritual was after he returned on the Greyhound bus from a trip to Portland to see medical specialists. Upon arriving home, he drove over to the Kerby general store, bought a gallon jug of wine with a screw-on cap, returned home and proceeded to try to drown the cancer with purple alcohol. Drinking the cheap booze had no appreciable impact on the disease but it made for one pickled parent that memorable night.

When you have a father who doesn't generally chat with his offspring, it was a shock to have him getting chummier with each tip of the glass. Mind you, that jug of wine would have laid out Huckleberry Finn's pap, a seasoned swiller who was no stranger to guzzling hooch. Although the brand name is lost in time, its color was reminiscent of concord grapes. Cheap it may have been but it produced a rich state of inebriation, one which included an impassioned spiel on politicians, religious hypocrites and the fine art of rolling your own cigarettes. His offspring was giggling until he wanted to strap on his wooden leg and lurch out to the car to go for a drive. In one of the rare moments in which our family acted as a team, we hid his keys, his wooden leg, crutches and the remainder of the nearly drained jug. Like most folks drinking to excess, he continued bloviating, then promptly fell asleep. As a drunk, he sorely lacked in expertise, something we all appreciated.

The next morning found him sitting sheepishly by the wood stove nursing a cup of steaming coffee as black as obsidian. Nothing was said about him being a drunken buffoon the night before. What we did talk about was his medical condition, albeit in whispers beyond his earshot. By then, we all knew what he had been told by the folks in white coats in Portland: he had cancer. None of us blamed him for getting stupidly drunk. Even as children, we understood he needed an escape from stark reality.

Shortly afterwards he went back to the hospital for an operation to remove the cancer. I assumed he would be cured. After all, here was a man who survived being crushed by a log and losing his leg. He didn't flinch when he sawed off the end of his thumb. As most children looking up at their father, no one could convince me that our dad wasn't the smartest, bravest man on the planet. He was definitely bright and courageous in many ways. He seemed invincible. A pansy little bug wasn't going to take down our dad. No way.

Turns out my faith in him as well as my prayerful entreaties to a higher power were on par with the innocent belief as a child that his leg would grow back. This belief was rooted in an episode in which I grabbed a lizard by the tail and little fellow scurried off, sans his tail. During one of his rare moments of friendliness toward his brother's rambunctious kids, Uncle Charlie explained the tail of a fence lizard would grow back. Losing a tail when grabbed by a predator and escaping helped them survive in the wild, he added. When I asked our older brother if Dad's leg could grow back like a lizard's tail, his answer was a sound cuffing. But I had stubbornly clung to hopes that it could happen.

The operation was not successful. The surgeons opened him up, found him riddled with cancer, performed a colostomy to give them something to do and sewed him back together. He returned home to die.

Before he became largely confined to a hospital bed squeezed into our small living room, he would stand in front of the kitchen sink, fill a glass with water and slowly drink it while gazing out the window at Eight Dollar Mountain rising to 4,001 feet above sea level some two miles to the north. He seemed to stand there forever, thinking. As a child, I often wondered what he was pondering as he gazed at the mountain. Now I have an idea of what was on his troubled mind. He wasn't physically staring at the impressive mountain. He was mentally looking at the world he knew: the Madstone cabin, his siblings, his family. He was staring at the end. He was thinking about the fickleness of life, about leaving behind five young children and a widow whose parenting skills were as questionable as his.

When he felt up to it, he would get on his crutches and make his way to the greenhouse. One day early in November of 1960, he asked me to accompany him. It was a singular honor, escorting Dad out to the one place he dearly loved. Since Dad had never before singled me out, I felt proud.

"I want you to take care of these plants for me until I get better," he told me when we were in the greenhouse. "Do you think you can do that?"

My nine-year-old head bobbed up and down. I followed him around the greenhouse as he talked about the different plants as though they were his children.

"With these orchids here, make sure the soil is always slightly damp," he stressed of the most beautiful of my green siblings. "You don't want to let them dry out. You test the soil with your finger. Don't worry so much about each cactus plant. Cacti prefer drier soil."

After all these years, I remember him using the word "cacti." Although he had only completed the eighth grade, he was self educated and an avid reader, particularly of botany books. He also had that rare trait of thinking before he spoke. Parenthetically, I grew up assuming his bearing reflected the thought processes and behavior of most adults, that responsible, reflective thinking was the norm in adulthood. Buttressing that assumption was the fact his friends were of the same ilk. I shed that mistaken belief when I reached adulthood. A wise old journalism professor of mine at the University of Oregon once dissected the word "assume" to illustrate it can make an "ass" out of "u" and "me."

During the tour of the greenhouse that day, Dad showed me how to bank the fire in the stove at night by stocking it with wood to keep the interior warm when the mercury dropped into the 30s. I already knew how to start a fire in a stove, using crumpled newspapers and kindling.

As we were leaving the greenhouse, he briefly put his hand on my shoulder. I felt my heart swell. In retrospect, I realize he chose me for the task, not because I had ever demonstrated the maturity to handle the job or had displayed any intellect beyond my years, but because I had frequently tagged along after him when he went to the greenhouse. He figured I cared about the plants and that some botanical knowledge must be taking root in my brain.

But the greenhouse duties quickly overwhelmed me. It took more than an hour to water the plants individually so I started spraying them to save time, resulting in some being overwatered while others received only a few drops. Some of the hanging plants I could not reach. On cold evenings, I would get the fire going well enough in the greenhouse but my wood-banking skills were poor at best. One morning before school I went out to check on the plants and found frost inside the greenhouse. When I turned on the garden hose to water the plants, no water flowed. The hose had frozen.

Within a few short weeks, the once overflowing jungle green of the hothouse was speckled with brown patches. Many of his cherished plants were dying. The orchids wilted. The bird of paradise drooped. The greenhouse looked like it had been afflicted with botanical mange as leaves began to drop. The only plant that flourished that holiday season was the barrel cactus whose Christmas cactus blossoms were thriving. I took some solace in its survival but knew, as a greenhouse caretaker, I had fallen woefully short.

One weekend morning early in January of 1961, Dad, already starting to look like a Dachau prisoner, summoned enough strength to pull himself up on his crutches and make what was for him a long forced march to the greenhouse. I meekly followed, knowing he wouldn't be pleased. I was right. He kept shaking his head as he inspected the dying plants he had lovingly cared for. "You let me down," he told me, his deep voice now only little more than a rasping whisper. Feeling miserable, I went outside, fighting a losing battle not to cry. Our dog Willy plopped down at my side, his muzzle resting on his paws. The pooch let out a long sigh to let me know he empathized. Our mother later gave me a hug and said I had done my best. "Your father is hurting right now," she said quietly.

Not long afterwards he gathered us around the hospital bed. I can't remember his exact words, only the feeling of panic that, as dire as things were, they were about to get dramatically worse. My brother Charles recalls what our father said that day.

"I'm dying from cancer," Dad said, according to Charles' memory which tends to be spot on. "Your mother won't be able to take care of you. You are going to have to take care of yourselves when I am gone."

Strong words for a father to use with his young children while their mother stood by with tears in her eyes. The reason I did not remember his words was that, as a notoriously stubborn youngster, I was probably standing there with my arms folded, refusing to accept what he was saying.

Besides, I had a secret weapon. When I crawled into my bunk at night, I had been whispering prayers, besieging a power on high to intervene. Had Uncle Alfred been around to guide me, my prayers would have likely been more professional since he was a faithful practitioner of the ritual. Like Moses in the wilderness, I was lost. But I had seen western movies at the drive-in theater in which a pious pioneer, before standing up to a bullying bad guy in the middle of a dusty main street of some little town, would begin a prayer with the first line of the 23rd Psalm. The prayer, with the aid of a smoking six gun, invariably worked. If such pleas could slay a bullying biped, I figured it could lay low an intimidating illness.

"The Lord is my shepherd, I shall not want," I would start out, then promptly beg for what I did want, namely a father who would continue to live and lead our family. Although I knew even then that our family was dysfunctional, I knew whatever functionality that it had would fade like steam from a teapot after he died. Sometimes my prayers were interrupted by agonizing moans coming through the thin wall separating our little bedroom from the living room as Dad writhed in wracking pain. Still, I pressed on with my quiet entreaties.

When our cousin Frank Cooke, a good fellow who was working as a cook in a local restaurant following a hitch in the Army, brought over an oyster dinner for Dad one night, I figured my prayers were working. After all, Dad sat up in his hospital bed and chatted while he ate. I remember going to bed that night believing the worst was over.

But the next morning found him barely conscious as we walked by his bed to catch the school bus. When I got to class, I couldn't focus on the subject at hand. I was worried and growing angry at the world. No omniscient entity had intervened.

By early February, Dad was receiving a shot of morphine each evening administered by a longtime friend, Arnold N. "Doc" Collman, a kindly naturopathic physician who was the first doctor in the Illinois Valley when he arrived in 1933. The dope worked well at first, putting Dad into a deep sleep. But towards the end it was only effective for a few hours, leaving him to cry out in pain throughout the night. Three days before he died, Dad acquiesced to our mother's pleas and allowed a minister to make a house call. Dad and the preacher man talked for a bit before the latter prayed over him and left. I fervently hoped his prayers would be more successful than mine. As for Dad's death bed conversion, I've always figured it was for insurance purposes.

Dad was not the only one suffering. For the rest of the family, life was also a living hell. Our mother cried continuously. Sleep became impossible; school offered no respite. I quit praying and wanted Dad's suffering to end, knowing down deep that death would be his only release. My wish that it would end left me guilt-ridden for years. I remember hugging Willy, burying my face in his fur neck and sobbing.

There must have been other times but I only recall once ever giving my father a hug. It was on the morning of Feb. 16, 1961, a day that dawned dark and drizzly. We quietly filed past his hospital bed en route to catch the school bus that would stop in front of our house. By then, the shrunken body that was our father breathed in labored gasps. I remember being afraid but, like the rest of my siblings, hugged him at the urging of our mother. She knew something we did not: he would not last the day. It was the last time I saw him alive, a memory which hangs like a shroud.

Unfortunately, the worst day of our childhood was about to get worse. I couldn't pay attention in class. During recess, I wandered around by myself, wondering if it would be better if Dad died. I immediately felt guilty and tears started rolling down my cheeks. When a friend came over to ask what was wrong, I walked away, unable to speak.

After school let out that afternoon, our bus headed north with its load of boisterous kids. It was around 3:30 p.m. that the bus began slowing down for our stop. Even before it stopped I could see what looked like a long black station wagon backed up to our front door. Curtains hung inside the rear of the sleek vehicle.

"What's that hearse doing at your house?" asked an older kid, tugging at my sleeve as I stumbled past him. I didn't answer the obvious.

Our mother and Delores, who had stayed home that day, came out to meet us brothers. As they all hugged in a little circle and cried together, I stood off to the side, my fists clinched and my jaw set, angry at our dad for not beating cancer and at a supposed loving god who could allow so much suffering. My disillusionment was complete. When I interviewed our mom when she was in her nineties, she said the funeral home had promised her the hearse would be gone before the bus arrived. It broke her heart when she saw the bus pull up while the hearse was still in the front yard, she said, adding, "I've always regretted you kids had to see that."

Many funeral experts—namely folks who sell funeral packages—will tell you the ritual is a healthy experience that provides closure. Although I have attended many funerals in which that is the case, our father's funeral was not one of them. It began with the same preacher who had visited him speaking for a few minutes about the deceased being a warm and loving father and family man who was bound for heaven. Never mind he didn't know the atheist in the open casket. While our dad was certainly a good man, the preacher's remarks dripped with insincerity. The organist offered some solace by playing "Twilight on the Trail" and "Indian Love Call," two of our father's favorite tunes. After the services, the family was invited to view the body, something Jim and I refused to do. A well-meaning maternal uncle grabbed us each by an arm and tried to usher us forward. I remember grabbing him by the leg and holding on while Jim tussled with his arms. Figuring a kerfuffle at a funeral was very bad form, the uncle wisely untangled himself and escorted our other willing siblings to the casket. Jim and I returned to our seats. Things didn't get any better at the graveside services, although I was proud to see that among the pallbearers were A. Donley Barnes, Keith Owen and Al Hobart, a botanist friend with whom Dad had spent many happy forays in the mountains. But Mother Nature was weeping prodigiously that day, having lost someone who cared about her plant kingdom. The rain pouring down on the cemetery filled the open grave with murky water, a sight which caused an involuntary shudder when I saw it. Knowing the sight of grown men trying to sink a bobbing casket into a water-filled grave was too ghoulish for five little kids to watch, the cemetery crew kindly waited until we left before plunging ahead with the job. All in all, it was a ghastly day offering precious little closure.

Our father's only siblings to attend the funeral were Aunt Laura and Uncle Charlie. Nary a word was heard from Uncle Alfred.

MADSTONE

NINE

Wild and Poor

L IFE WAS ALREADY GRIM ENOUGH BEFORE our father's suffering ended, but it quickly became apparent it was a stroll in the park on a sunny Sunday morning when compared to the ensuing stormy years of our childhood. As a single parent of five, our kind-hearted but poorly educated mom was woefully unprepared for the challenges ahead. She quickly became overwhelmed and withdrew into herself during that dark and dreary period, leaving her offspring to fend for themselves.

In all fairness, her unpreparedness was in part because our father had never let her voice be heard when it came to making decisions which would impact the family. In turn, he was simply following in the footsteps of Fattig tradition. His father, reputedly a fellow of strong character who did not tolerate second-guessing from women folk, firmly believed the man of the house was the sole decision maker. In his world, women cooked, bore children and did housework. Like his forefathers before him, Dad, despite being progressive in some ways, had been a natural-born Neanderthal when it came to family governance.

To his credit, our father managed to balance our exceedingly tight budget of some $200 a month from his Social Security income and the occasion plant he sold from his little nursery during the last years of his life. With seven family members, that was no small accomplishment, even for the late 1950s and the dawn of the '60s when prices were far lower than today. However, to reiterate, his lone management style of keeping his significant other in the dark left us all in the lurch.

Ignoring the injustice in the autocratic father-knows-best approach—my wife and daughters would have removed body parts sans painkiller had I even joked about following such a cretin path—there is the very obvious problem: the family unit collapses into anarchy when the lone decision maker is no longer there. Having been treated as little more than a child, our mother was like a deer caught in the headlights of life. While she tried to cope, she was quickly overwhelmed.

Yet she did her best to improve our financial status, including some babysitting to help make ends meet. Unfortunately, the ends seldom met. Since Mom didn't know how to drive, she sold the ugly Plymouth to raise a little cash shortly after Dad died. A trusting and naive soul, she gave the keys, title and car to a weasel of a fellow who assured her he would pay for it with his next paycheck. You guessed it. Snidely Whiplash never got around to paying the widow Fattig with five young children. But she just knew in her innocent heart that he would one day be good for the debt. Had there been railroad tracks running through Kerby, Mr. Whiplash would have gleefully tied her to the rails.

When you are poor, life is largely by rote. Each destitute day is as bleak as the one before. Like some suffering dog that has been beaten by its cowardly owner, you cower throughout the day. There is little to look forward to, nothing to keep hope alive. When your clothes wore out, you continued wearing them. We would wear what our sister called "talking shoes," footwear whose soles flapped after separating from the upper portion. Our knees peeked through our pant legs. When the weather was really bad, I had to stay indoors during recess at school because I didn't have a jacket.

But my worst memory of being poor popped up during a Christmas play directed by Eileen Orton, one of my favorite elementary school teachers. I was proud when she gave me a small part which called for me to step forward and declare, "This play has been brought to you by Sog, the soggy breakfast cereal." At that point I would then whip out a concealed arrow, pretend to have been shot and flop down. I loved that line. But, as with all things related to arrows in my young life, it did not have a happy ending. The day before the play was to be performed, the well-meaning teacher announced that all the boys in the play had to wear white shirts with collars. I had no white shirt, except for a T-shirt that was originally white but had turned creamy over time. When I told our mom I needed a white shirt, she sadly responded we could not afford one. As a result, I didn't show up for the play that evening. The next school day a concerned Mrs. Orton asked me why I wasn't there. I told her I was sick, too embarrassed to tell her we were too poor to buy a white shirt. In retrospect, she must have guessed the truth.

There were few jobs to be had for kids in Kerby but Jim bucked hay on the Sauer ranch during the summers and we three smaller brothers were hired out to pull weeds from neighbors' gardens and flower patches. The princely weeding wage was .25 cents an hour. I was fired from my first weeding job for lack of progress but Charles was a weed-pulling phenomenon whose reputation for tenacity grew like, well, a weed. Weeds all but jumped out of the ground and fled at the mention of his name. We also filled gunny sacks with bottles found along Highway 199, lugging them to the Kerby general store to exchange them for cash, the same place where our draft-dodging uncles had traded in fur and gold for groceries during their Madstone years. Parenthetically, the Oregon Bottle Bill of 1971, requiring all pop and beer bottles to be returnable with a minimum refund, stopped many folks from thoughtlessly tossing bottles from speeding cars. It helped clean up Oregon's highways and byways, albeit probably left some gunny-sack toting kids grumbling.

Our family remained among the poorest of the poor, no mean feat in a time and place where the breadwinner was invariably a logger or sawmill worker doing hard time in the physically demanding toil of converting trees into lumber. These were tough men with calluses on their hands as rough as coarse sandpaper. Many of them worked hard, fought hard and drank hard. Only those who didn't let booze dictate their lives were able to carve out a decent life in the woods or mill for their families.

Without a breadwinner, drunk or sober, we were destitute. He would have been a better student had he not been too poor to pay attention, our wisenheimer older brother liked to quip. The humor helped. Besides, he could poke fun at himself because he was an apt pupil when he applied himself.

When the weather was as cold and bleak as our existence, books became our escape. Dad had left a number of botanical books but his little library also contained several volumes of literature, including Homer's Odyssey. Although it was the English translation, the epic poem proved hard slogging for my limited juvenile vocabulary, sometimes requiring several attempts at a passage before I got the gist. But it was a good read once I started down the trail of the 3,000-year-old adventure and got the cast of characters and gods relatively straight in my mind. Kerby was my Ithaca; Oregon my Greece. But I wondered why Penelope didn't demand that Odysseus quell his wanderlust or get lost permanently. At the very least, I expected her to boot out the suitors and become a strong queen. Sadly, it seems ancient Greeks subscribed to the same school of thought as the patriarchal Fattigs of yore.

Upon having read everything at home, I pored over the books in the little Kerby Elementary School library. Mrs. Orton often served as the librarian during our lunch break and was always happy to suggest a book to take home on a Friday. I spent many a wet winter weekend happily escaping reality with Tom Sawyer and Huckleberry Finn. As a fan of Mark Twain, I was thrilled when brother Jim, then a sophomore in high school, brought home a copy of *A Connecticut Yankee in King Arthurs Court* from his school library. When he finished it, I surreptitiously borrowed it and began reading. After a few days, he started looking for it because the book was overdue. I kept it hidden until I was done reading it, then placed it strategically behind a couch cushion where a puzzled big brother would discover it and sheepishly return it to the library. It wasn't Twain's best but it was excellent reading for a young lad desperate to escape the confines of Kerby.

By now, you're probably thinking I must have been a good student. Not so. I was just a daydreamer who loved to read when I wasn't fishing or camping. Homework was largely ignored. Give me Jack London's *White Fang* or John Steinbeck's *Travels with Charlie* and I focused on the subject at hand. But Lorna Byrne's math class and Don Orton's English lessons left a jumbled pile of long division and dangling participles clogging my mind. Good teachers both, they no doubt rued the day I came to class.

Without books, we were little more than doing time in the little gray house that was our prison cell. Since we had no television at the time, I always pretended to know what the other kids were talking about when they mentioned a popular TV program. It wasn't until our maternal grandmother bought a color television that she bequeathed her old black and white one to us. Chuckle all you want but we thought we were in the money.

For entertainment at school, playing marbles during recess was one of my favorite entertainments. Because we had no toys to speak of at home, I took playing marbles seriously. I performed well enough to not only keep my marbles but acquire more. I can honestly say I didn't lose all my marbles until adulthood. Kerby marbles were usually carried in a spare sock, preferably a white gym sock, although most of them had long lost their whiteness. These socks tended to get a little gamey, especially down around the toes.

The rules of the game were somewhat flexible, depending on the whims of the kid who was the biggest and baddest. Not being either, I didn't make the rules. The game always started with someone drawing a circle on the ground with a stick. The goal was to use your favorite shooter to dislodge the marbles each player put in the circle. It ended when all the original marbles were knocked out of the circle or a fight broke out, whichever came first.

The language of those who played with marbles could best be described as onomatopoeic, albeit hinging on sight rather than sound. The marble's moniker reflected what it looked like while the name of the play reflected what was happening. For instance, "aggies" were marbles made of agate. A glass marble made to look like agate was called an "immie," short for imitation. Clear glass marbles were called "clearies," steel marbles were dubbed "steelies." If you were playing for keeps, it was called "keepsies." That was for all the marbles. On the other hand, if you weren't playing for keeps, it was just "funsies." An angry kid losing the game often suddenly insisted at the end that it had only been for funsies all along, triggering a fight. It really smarts to be smacked in the face by a sock loaded with marbles, by the way.

When Kerby kids were not playing marbles outside in the late 1950s, they were farther afield in the great outdoors, including the river and the rugged mountains. Since we had no supervision at our home after Dad died, we were left to explore the wilderness behind our back door at will.

Sometimes our wayward ways required a visit to Doc Collman for a little stitching or have a foreign object removed from our person. Had you been paying attention, you would have remembered him as the elderly fellow who kindly visited our father in his dying days. George once sliced open his belly an inch or two during some wild adventure and, while there were no protruding intestines, it was decided he be taken to the good doctor to have it stitched up. The problem was that he—the doctor, not George—had been imbibing a bit as was his habit. George was too scared to watch the sewing process and was heartened when doc told him he was just about done. That's when George looked down and saw there was no thread in the needle. The process was repeated, this time with the requisite thread. Doc Collman also cut a fishhook out of my head following a particularly bad cast by yours truly. We were both sober at the time of the hook removal.

As for drinking booze, I did not get drunk until I was at the ripe old age of twelve. A friend of Jim's named Tom—no last names, given our society's litigious nature—gave my twin and me a ride in his car and figured it would be entertaining to offer us a nip or two from a cheap bottle of wine he happened to have. By the time he dropped us off at our house that evening, Jim's youngest twin siblings were snockered. I didn't think it was all that fun, particularly the projectile vomiting. That episode could be why I was never a big fan of alcohol, although, much to my regret, I would periodically abuse it through my teenage years. Nor was our mom impressed that evening, although she looked after us until we slept it off. I could tell she was very upset because she swore several times. Her swearing consisted of, "Oh, poop!"

Not a few of our neighbors watching us through windows from behind their locked doors during those years assumed the Fattig boys would be doing ten to fifteen in the state pen one day, providing we somehow managed to survive our teens. Delores was not a troublemaker, I hasten to add. I am proud to say that only two of us ever did any time behind bars. We'll get to that in the following chapter.

While we won't go into all of our juvenile shenanigans—we'll save the teenage years for another book—I'll wet your whistle with one telling anecdote which you should never, ever try to duplicate. Don't try it at home, don't try it anywhere. It was idiocy on steroids.

Jim had acquired another bow and a quiver of arrows but didn't play William Tell with them, something one of the younger twins really appreciated. However, he found another pastime that was arguably more dangerous. Through some illicit means, he became the proud owner of several sticks of dynamite, complete with fuse and caps. A creative fellow, he figured dynamite could provide interesting amusement. Admittedly, his younger brothers were enthusiastically culpable in this dangerous endeavor. Thus we were eagerly anticipating the New Year's Eve in which our version of a proper celebration would be launched.

We retreated a little toward the river, not out of concern we may blow out the windows of the already nervous neighbors, but to give us a chance of escaping into the woods should the law be summoned. Jim obviously had no expertise as a powder monkey—the fellow who blows up stumps in the logging woods with dynamite—but someone apparently told him how to set off the dynamite. Or he may have just winged it. He cut a slice off a dynamite stick, shoved a short fuse into a cap and pushed the cap into the dynamite. Encouraged by the fact he had not lost his hands in an explosive flash, he then taped the explosive device onto the business end of the arrow. You can guess where there is going, right? The young archer took up his bow, attached the arrow and pulled back, holding the position while one of us—I believe I was the only one dumb enough—lit the fuse. He let fly.

If you were watching from, say, a quarter of a mile away, you would have seen something sparkling streaking into the night sky, followed by a flash and bang. Ah, New Year's Eve fireworks, you would have concluded. It would have impressed folks who go in for that sort of thing. We juveniles were thrilled.

While we were not acquainted with the laws of physics, we had deduced that if one small piece of dynamite provided a small bang, a larger chunk would result in a bigger bang. Call it our Kerby version of the Big Bang theory. We were up to about a half stick of dynamite when it happened. Once again Jim pulled back and let fly. Only this time there was no sparkling streak across the dark sky. Even the dynamite challenged among us knew this was not a happy development. That's when we heard the telltale sound that is somewhat reminiscent of a hissing cat, a very angry hissing cat. Most troubling was the fact the sound was coming from the ground upon which we stood. The dynamite had not been properly taped to its mother ship for the short flight. The fuse, still firmly attached to cap and the half stick of nitroglycerin, was hissing at our feet.

The young Fattig brothers ran shrieking into the night, scrambling through brush and over rocks to get away from the imminent explosion. Kaboom! Standing perhaps 100 feet away, I didn't not know if all, or any, of my brothers survived. Jim called out. We all answered, although I believe George was a little deaf for a time, having run into a wall of brush which didn't allow him to get far enough away from the thunderous noise.

I would like to say we stopped our dangerous enterprise then and there but that was not the case. We experimented with dynamite a bit more, including employing it to fish for salmon. Like all poaching scofflaws, we referred to a stick of nitroglycerin as a Dupont spinner. Again, I bring this up only as a gauge of our unbridled childhood and am not suggesting such behavior be emulated. I do not look back on it with pride.

Nor am I proud that we often hunted out of season, albeit out of necessity. When the cupboards were bare, Jim, with his three younger brothers tagging along to serve as hunting dogs, would go in search of game. The local game warden, no doubt responding to complaints of deer poaching, would periodically stop at our house to inquire if we had been hunting illegally. He was polite enough, just doing his job. He once asked me to open the refrigerator which I did. When he glanced in, he saw nearly empty shelves, a sight that caused him to shake his head and leave. Fortunately for us, his timing was always off.

You get the gist. Unless Donald Duck and Mickey Mouse have taken to carrying firearms and playing with dynamite, our childhood on the edge of the Madstone country was no Disneyland.

But I was proud of our ability to hike into the mountains and survive with little more than a rifle or fishing rod and a few matches. OK, we did cheat by carrying one blanket. We would cut some boughs to serve as a mattress and share the blanket. If you were in the middle, you were relatively warm. But the little brothers on the outside usually woke up shivering with no blanket, unless a skunk or porcupine decided to cozy up to us. We would tell our mother roughly where we were going and approximately when we would return, give or take a few days.

While most of our trips are lodged only in our memories, one can be found in the Sept. 24, 1962, issue of the *Medford Mail Tribune.* It happens to be the paper I would retire from more than half a century later.

"Charles, George, Paul and Jim Fattig and Charles Hoover of Kerby, together with Jim and Doc Cooke of O'Brien, made a 'survival' trip into the Baldface Creek area week before last," wrote Illinois Valley correspondent Letha Cooke in the page six article. "It was a survival trip because the committee in charge of groceries and supplies forgot to bring bread and hot-cake flour, the two most important staple items."

As mentioned earlier, Letha was our aunt married to Jim Cooke, our favorite maternal uncle who periodically took us hunting or fishing. He was the one who forgot the aforementioned items, causing us to fast a bit in the wilderness. Their son, Jim "Doc" Cooke, was our cousin. A couple of months younger than me, he was a childhood chum during my formative years of hunting and fishing.

The Baldface Creek drainage was also an area that our draft-dodging uncles periodically visited during their forays away from the Madstone cabin. It should be noted they rarely had bread or pancake mix.

On one camping excursion, we hiked to the top of Canyon Peak where a fire lookout stood, although the U.S. Forest Service no longer used it and would later move the lookout building to another peak to the southeast. As we stood on the decking skirting the lookout, Jim pointed to a distant spot across the rugged terrain. That was where our uncles had hid out in the remote Madstone cabin to escape the draft during World War I, he said. We talked about hiking to the area but, in one of our rare moments, let common sense dictate our decision. The cabin site was more than a dozen miles to the west by foot over extremely rough country and we were already that far from home. We looked at the blue-green mountains in the distance for a while and talked about how they must have lived nearly half a century earlier. With that, we started hiking down our back trail.

But I told myself that one day I would explore that rugged country and find the Madstone cabin.

TEN

Running Away to Madstone Country

"RUNNING AWAY" IS A MISNOMER. It's a fair bet that most urchins don't run away from home when they decide to flee the nest. Even as a kid, you realize that running on a long journey is not practical. So you throw a few clothes into a small bag—in my case it was a musty gunny sack—and simply walk away, knowing full well it is going to take a while to find a better life. You take it one step at a time without giving a lot of thought about your ultimate destination. Nor do you have a precise idea of what you are going to do. There is no strategic plan.

All you know is that one morning you wake up and decide you cannot stand one more day in purgatory that is the confines of your impoverished childhood home. That is the morning you walk away, afraid yet optimistic you can improve your lot in life.

For the Fattigs of Kerby, the early 1960s was filled with a series of terrible events: our father died in February of 1961, the Columbus Day storm of 1962 devastated the region, President John F. Kennedy was assassinated on Nov. 22, 1963, and the massive December 1964 flood brought four feet of water into our house when the Illinois River flowed in for a visit. We'll overlook the other lesser calamities and misfortunes, all mired in a quagmire of unrelenting poverty.

Chief among the physical disasters was the flood which caused us to move in with our compassionate cousin Frank Cooke and his young family in downtown Kerby, no doubt causing them discomfort and hardships. After two long months, our mom found a small house for us to rent in Kerby. We were shaken by the flood but back in our own house by late spring, quietly resuming the status quo of poverty. Unlike a fire which leaves little more than ashes, a flood doesn't play for keeps. Our ramshackle house and its ratty contents survived the floodwaters. A half century later, we still have flood-stained ancestral photographs. Unfortunately, we don't know who most the people in the old pictures are because no one thought to write identifications on the back. Judging from the furrowed brows, they appear to be relatives in the form of either Fattigs or Cookes prior to our parents' arrival on the planet. Hopefully the unidentified ancestors were not married since that would point toward cross breeding in the family tree, something frowned upon even in Kerby back in those distant times.

Throwing JFK's murder into the mix may seem like a reach but the charismatic and sophisticated president offered a rare ray of sunshine for a young country bumpkin out in rural Oregon. Kennedy was vibrant, confident and full of optimism. I was ecstatic he had been elected. Never mind that our father, a staunch Democrat, had turned away from the party of his choice and voted for Richard Nixon in the 1960 general election, the last vote he would cast. His concern was that Pope John XXIII would hold sway over Kennedy's presidency because the Democratic candidate was Catholic. Although I was a kid who didn't know squat about politics, I recall raising my young eyebrows over Dad's rationale. Even to a child, it seemed irrational.

From my perspective, one ray of sunshine shining through during this dark period was the congressional passage of the 1964 Wilderness Act which included the Kalmiopsis Wilderness Area whose later expansion ultimately covered some 180,000 acres in southwest Oregon. This spanking new wilderness area was just out our back door, after you forded the river and climbed a few mountains, that is. It fairly beckoned anyone with a yearning for the wild.

As usual with legislation which seeks to preserve a natural area for future generations, it caused a rift in the local social fabric. Some folks, particularly those who wanted the area left open for mining and logging ventures, were incensed. But others, including hunters, hikers, fishing enthusiasts and those interested in indigenous plants, were tickled since it meant that not all federal lands in southwest Oregon would be opened to large-scale resource degradation. I recall my older brother, a future logger and the one from whom I took my political cues at the time, supported the new wilderness. Tacking the label "wilderness" onto an area definitely adds a certain gravitas as well as a protective regulatory shield. Uncle Alfred fairly beamed when Jim and I told him about the wilderness encasing the upper reaches of the Chetco River where he once roamed as a wanted man nearly seventy years century earlier.

For smack in the middle of the wilderness is the Madstone cabin site. By 1965, with the wilderness' designation in place, my desire to explore that wild country, already pushed by my longing to escape from our family's prison of poverty, was bursting at the seams.

Like all juveniles who opt to leave home, I didn't give any thought to the consequences. I did not think about how our gentle mom would worry or if my siblings would feel abandoned or embarrassed. I knew that Jim, who had become our father figure, would be concerned, although he had graduated from high school the previous spring and had fully fledged the Kerby nest. Having outgrown his penchant for shooting arrows into the head of one younger brother and playing with dynamite, he was well on his way to becoming a decent fellow. After having been presented the scenario and mulling it over at considerable length with chin in hand, a veteran psychologist would likely come up with the theory that losing the second father figure triggered my juvenile decision to leave. I don't know if I would buy that white-coat conclusion but I know I felt free to hit the trail. Constraints I had none.

In retrospect, I had no practical plan of action. There was no realistic strategy for eating regularly. I didn't even consider how a police officer might react upon spotting a youngster with a gunny sack slung over his back hiking along a road while everyone his age was in school. I just assumed that my excursion, like our camping trips to the edges of the wilderness, would somehow work out.

After all, among the books our dad had left was an old hardback—its title has long been lost to memory—by a fellow who preached the benefits of camping without the comforts of a sleeping bag, cooking utensils or packaged food. The author, whose likeness was revealed in the book with a drawing depicting an elderly gentleman with a long gray beard, built a little lean-to covered by conifer boughs over a nest of leaves and grass. His mouth-watering meals were roasted on a wooden spit over coals or in tightly woven baskets placed on rocks near the campfire. Abundant food was out there, from trout caught by a net woven from vines to edible plants growing wild, he promised the reader. He made it seem as though the woods teemed with rabbits just waiting to hop in a snare for your dinner.

With Gray Beard's literary guidance, my cross-country trek looked astonishingly easy. You took a few minutes to make a comfortable camp, spent a few more minutes gathering food and cooking it, then napped or explored the day away. Nothing to it. Here was a fellow who could have taught that Huckleberry lad a thing or two about living in the wild. His life was nothing more than free shopping at Mother Nature's supermarket, followed by cooking a natural barbecue on glowing orange coals and slumbering under the conifer bough canopy. As a youngster, I figured that's how my uncles lived while out on the trail before returning to the luxury of their mountain retreat. I could just imagine the two cooking bountiful meals, discussing deep philosophical questions in front of a crackling campfire at night and happily falling asleep in comfortable beds under the twinkling stars. While poring over the book, I couldn't wait to emulate Gray Beard's approach to roughing it.

I conveniently overlooked the fact most of the childhood camping forays with my brothers were invariably hair-raising affairs in which we staggered home hungry, bruised and scratched as well as a little shocked we had once again survived. We had gone hungry, slept miserably and had occasional brushes with fear in the form of a feisty rattlesnake or an unseen menace in the darkness lurking beyond a smoky campfire. Nor did I give any thought to the fact I was not a particularly brave soul, especially when it came to camping alone deep in a wilderness.

Yet I would not be alone. I would have a companion in the hairy form of Willy, our little red dog. He wasn't much bigger than a red fox he resembled but the lion-hearted mutt was always eager to trot off on an adventure down the Illinois River or into the rugged mountains. His furry face would break into a tongue-lolling, idiotic grin, his tail would wave like someone hailing an old friend and his ears would perk up like a rabbit's every time I called him for a walk into the woods. He had a happy-to-be-here attitude. He loved me. And I loved my furry pal.

Like all creatures, including humanoids, Willy had a few troublesome traits. His greatest delight in life was rolling in a pile of cow flop, the riper the better. If there were no bovine pies to be found, his other relished activity was leading me on fishing and exploring excursions. But this time we were going beyond the nearby Illinois River deep into the mountain wilderness to follow the remote Chetco River through the wilderness to the ocean. Had he known this, the knowledge would have sent him chasing his tail with excitement until he collapsed from exhaustion with a cow-pie eating grin on his face.

But he was a game little guy. Back in the Kerby Elementary School library, I had read books by the likes of Jack London and John Steinbeck which featured dogs. Willy was no White Fang, wild dog of the north, but he was a fearless little fellow. I knew he would stand beside me in times of danger. In Steinbeck's *Travels with Charley*, the author and his dog Charley traveled in a pickup and jerry-rigged camper, a man and his pooch off to become reacquainted with the Lower 48 in 1960. Willy may not have been a pureblood in the form of a French poodle but he was an all-American mutt. If the writer and his French friend could try to discover the real America on a country-wide trek, I figured a juvenile country rube and his mongrel on their six feet could go in search of the elephant in southwest Oregon.

Willy was about six years old at the time, making him roughly forty-two in human-year equivalency if you accept the theoretical 7-to-1 ratio of aging between boy and his best friend. Being that I had turned fourteen that summer, it would follow that I was two years old in dog years. Therefore, it should be obvious to any fair-minded adult that it was the forty-two-year-old canine smelling strongly of fresh cow pie who led the wide-eyed biped pup astray.

And so it was in early September of 1965, I walked away from home in hopes of finding a better situation. For the first time in my life, I was facing the world alone. There were no twins around, no big brother, no parent. It was with mixed feelings of exhilaration and excitement coupled with trepidation and vulnerability that I left. With Willy trotting ahead of me, occasionally stopping to whiz on a bush, I stepped out, hoping for the best. One thing I knew was that once I made my mind up, there would be no turning back. Stubborn was my middle name.

Yet I felt I was finally tough enough to survive my long-awaited quest into the Madstone country and beyond. As I walked, a makeshift plan began to form in my teenage brain. After checking out the cabin, perhaps staying there for a bit, I would head north to Alaska where my father and uncles had lived in the 1930s. Perhaps I could track down my great uncle Jay Cooke whose wife, Fanny, was a native lady from Alaska. He had made a name for himself—at least within the family—as a world-class dog musher and trapper. They had visited our house about a year earlier and had been very friendly. The old musher and his pleasant wife had cheerfully answered my barrage of questions about the Last Frontier. Maybe I could stay with them until I got on my feet, I thought. Then, having made my fortune in the Last Frontier, I would send money to our mom back in Kerby.

As it happens, when my brother Charles took a solo hike to the Madstone cabin site in the early 1980s, becoming the first Fattig to return to the area since our uncles left it shortly after World War I, he found the cabin long gone. There were only a couple of charred logs, a rusting frying pan and bits of broken glass turning purple with age. Charles had corresponded with Alfred via letters for several years before I began communicating with our uncle. I would not hike into the site until the late 1980s, accompanied by a wilderness ranger for the then Siskiyou National Forest. Later, I survived another forced march into the site with brother Jim and his son, Todd. Later still, during my research for this book, I would learn the cabin had likely been destroyed by fire, probably during the 1940s or early '50s. In addition, not only was the Madstone cabin no longer there when I ran away from home, but Jay and Fanny Cooke had already moved down to Seattle where they would live out their retirement years.

Of course, I knew none of this back in 1965. Like Gray Beard's book, my provisional plan didn't have any flaws as it flitted happily through my immature brain like a butterfly floating on a warm spring breeze. Unfortunately, as I learned in college French, reality has a nasty habit of nipping one on the derrière.

It wasn't just the big things that would cause problems. Even a cub scout could have told me I wasn't prepared when it came to the bare necessities needed for surviving in a wilderness. But I would have waved off such concerns. Flashlight? Now why would I bother with a flashlight when I had campfire light? Map? Pshaw, I didn't need a map. All I had to do was follow the headwaters down to the Chetco River, spot the cabin and rest for a bit. Surely there would be a sign reading, "Madstone Cabin 200 yards." After resting, Willy and I would saunter down river to the ocean where we would turn right and stroll up north to Alaska. How would we get there? Again, mere details. Yep, everything was going to work out just fine.

What I did have was a cheap fishing pole and spinning reel with a few lures, a frying pan, a small hunting knife, wooden matches, a small container of salt and an old sweater should the weather turn cold. I was wearing old tennis shoes, worn blue jeans and a T-shirt that had once been white. I was not prepared for a picnic, let alone a cross country trek through a rugged wilderness. Along with my four-legged companion, what I did have in over-flowing abundance was doggedness.

Having cast prudence and common sense aside, I looked forward to the adventures waiting around each bend of the distant Chetco River tumbling through the mountain wilderness. With the warm Indian Summer sun on my back and Willy trotting alongside, I almost felt giddy the first day out.

But that feeling faded to hunger by late that afternoon. Grey Beard may have made it seem like you can feast every day in the wild but he apparently didn't account for a boy and his dog, both of whom are little more than walking stomachs. And both our stomachs were growling.

We were on the side of a mountain halfway to Babyfoot Lake, a small lake carved out by a glacier during the last ice age. I knew I could catch some trout at the picturesque lake but we wouldn't reach the body of water until the next day. Those fat trout would have to wait.

So I sat down to rest and mull over our situation under a small oak tree as the sun began to drop behind the mountain. A large Stellars jay, the kind with the dark blue topnotch reminiscent of a punk rocker, flew into the branches just above me. He kept hopping around the tree and peering down, checking out the young humanoid and his hairy little companion. Apparently not impressed by what he saw, the cocky fellow began scolding us in the slightly annoying way unique to jays.

It was not the scolding but the thought of fried drumsticks which fired me up. I picked up small rocks and started hurling them at the bird which continued to reprimand us while hopping from limb to limb. He seemed curious as the missiles whistling past, sometimes cocking his head as if to question the strange actions of the lad standing below him. After years of practice, I had a good throwing arm. It wasn't long before my aim was true. The cold-cocked bird literally fell at my feet.

I started a campfire and proceeded to pluck and gut our dinner guest as Willy looked on. After washing the carcass in a little spring whose waters ran clear, I cut out the drumsticks and the breast meat. It wasn't much but it fried up rather nice, smelled good and helped satiate our appetites. Yes, it tasted like chicken, albeit a very small chicken. Make that a squab.

Fast forward to the future and Uncle Alfred would tell us of lean meals during his stay in the wilderness but he never mentioned having feasted on a jay. Perhaps he had pushed such memories to the deep recesses of his mind. My recollection of eating that small fowl never took flight. Nor would I ever forget my disillusionment with Gray Beard and his false promises. I quickly lost my fussiness when it comes to gastronomic fare that I would have ordinarily have never munched on, including blackberries that were well beyond ripe. Willy started glancing at me over his shoulder, probably worried his young master would suddenly develop a taste for leg-of-canine grilled over a campfire.

We were exhausted when we reached Babyfoot Lake the second day out but I caught half a dozen Eastern Brook trout which had been stocked in the lake years before. These are fine fish with pink flesh. Although the ones I caught were not large, they were plentiful. We both ate our fill that night. I had no butter or cooking oil but I found that the trout cooked with a little water in a frying pan were edible, albeit a bit mushy. The salt helped, of course.

Having stepped in fresh bear scat on the trail leading to the lake, I was apprehensive about an uninvited visitor as darkness descended. I dragged a couple of small logs up near our campfire and made a short wall. With the campfire in front and the logs behind me, I felt somewhat protected. Despite being appointed to stand guard duty, Willy curled up and slept beside me on our bed of green boughs.

After catching a few more trout the next morning, we left the lake, heading down the trail to an old jeep road which led to a high shoulder on Canyon Peak before dipping down into the Little Chetco River drainage. It was the road my brothers and I had taken to Canyon Peak lookout a few years earlier.

Upon reaching the jeep road, I could hear human voices coming up from the canyon floor several hundred yards below. Peeking over the edge of the road, I saw two men panning for gold in Babyfoot Creek which flows out of the lake and eventually into the little river. They seemed to be arguing, probably having growing tired of each other's company. The smaller one was badgering the larger fellow unmercifully but the big guy was giving back nearly as good as he got.

Miners or not, I didn't want to be confronted by the two fellows since they may have wanted to take me and the pooch back to Kerby. Minding me for once and refraining from barking, Willy was ready to move on when I quietly turned and whispered for him to follow me up the road. A couple of hundred yards farther along, we came upon the miners' campsite, including their tent. No one was around.

Already hungry from our morning hike, I decided to check out the miners' lean camp for any food they may not need. When I stepped inside the tent I saw what I considered a veritable feast: two loaves of white bread along with several cans of sardines and a couple of cans of chili. In addition, there were two cots with sleeping bags on them, a flashlight, an open carton of Marlboros containing two packs of cigarettes and a few other grocery items.

I'm not offering it as an excuse, but the dog and I had not had anything to eat beyond blackberries, trout and jay since leaving home. With Willy egging me on, I decided the miners did not need one loaf of bread, three cans of sardines and a can of chili. I looked longingly at a sleeping bag and the flashlight but figured that was moving from misdemeanor thievery to felonious behavior. However, having been told that a cigarette will take the edge off hunger pains, I used my light-finger discount in the tent to purchase one pack of Marlboros. My rationale that it would reduce the miners' chances of getting cancer did not quell my conscience.

With our ill-gotten gains in the gunny sack, we hotfooted it up the jeep road, heading deeper into the wilderness. There had been no vehicle near the tent but the miners may have had one parked a mile or so back down the road at the locked gate intended to block motor vehicles from entering the wilderness area. Back then, just as they do now, scofflaws often drove around locked gates to access protected areas.

It would have been interesting to have been a fly on the tent wall when the miners returned that evening to discover the missing items and started accusing each other. Chances are the bickering reached fisticuff stage. I hoped it didn't come to gun play.

Within a few hours, we reached the point where the road crested the north shoulder of Canyon Peak, which rises to 4,903 feet above sea level just inside the eastern edge of the wilderness. As I rested, I recall looking at Pearsoll Peak, another high mountain with a fire lookout some seven miles north as the crow flies. Although I had not been to the lookout at that point, I knew my father had helped build Pearsoll Peak lookout around 1930. The thought gave me some comfort.

Unbeknown to me at the time, my name was chiseled deep into a rock the size of a refrigerator a few feet east of the lookout. When our dad and longtime friend Art Cribb—whose home Dad visited when he was trying out his driving prowess in the Plymouth after losing his leg— were fellow U.S. Forest Service employees around 1930, they were deployed to the mountaintop to help build the lookout. While waiting for mules to haul lumber to the mountaintop, which rises to 5,098 feet, they had time on their calloused hands. They also had tools, including hammers and chisels. The young men began carving their names into the large boulder. As one named after his father, although I never attached the junior appendage to my by-line while working as a journalist, I would appear to anyone visiting the lookout years later as the culprit. While working as a journalist in the region, I periodically got a call from an unhappy Pearsoll Peak visitor asking why I had the impudence to carve my name on the prominent peak. I would explain the graffiti was done by my father but it never seemed to lessen the anger on the other end of the phone.

As an aside, I have a photograph of our father taken during the same era he and others built the lookout. He was working in the then Siskiyou National Forest in what is now the Wild Rivers Ranger District. The black and white shot shows him decked out in a tight-fitting ranger's jacket and jodhpurs, those funny-looking riding breeches that blouse out above the knees and are tight from the knees to the ankles. He is wearing a light-colored shirt with a dark tie. The photograph is faded and torn, the result of having been soaked in the 1964 flood and packed and unpacked countless times over the years. But I remember the now missing bottom portion showed that he was wearing knee-high leather boots. Capping his attire is a Smoky-the-bear hat that is slightly tilted, giving him a somewhat rakish appearance. With those jaunty jodhpurs, he looks a bit like Dudley Do-Right about to give Snidely Whiplash a severe thrashing in anticipation of the dastardly deed the villain would play on the widow Fattig some thirty years later. Even today, the photograph makes me smile.

Taking one last look at Pearsoll Peak, I turned and headed west down an old jeep road toward the Chetco River, an area where I had never before stepped foot. I was looking forward to exploring the Madstone country, yet fearful of what I might encounter.

We spent the night in a broken down cabin a few feet off the road about two miles beyond Canyon Peak, supping on the stolen chili and white bread, courtesy of the bickering miners. There was an old mining adit into the side of the mountain but we didn't enter it. Even if we had the miners' flashlight, I would have avoided the tunnel. The silent maw in the mountainside was creepy, particularly as nightfall descended. Besides, Willy was tooting from the chili and I wasn't about to get inside a confined space with him. A night spent in a drafty old cabin with my stinky buddy was bad enough.

After breakfasting on sardines and the last of our white bread, we hiked down the road that was now little more than a jeep trail to a point where we left it to hike along the Little Chetco River. We skirted an occupied site known as Emily Cabin since I didn't want anyone to know we had come that way. The scuttlebutt at the time was the cabin had been purchased by a retired college professor and his wife from California. If he was seeking to avoid college students, he could not have found a better retreat. I recall looking longingly at the smoke floating up from the chimney. I knew we were about to leave the last vestiges of civilization behind.

Had I a map, I would have known we somehow missed the Madstone Trail which connects with the trail along the little Chetco River near the confluence of Copper Creek. At the time, not only did I not know the trail existed but I saw no Madstone Trail sign. So we walked blindly on down the Little Chetco River to the Chetco River, finding nothing pointing the way to the Madstone cabin. As it turns out, we came to the Chetco River about three miles downstream from the cabin site. I was completely lost when it came to finding the place where my uncles had hid out nearly half a century earlier.

Our first night on the Chetco was spent on a sandbar beside a roaring fire. It wasn't a particularly cold night but I wanted to let any large fierce creatures in the vicinity know that we had fire and knew how to use it. I made a little bed in the sand near the fire and slept relatively comfortably for the first time on the trip. In retrospect, it was the only time I had a good night's sleep as a runaway.

Not only had I a soft bed and warm by the fire but we had full stomachs. While we had one can of sardines left, I decided to save it as an emergency ration. When we got to the river that evening, I had taken a couple of casts into the riffles, using an old spinning lure that had seen better days. I was hoping to at least catch a couple of small fry. Just when I started to lose hope of catching anything, a strong jerk on the line told me I had a fish on and a large one at that. Normally as a kid who loved fishing, I got excited when I latched onto a lunker. But I was cool and calm that evening. Catching the fish meant the difference between eating fresh trout or consuming our small emergency ration that night. This was serious business. I carefully pulled the fish to the water's edge before quickly hoisting it onto land.

It was a fat rainbow trout, at an estimated eighteen inches the biggest I had ever caught at that point. Even with the head cut off, the fish was too large for my frying pan so I had to cut the body in half before it would fit. Gray Beard would have been impressed by the dinner although I wouldn't have complained about a large slice of one of Mom's apple pies that evening. I would have even settled for a slice of the infamous cherry pie, pits and all.

The next morning I caught a few more fish, but none as large as the whopper we had eaten the night before. Still, we had breakfast and, after a dessert offered up by some nearby berry bushes, we were in relatively good shape. Willy ate blackberries, providing I hand fed him. He was spoiled that way.

After breakfasting, I had a decision to make. Head upstream in search of the Madstone cabin or go downstream to eventually end up at the ocean. Although I knew the cabin had been built along the upper Chetco, I didn't know whether it was upstream or downriver from where we stood. We weren't exactly lost but we didn't know precisely where we were, other than on the Chetco River. Since the river ultimately drained into the ocean and that was our next goal, I decided to head downriver, following an old trail along the south bank. The trail had likely once been used by miners, trappers and no doubt my uncles but it was in poor shape. In some places it simply disappeared, leaving us to average out the path as best we could.

It was on the second day of our downriver journey that we had our close encounter of the large hairy kind. That would be hairy as in a bear far more curious about us than we were of him.

We were at a point where the trail made a short detour away from the river and had climbed over a small ridge before heading back toward the water. As we crested the ridge and started down the steep grade, I saw a big bear plodding nonchalantly along the trail ahead of us. From behind, he looked like he was wearing furry bedroom slippers. I yelled just as Willy sped off toward the bear in full attack mode. The bear whirled around, prompting Willy to follow suit and hightail it back my direction. If I hadn't yelled, Willy would have latched onto the bear and died, of that I am dead certain. The big fellow would have easily crushed him with its jaws or swatted him like Babe Ruth hitting one out of the park.

With a look of fright on his little face, Willy was now running back towards his young master who was equally terrified. When you are a boy in the wilderness and armed only with a small dog, confronting a large and potentially fierce creature is not something you want to happen. Still yelling, I ran off the trail and scrambled up a tree which I believe was a madrone, although it may have been a live oak. I distinctly remember it was not a conifer because it had open limbs which I could easily climb up to about fifteen feet. However, given my sense of urgency to get out of reach of the bear, I could have probably scurried up a telephone pole.

But the bear did not charge. Instead, it began walking slowly toward us. It stopped and rose halfway up on its hind feet, sniffing the air. The bear then dropped back down on all fours and continued to peer as though he couldn't figure out what kind of creatures were before him. It may have been his first encounter with a humanoid, let alone a barking canine. He was downright inquisitive, continuing to sniff and peer at us through pig eyes. He—I use the term loosely since I didn't have a chance, or inclination, to determine its sex—didn't seem afraid at having encountered a human.

The bear was undoubtedly a distant descendant of the bruins Alfred and Charlie Fattig met while roving the Madstone country. Of course, they—the brothers, not the bruins—had firearms and the bears didn't wait around to see if they were loaded. Although ours was definitely a member of the black bear species, his fur was not black. His tan coat was only slightly darker than the blonde grizzlies I would see in Alaska while living there in the mid-1980s.

While the bear was checking us out, Willy continued barking as I yelled from the tree for the stubborn pooch to stay back. The mutt ignored me, of course. He would take a barking rush to get between me and the bear, then beat feet when the bear looked like he was about to charge him. Whatever Willy's game was, it wasn't helping the situation.

More than anything the bear seemed puzzled. He couldn't decide whether we were food or foe. Finally, the bear turned around and resumed his leisurely stroll down the trail, periodically stopping to glance over his shoulder to see what his loudmouth tormentors were up to. He padded off down to a bend in the trail where he plunged off into the underbrush. He had enough of the yelling biped and the oversized red fox with the pestering bark. Willy and I waited until we saw him climbing the next ridge before hurrying on down the trail. Our curiosity regarding large creatures with long teeth and claws was more than satisfied.

That evening I came across an old cabin that was falling down on the south side of the Chetco. The cabin's shingle roof had rotted through but about twenty feet up the hill from it was a small shed used as a smokehouse. In the center of the smokehouse's dirt floor was a hole which was apparently the upper end of a rock-lined flue from the cabin. The smoke from the fire in the cabin had been filtered up the hill to the smokehouse. If it worked as intended, it was ingenious.

Since the smokehouse was in relatively good shape and unoccupied, we took it as our room for the night. It also had a little door which I appreciated since it wouldn't provide easy access by a large furry creature. When rain began to drop along with the temperature, I lit the wood a packrat or some other considerate creature had stored in the top end of the ground flue.

If you have a smidgen of common sense, you know where we are headed here. Although I am not endowed with a huge amount of horse sense as an adult, those who knew me back then will tell you I had virtually none as a newly-minted teenager. I did not give a second thought to the fact I was lighting a fire in a smokehouse where I was also spending the night.

Before long, our little house was warm but it was also filled with smoke. That was the only time I saw a dog cough like an old smoker hacking up a lung. We found there was somewhat breathable air if you kept your nose no more than a foot above the dirt floor. We somehow managed to survive the night but we both smelled like smoked jerky the next morning. If we met the blonde bear that day, he would have likely decided we were food after all.

Yet a far worse night was ahead. The next morning we encountered a section of the river in which the trail petered out. At this point, there were rock walls on each side on the river. We had to climb ridges to skirt the walls in some places. In one steep spot where we could not scale the walls or find a way around them, we swam down the river. Actually, Willy swam while I bobbed along the edge, clinging to the rock face. The water was chilly but we needed a bath.

Having made little headway that day and finding no old cabin to stay in as dark clouds began to blow in from the Pacific, I walked up a narrow draw, seeking shelter from the coming storm.

Had the Kerby Elementary School library contained a larger selection of reading material, I may have read the works of Shakespeare in which he unwittingly foretold the meteorological fate of runaways.

"It is the stars, the stars above, governs our conditions," the Bard penned in "King Lear." True, he wasn't referring to the weather, but as an avid camper I would have assumed back then that he was simply making a observation concerning the chance of rain. Seeing the stars at night is a good thing when you are camping with no shelter in coastal mountains. No stars means clouds, and clouds off the ocean carry the potential for really nasty wet weather. Did I mention I had no sleeping bag, much less a blanket? A rain jacket? Surely you jest, as the Bard would say.

There would be no stars showing that extremely dark night. The only protection I could find was underneath a large cedar which had fallen across the head of the draw. Rain started to drum down on the surrounding forest, filling it with the sound of dripping water. I hastily made a little camp under the log which was about four feet over our heads. The pickings were slim but I was able to gather some firewood before it got dark. We ate the last can of sardines but were still hungry. I lit a cigarette, drew in a deep breath as I had seen real smokers do and nearly upchucked a sardine. It worked as I had been told since my hunger pains were gone. From that point on, I never inhaled another cigarette during the trek. Just puffing on one killed my appetite.

At first, the rain was coming straight down and tolerable because the log, maybe three feet wide, offered some protection. When the wind picked up, the rain came in at a slant. I was able to keep the fire alive by pulling strips of bark from the log. But we were still cold. Willy balled up between me and the fire and I curled around him. Misery loves company, especially when you are wet and shivering. I did not care one whit if I smelled like the hair of a wet dog.

When the fire started to die out, I reluctantly left our tiny sleeping spot to find more bark to keep the flames alive. With no watch, I had no idea what time it was. It must have been close to midnight. I had gotten all the bark up close so I had to go about ten feet from the fire where the north end of the log rested on the mossy ground. There wasn't much light but I could see a little. Just as I was pulling hard on a piece of bark, a loud scream pierced the black night. I nearly wet my pants already damp from the rain as I scrambled back to the fire. Never before or since have I been so scared. The eerie sound was a cross between the scream of a terrified women and the aggressive roar of an hungry creature looking for a pound of flesh. I hugged Willy who was trembling, too afraid to even growl. At that point, I would have gladly exchanged my little friend for a barrel-chested White Fang. The scream seemed to have come from our side of the river and a bit farther up the mountainside. There was no way to tell how far away the beast was but its owner certainly seemed close enough to drop in for a visit. It must have been a cougar but I also had mental images of a towering Sasquatch striding through the darkness toward our little campfire. If it did come into the camp, I figured I would run down the ravine and jump into the river. Drowning seemed preferable to being eaten alive.

As boy and dog huddled together, shivering away the wet night, the night seemed to exist forever. We were chilled to the bone marrow. But it wasn't just the cold that made us tremble. Although it was emitted just that once, we could still hear the blood-chilling scream in our minds. When the gray dawn finally arrived, I was largely in a somnambulistic state, nearly dead from hypothermia yet still petrified with fear. But the dog and I headed downriver at a double-time pace that would have impressed my fellow jarheads later in life. Our motivation was to get as far away from the source of the scream as possible. Trail or not, we plunged ahead, intent on reaching civilization as soon as we could. Indeed, after that horrible night, my interest in exploring the Madstone country was gone.

During our visit in Texas, Uncle Alfred insisted he had never heard a cougar make a sound in the Madstone country. However, other wilderness veterans have assured me that panthers of the night do scream. To my last breath, I will believe a cougar screamed that dark and stormy night in the upper Chetco River drainage. Whatever it was, it was not human. I still shudder when I think of the night of the scream.

It would take us about four more days of forced marches and three sleepless nights to reach the seaside town of Brookings, a pleasant community nestled on the north bank of the Chetco where it meets the Pacific Ocean. Willy and I had started following a mountain road on the last morning, and caught a ride to town with a friendly older man and woman in an older pickup truck. With nary a word questioning the presence of a grubby boy and his equally grubby dog in the middle of the mountains, they dropped us off early that afternoon along Highway 101 at the edge of town and drove off.

Whatever was left of my already shaky plan fell apart at that point. I had no idea how to reach Canada, yet alone Alaska. So I swung my gunny sack over my shoulder and started walking north along the edge of the coastal highway with Willy hard on my heels. A police officer driving in the opposite on the other side of the highway slowed down, gave us a long stare and made an abrupt U-turn. I jumped off the road and ran into a group of trees with Willy following suit. As I did when facing a bear of another stripe, I climbed a tree.

Unlike the first bear we faced, this one could talk. "If you don't come down right now, I'm going to shoot your dog," the police officer called calmly up to me in a nearly conversational tone. I know now the officer would not have heartlessly shot my dog. But I did not know it then. I meekly climbed down the tree and surrendered. "It was the only way I could talk you down—I wasn't about to climb that tree after you," he explained before herding Willy and I into the back seat of his police cruiser. He checked out my gunny sack before placing it in the trunk.

It was the first I had ever ridden in the back of a police car. I figured my life was over. I was prison bound like my ex-con uncles. I would probably be covered with self-etched tattoos by the time I was twenty-one.

But when I was asked what my name was and where I was from, I refused to tell the officer because I knew I would be taken back to Kerby. Since I had no identity on me, he was left clueless. We were placed in a cell in the town's small jail.

The officer later brought us both a hamburger, something we both made short work of. Mine was accompanied with fries and a glass of water; my jail mate's water came in a bowl but he seemed content. He curled up on the floor and fell asleep. I sat on the lone cot and tried to figure out what to do. The small police department obviously didn't know what to do with me, let alone my dog. We weren't charged with any crime against society. I thought they might even just let us go. I convinced myself if my frail Uncle Charlie could survive a little jail time, so could I.

That night the jail was eerily quiet. No one seemed to be around. But a chubby officer I had never seen before, apparently the one on night shift, came in and walked over to my cell. He immediately accused me of having broken into a local store. "We know you did it," he kept saying, ignoring my denials. "It'll be easier for you if you confess." I kept protesting my innocence; he kept insisting I was the culprit.

Although it was the first—and only—time I had ever been arrested, I knew the cop was not the brightest fellow on the force. After about an hour of haranguing me, he left and never returned. As tired as I was, I didn't sleep much that night. I figured I would be charged with whatever local unsolved crimes were on the books and I would be headed upriver. I would be an old man when I got out. It wasn't quite as bad as the night of the scream but it was mighty unsettling.

My worst fears appeared to be confirmed the next morning when a tall Oregon State Police trooper arrived and told me he was taking me to the county jail in Gold Beach. Once again Willy and I were placed in the back of a police cruiser, unsure of our fate.

However, before we left town, the trooper stopped at a restaurant where he bought me the breakfast special: two eggs over easy, hash browns, toast, sausage and a cup of hot chocolate. While the kind officer patiently sipped coffee, I wolfed down what even today remains the most memorable breakfast I have ever had. I felt guilty Willy was still in the police car and wasn't there to share it with me. But I saved a sausage for my little chum.

Gold Beach is the Curry County seat nearly thirty miles north of Brookings at the mouth of the Rogue River. While the trooper was pleasant, he said little during the half hour drive. Although a small town, Gold Beach's courthouse and jail looked to me like a towering San Quentin. The trooper took me into the facility and turned me over to the Curry County Sheriff's Department. Before leaving, he wished me good luck.

In the small world department, an Oregon State Police (OSP) trooper based in Gold Beach at that time was James Allen Choate who—fast forwarding half a century—happens to have been my wife's paternal uncle. He had joined the OSP in 1963, starting out in Gold Beach before being transferred to eastern Oregon in 1979. The officer, who would retire from the OSP as a first sergeant after twenty-seven years on the force and pass away in the fall of 2013, may have very well been the officer who took me to Gold Beach that day. Unfortunately, I never had a chance to ask him. If he was able to confirm it and I told him I had become a journalist, he probably would have shaken his head and said, "I knew you would come to no good."

Back in the slammer in Gold Beach, I was placed in a cell, one of several in the facility while Willy was taken to the local dog shelter to do his time. For me, the door clanked shut with the finality of a judge's gavel.

"Hey, man, you got a cigarette?" a disembodied voice called out to me from another cell.

"I'm sorry, I don't smoke," I timidly replied to the fellow who I could not see. This was true. I couldn't even smoke the borrowed Marlboros to stave off the hunger pains. As a criminal, I was an abject failure. There was a grunt, followed by silence.

"How old are you?" the gravelly voice asked again. I told him I was fourteen and had run away from home.

"Starting out young," he said. "You'll be going to MacLaren. That's where I started out. It's better here. But they got me for stealing a car this time. I'm going to be doing hard time now."

He was referring to what is now the MacLaren Youth Correctional Facility in Woodburn in northern Oregon, originally called the MacLaren School for Boys. His observation sent chills through my body. When we were living along Waters Creek, a boy named Billy James ran away from his home just upstream from our house in the mid-1950s and was sent north to a youth correctional facility for his troubles. He was a tough kid but he was killed when another youth hit in the back of the head with a chair. I seriously did not want to go to a juvenile facility.

The stark reality of my predicament hit me hard. I sat on my bunk with my fists and jaw clinched fighting the tears that started running down my cheeks. It was embarrassing but I could not help sobbing. "Hey, man, I'm sorry," the voice yelled again.

Later that afternoon, a man who was not in uniform came to my cell and talked to me for a while. When he asked me again for my name and where I was from, I was polite but again refused to provide the answer. He didn't react angrily. Instead, he told me my dog was being well cared for and that I was being held until the powers that be could decide what to do with me. He shook my hand and left.

Not long afterwards a deputy took me out of the cell and led me to a small room with a bed and a bathroom. "You don't belong in a cell with the rest of the inmates," he told me. The door was locked from the outside but there were no bars.

Although I have read plenty of horror stories about small-town jails, I was treated well. Like the state trooper, the deputies were not threatening. But the unseen inmate's comment about me being sent to the juvenile detention facility continued to gnaw at me. I was afraid I would never see Willy again, let alone my mom and siblings. By day three, my resistance no doubt softened by the decency shown me by the deputies, I squealed on myself and told an officer who I was and that I had walked through the Kalmiopsis Wilderness to the coast.

"Are you serious? You hiked through those mountains by yourself?" asked the incredulous deputy. Clearly, he was dubious about my story. But after calling the police chief in Cave Junction and my mom back in Kerby, he came back convinced.

"Your story checks out," he said. "Your mom is relieved you are safe. But she says you sure are stubborn. Anyway, your older brother is coming over to pick you up tomorrow."

Before leaving, he turned around and looked at me again. "If being obstinate was a crime, we would have locked up you up for life," he said with a chuckle.

Before leaving this chapter, it should be observed that my two paternal uncles and I were not the only Fattigs who did jail time. The fourth one you've already met: my big brother Jim. You should know he has been a teetotaler since early adulthood and has long been a responsible family man walking the straight and narrow. Moreover, the crime that put him in the slammer wasn't anything that would impress the criminal mind.

However, in the summer of 1965 he and a buddy we'll call Tom—his real name—were tooling around in Gold Beach not long after they graduated from high school. Although they were underage, they acquired a few bottles of beer and began sampling the brew.

"I spent ten days in the Gold Beach jail because I threw a beer bottle at a mailbox," Jim recalled. "Two hours after they pulled us over we had been taken before a judge and were behind bars. They made me a trustee so I got a little more freedom but it taught me a good lesson. Anyway, it's all part of life and probably helped us mature a little.

"It's funny what a little alcohol can do to you," he added. He was not referring to the humorous version of the word.

Still, we both drive carefully and abide by all laws when venturing into Curry County these days. One visit apiece to the county lockup was ample for the both of us.

Moreover, that combined thirteen days in the stir is the extent of my and my siblings' penal past. We just didn't have the criminal chromosomes crouching in our genes necessary for major transgressions of the law. At best, we were featherweight jailbirds. Our uncles, on the other hand, were heavyweights who did harder time. They broke both bread and rocks with would-be ax murderers and assorted human hackers.

ELEVEN

The Nature Man

A LFRED AND CHARLIE FATTIG ESCAPED INTO the southern Oregon
mountains to avoid killing other men in World War I; I fled our
prison of poverty by following their footsteps nearly half a century later.
For the brothers, their mountain retreat was a safe bastion until they could
no longer stand the solitude and each other. Alfred would make his point
during his fifteen minutes of fame, thanks to newspaper coverage nationwide,
and serve his time. I was overcome by the solitude after a few days and,
inspired by the scream in the dead of night, fled the wilderness. That
immature escapade was quickly forgotten by everyone but the immediate
family, although Willy probably dreamed of our long walk on the wild side
every time he took an afternoon snooze. My sole accomplishment was
discovering I did not want to ever be behind bars again.

However, before returning to the brothers and their cause célèbre, we
are going on one more southwest Oregon wilderness adventure with a
stranger. At first glance, it would seem to be an odd digression but the
tale ties in with both the war and the wilderness. It also sets the scene by
depicting the region at the onset of the war.

In the summer of 1914, a colorful character named Joseph Knowles
walked into the Siskiyou Mountains of southern Oregon purely for fame
and fortune. What's more, he entered the wild country with far less than
I carried in my gunny sack. In fact, he was nearly stark naked.

While Europe was about to explode into war in the weeks following the assassination of Archduke Ferdinand in Sarajevo on June 28, 1914, Knowles was stripping down in the Siskiyous. Save for a loin cloth, he was about to walk au naturel into the forest as a national stunt to demonstrate man could survive in the wilds on wits alone.

Before walking off barefoot on July 21, 1914, wearing only what amounts to a hairy bikini bottom into the mountains near the Oregon Caves, Knowles boldly announced he would take no firearm, no knife, no matches. It wasn't the first time he had gone naked into the arms of Mother Nature. He had done the same thing in the Maine woods the previous year, drawing national attention. He was known as "The Nature Man" or "The Yankee Tarzan." Knowles' adventure was 1914's version of a reality show. As many reality show stars are wont to be, he was a combination blowhard and con artist with just enough gravitas to attract a following.

His West Coast adventure was financed by American newspaper tycoon William Randolph Hearst who was looking to gin up some copy for his vast network of domestic papers. Hearst was no stranger to taking liberties with the Fourth Estate to boost circulation. Remember, back in the day, newspapers were *the* source of news. This was before television and the advent of the internet, of course.

It was no coincidence that Knowles began his much-touted wilderness adventures the year after a novella by Edgar Rice Burroughs was published. Perhaps you've heard of *Tarzan of the Apes*. Jack London came out with *The Call of the Wild* in 1903, followed by *White Fang* in 1906. Americans were definitely interested in back-to-nature stories as they entered the 20th Century.

In fact, Teddy Roosevelt was cautioning Americans not to get soft, what with automobiles and telephones and other new fangled contraptions making us forget our caveman roots.

"Unless we keep the barbarian virtue, gaining the civilized ones will be of little avail," Roosevelt told America. Our twenty-sixth president had obviously never been in the Illinois Valley where barbarian virtues were the norm a century ago. As you have read, it even had its barbarian runaway in the mid-1960s. You also know it is extremely rugged country even when you are dressed for it. Summer or not, it would also be chilly country for one wearing only a loin cloth.

Knowles was no Tarzan, of course. He was 5-foot-9 and weighed about 180 pounds. He was forty-five years old and already fighting a paunch. Although a grade school dropout, he had natural talent and had become a professional illustrator for the *Boston Post* newspaper. When he wasn't illustrating, he had a penchant for hanging out in Boston bars. He liked to tell whoever was slouched on the adjacent stool about having been a trapper and hunting guide in the Maine woods back in the 1890s.

The Nature Man hailed from Wilton, Maine, a tiny town some eighty miles northeast of Portland. His father was a disabled Civil War veteran whose wife supported their four children by making and selling moccasins. The family also sold firewood and berries gathered in the nearby woods. So there is no doubt that Joe Knowles had some knowledge of the back-woods.

But there is also no doubt his wilderness acts in both Maine and Oregon were publicity stunts.

In 1913, Knowles talked Charles Wingate, Sunday editor of the *Boston Post*, into sending him out into the Maine wilderness to create a melodramatic man-against-nature series of articles. Back then, there were ten newspapers in Boston, making it a very competitive market. Wingate agreed the stunt could boost circulation. Knowles told Wingate that he would stay out in the woods for sixty days, living off the land. He would leave charcoal messages and illustrations on bark at a designated site for the fawning press.

The 1913 stunt drew attention from coast to coast. The modern primitive man reported incredible tales of wrestling a deer to the ground with his bare hands and killing a bear with a club. His reports told how he lived on roots and berries and made sandals out of bark. He also reported that he made his clothes and moccasins out of the skins of the bear and deer he had killed.

The wilderness saga proved to be a huge boost to the paper's circulation.

The Post later reported that its circulation rose from some 200,000 to more than 436,000 between August and October of 1913, the period Knowles was out in the wilds. That was a tremendous amount in those days just as it would be now. The competing *Boston American* published several articles discrediting Knowles, labeling him a fraud. Of course, that controversy didn't hurt the circulation of either paper.

As it happens, the *Boston American* was owned by Hearst, a fellow who knew a good publicity stunt when he saw it. That is why, a year later, the *San Francisco Examiner*, another Hearst newspaper, sponsored Knowles' excursion into the rugged Siskiyou Mountains.

But Hearst, knowing there would be scoffers, hired two so-called experts whose stated responsibility was to be the Nature Man's judge and jury. Presumably, they were to report any skullduggery.

The *Examiner* promoted the story big time. "WILD BEASTS ROAR INVITATION TO JOE KNOWLES," shouted a page one headline above the fold on the day he strode into the wilderness. The story did not make it clear just how the *Examiner* determined these were invitations and not threats.

Oregon papers also joined the 1914 chorus. Leading them was the *Oregonian* which included several articles on July 21, the day of Knowles' departure from a site in the mountains just southeast of Holland. Incidentally, we're not talking about the Holland with windmills and wooden shoes. This Holland was a small community named after a family of settlers in the Illinois Valley. Back in 1914, the metropolis of Cave Junction did not exist.

"WILDERNESS WAR" screamed the front page *Oregonian* headline. "Battle for Life for 30 Days Is Started," added a subhead. "Indian Loin Cloth Worn," read yet another. You get the gist. It was to be a smack down between the Nature Man and Mother Nature.

"Joe Knowles entered the woods of Southern Oregon and Northern California this morning as the primitive man, on a test for 30 days or more to demonstrate that the resourcefulness of the man of the present day is sufficient to cope with nature and to prove that, unclad and unarmed, without any of the implements of modern times, he can wrest a living from the woods, and return to civilization dressed in clothes he has made in the woods, well fed and in good physical condition," read the lead.

"There was but little ceremony about the departure," the story continued. "It had been planned by the people of Grants Pass to give the primitive a send-on, and a party of more than 60 had planned to see him off, but the location, practically picked out by Professor Waterman of the University of California who is to observe the 30-day test from a scientific standpoint, made it impossible for the party to get to the point where Knowles made his departure. Knowles was naked with the exception of an Indian loin cloth, and this he will bring out of the woods with him at the end of the test in the same condition as when he entered."

I don't know about you, but I figure that is a little too much information. I would just as soon he left the loin cloth back in the woods. We don't need to get into the physical hygiene issue here. Yow.

"He says if he cannot get a bear skin for a coat, then he will weave one from moss that hangs from almost all the trees in this forest," according to the article. "Knowles will begin leaving his reports so that they may be found and sent to civilization as soon as he makes something to cover his feet and has found a place to sleep."

Down in Josephine County, the *Grants Pass Daily Courier* also covered the story.

"If I do not meet a bear, a cougar or other wild animals I would regret it very much and should any of these animals show themselves, they will not get away," Knowles told the *Courier* in an article printed July 22.

"Knowles will take up the battle with nature, providing himself with food and clothing from the mountains and streams," it continued. "Traps and snares he must make with his unaided hands. Fire he must kindle by methods he says are easy without matches, without flint and steel. Fish he will get without hook and game without steel traps."

The nights would be cold but Knowles claimed "he would sleep as comfortably in his bed of moss and leaves with his friction-made fire as he does at the hotel with artificial clothing," the *Courier* added.

The *Oregon Observer*, a weekly newspaper out of Grants Pass, got into the act with a front page article on Knowles departure which also ran July 22. "Grants Pass Gave Knowles God Speed," read the headline.

"I shall tell you now, if I have the good fortune to run up against a bruin, I shall come out of the woods dressed in his skin, and shall live like a millionaire camper while the meats lasts," he told the *Observer*. "Mountain lions? I would tackle them as a bear and they deserve no more mercy than they show to a deer and their little fawns. I shall have to fight for my food, and it will be a fight of wits."

Before walking barefoot into the woods, the *Oregonian* noted that Knowles shook hands with members of the party, including Professor Waterman and Charles L. Edwards, head of the nature study department at the Los Angeles high schools. The two experts were hired to follow his progress while staying in a nearby abandoned miner's cabin. It specifically notes he shook hands with the *Oregonian* reporter. What it doesn't mention was that he also shook hands with the reporter for the *San Francisco Examiner* who was present. Newspaper rivalry, you understand. No need to mention your competition.

"After he had stripped he was searched, searched so thoroughly that everyone was convinced he had nothing concealed about his person," according to the story. "There are but two things he carried with him, his brains and his woodcraft, that is a second nature to him...He has gone into the woods to fight for his life alone and with help of no kind.

"It was a minute, perhaps, as he swung across the little clearing, his arms working and every muscle of his great body in play, and then it was swallowed up by the forest," it read. "He disappeared, it seemed, as though he had drawn back the deep curtain of the forest and made his exit. The first act in the Knowles drama had ended."

Of course, there was a little sidebar to go along with the main story, much of it redundant.

"The scene was worth traveling miles to see and experiencing all the discomforts that attended the trip," the reporter wrote in the sidebar. "The Knowles camp was pitched so far in the wilderness that it practically is inaccessible. The trail was broken through an absolute wilderness from the ridge that runs over the Siskiyou Mountains from Oregon into

California....Had it not been for the surefootedness of the ponies and pack animals, one might have dropped thousands of feet to the creek below."

That last sentence was unadulterated hyperbole. The slopes may be steep but we're not talking about the Grand Canyon. It would be difficult to drop 100 feet at best, although that would certainly snap a few bones.

The *Oregonian* reader that morning would also find an article written by Knowles, one headlined, "All My Clothes Now Are Off, and Now I'm Off, Naked."

"When you read this I shall be in the forest of the mountains, the primitive man," Knowles wrote. "In about twenty minutes I shall make my start from this little cabin, nestled here between the towering mountains of this range. Mount Bolan rises above me to the north with its lake almost at the summit, which looks like the crater of an old volcano, and maybe it is. While to the south as far as the eye can reach, stretch the tumbling tops of the great Sierra Nevada range."

I can tell you with 100 percent certainty that he could not see the Sierra Nevada range from where he was. Best he could do was spot the tip of Mount Shasta to the east and the Marble Mountains to the southeast. As for Bolan Lake, the depression it sits in was carved by a glacier, not blown out by a volcanic eruption, according to scientists who study those things. But we can forgive Knowles that geologic fantasy. As a kid, I always thought it was of volcanic origins. Besides, we are interested in his nature notes here, not his scientific theories.

"I do want to be let alone," he wrote. "That really is the only request I have to make of those whom I leave behind. I want to hear nothing from the outside world. I have insisted that, even should there be a death in my family, even should my dear old mother die, I not want to know it. It would do me no good to get the information. I could not go back East to do anything and it would break me up to such an extent that I probably would be unable to complete the test."

"I have promised all along that I would come out of the woods in the garb of a wild man, with the skin of deers and a bear for my clothing," he continued. "That is my ambition, but if I am not fortunate enough to secure these animals, I shall not return unclothed. I shall have a suit even more unique than either the deer or the bear skin would make. There are masses of fiber in the forest which I believe I shall be able to weave, as one weaves cloth, into a fairly good reproduction of the tailor's art. White cedar seems to be more or less plentiful, and that will be of immense value to me. From the inner bark of these trees, and with other fiber which I shall find, I shall come forth clad in a good-looking suit."

I suspect that a bear, a cougar or even Sasquatch would scream and run the other way when confronted by what looked like a hideous creature from the underworld lurching towards them in the forest.

As for human visitors, Knowles cautioned them to stay away.

"I want to warn those who may come into the forest and begin a search for me," he wrote. "They are liable to get into trouble for the snares I shall make for the wild animals of the forest will be sufficiently strong to jerk a full-grown man into the air and hold him there, and there won't be any getting down until I come along. I don't want to have to cut anyone down from that position. Besides, I won't have the opportunity to apologize. He won't care whether I do or not."

In other words, death awaited those who ventured into his survival-of-the-fittest world, warned the pitchman for the primitive.

"It's off," he concluded. "Tonight I shall sleep in a bed of moss. I shall have made some kind of shoes that will protect my feet temporarily. I shall be busy with the small snares for the little game of the forest and with the fish in the creeks. Then I shall begin my big snares for the larger game, and I do hope that I shall get one of the wild animals of this forest. I am so anxious to produce a bear and a couple of deer that I cannot get it out of my mind."

To its credit, the *Oregonian* carried another Knowles article that day, one which acknowledged the *Boston American* had reported that Knowles was a fake.

"The attack upon the good faith of Knowles was made on the authority of one Allie Deming, a Maine guide, who says in the *American* article that Knowles is a faker and did not carry out in good faith his Maine woods experiment or living for 60 days solely upon the resources or nature," it stated.

Hearst knew a little controversy was good for circulation. He also knew that a lot of controversy was great for circulation. He was simply stoking the fire.

The *Oregonian's* next story came on July 27, page three. It was written by Professor Edwards of the Los Angeles schools with a Grants Pass dateline.

"Joe Knowles' first message from the wilderness was written with charcoal upon three flat pieces of dry-rotted white fir," it began, then quoted the messages, " Slept before open fire first night. Country full of miners. They are fishing or hunting all the time. If I can avoid the prospectors and get a living I will do well. I have seen five prospectors and one has seen me. This will be very hardest week. It is hell. You will hear from me Saturday. JOE."

Edwards wrote that Knowles' message was left by the trail at a pre-arranged spot one-third of a mile down the valley from their cabin.

"It is obvious from the message that Knowles is having a test severe enough to satisfy anyone," Edwards concluded. "In Maine the forest is much more open, while here, in the Siskiyous, there is a dense growth of underbrush, which makes extremely difficult going for those of us who are well clothed. What then must the hardship be for Joe until he can manufacture some kind of clothes? We in the forest are well able to realize the severity of this test."

Unfortunately for Knowles and Hearst, a much greater test was taking place on the other side of the planet in the aftermath of Ferdinand's assassination. On July 28, a week after Knowles went caveman, World War I began and the tenuous peace among Europe's great powers collapsed. Austria-Hungary declared war on Serbia. Russia, Belgium, France, Great Britain and Serbia lined up against Austria-Hungary and Germany. The United States would enter the war three years later.

The world war naturally took the media spotlight off the Nature Man. After all, this was a time when many Americans still had relatives living in Europe. Who cared about a buck- naked guy living off the land in the Siskiyou Mountains? The news was now focused on the war.

Oregon papers still covered Knowles but their enthusiasm definitely had waned. He fell off the front page of the *Oregonian*. Yet there were still a few blurbs. Knowles apparently stumbled upon a deer killed by a mountain lion, according to the weekly *Oregon Observer* on Aug. 5th. "Cougar Kills Deer for Joseph Knowles," read the headline. "The skin will make covering, the sinew thread, the bone tools," added the sub head.

On Aug. 11, page five, the *Oregonian* had a short article by Professor Waterman expounding on Knowles hard life in the wilds.

"Anyone who thinks Mr. Knowles is pretending, or living in luxury somewhere on the quiet, should have the chance to inspect him as *The Morning Oregonian* party did Thursday," Waterman wrote. "We found him in his hole very snugly stowed away at the foot of a big tree on the side of the mountain, a hundred feet or so above the brook."

He described the hole as covered with a slab of bark. The hole itself was down in a hollow, he added.

"This is the correct scientific principle," he wrote. "A person down in the ground is away from the wind, and that of course the main thing. A wind blows the warm air which accumulates around the body away."

Waterman reported that Knowles was living mainly on fish, berries, nuts and roots, and that he had another camp farther up the mountain. The mountain man also reported his feet had become swollen and infected. He healed the injuries with herbs made from local plants and a balsam extracted from fir trees, according to Waterman.

The next *Oregonian* article appeared on Aug. 13, page twelve.

"Joe Knowles has caught his deer and success now is assured the man who entered the Klamath National Forest naked three weeks ago," it read, noting this was known by more bark messages. Knowles also kindly left some venison for the press and the professors.

"Last Friday night roped a deer in one of the trails by moonlight," Knowles wrote. "Will tell you all about it when I get out."

He said he would use the hide to make clothes and the meat he kept would last him the remainder of the test.

"I am leaving one hind and one front quarter of the deer with this report," he added. "Don't turn your nose till you try it, as it ain't half as bad as it looks."

According to B. E. Lambert, a photographer on the mission who was also a friend of Mr. Knowles, the woodsman had fashioned a rope out of cedar bark and snared the deer, the paper reported.

"What happened is not reported, but Knowles probably used a heavy club or broke the deer's neck with his hands," the article surmised. "The deer are small in this part of the mountains and to lasso one in this fashion would be easy for Joe Knowles."

The story of precisely how he captured the deer never materialized, at least not in my research. But I have a gnawing feeling that something was suspect.

The *Oregon Observer* noted on August 26th that Knowles received a hero's welcome when he returned to Grants Pass and the Oxford Hotel where he stayed on August 25th. He was greeted by the Moose Lodge band on Sixth Street, it noted. Knowles later toured the town in his deer skin suit that day, it added.

"There is no doubt in the minds of the people who witnessed his return that he made good in his endeavor to brave the weird and beautiful wilds of southern Oregon," the reported declared. "Both men who were able to watch him are satisfied that he was honest in his experiment."

The other papers, the *Oregonian* and the *Daily Courier*, also reported that Knowles had left the woods on August 21, receiving a warm welcome in Grants Pass. There were a few letters in the *Oregonian* questioning Knowles' authenticity. But there was never really any journalistic investigation, probably because people had lost interest.

For any kind of investigative journalism regarding his nature forays, we have to go back to his Maine excursion a year earlier. In late October of 1913, the *Hartford Courant* newspaper ran an editorial which asked whether "the biggest fake of the century has been palmed off on a credulous public."

And on Dec. 2 of that year, an investigative piece in the *Boston American* labeled Knowles a liar. It noted that he supposedly caught a bear in a pit but that the pit was apparently four feet wide and three feet deep. In other words, the pit was too small to hold any bruin, save a

Teddy Bear. As for the club he supposedly used to kill the bear, it was made of rotten wood, the paper reported. Knowles had spent the two months in a cabin owned by a friend, except for the time he went to another cabin to entertain a lady friend, the paper added.

In 1938, nearly two decades after Knowles first went on a publicized wilderness adventure, the *New Yorker* magazine took over where the *American* left off. It concluded that the Nature Man stunt was dreamed up by Knowles's drinking buddy, Michael McKeogh, a freelance writer for the *Boston Post*. The idea for the stunt was apparently arrived at after the two had consumed a number of brewskis one night. The magazine reported that McKeogh had a cozy cabin in the area in Maine near where Knowles purportedly went into the wilds. It was well stocked with Knowles' favorite brand of bottled beer, it added. As for the bear he supposedly killed, its hide had four bullet holes, the *New Yorker* observed.

Furthermore, MeKeogh referred to his old buddy as a melancholic louse, according to the magazine. For whatever reason, McKeogh and Knowles were no longer pals after the Maine excursion. I believe that may have had something to do with the fact McKeogh went into town where he brought back food to the cabin, including an apple pie. Knowles purportedly ate the entire pie, leaving none for his buddy. On my childhood camping excursions where food was always scarce, anyone eating an entire pie—as if we ever had one—would have met with an unfortunate accident.

Still, bad publicity never seemed to hurt Knowles. He did a five-month stint on the vaudeville circuit as the "Master of Woodcraft," earning what was reported as $1,200 a week. That was big bucks in those days. Not too shabby for many people today, come to think of it. Knowles also published a memoir, *Alone in the Wilderness*, selling about 30,000 copies. And he starred in a silent movie in 1914, a flick also called, *Alone in the Wilderness*.

In 1916, he attempted one more wilderness adventure. At Hearst's behest, Knowles joined up with the *New York Journal* whose staff would cover the Nature Man's planned two months survival in the

Adirondacks. But Hearst added a twist. This time he would share the billing with a lady to be known as the "Dawn Woman." The lady chosen to strip down was Elaine Hammerstein, a silent film actress and daughter of Broadway producer Arthur Hammerstein. If the surname rings a bell, it is because her uncle was the famous composer Oscar Hammerstein, as in Rogers and Hammerstein.

After Knowles trained her in rudimentary survival skills, they entered the woods at the same time but in different locations. Apparently a nearly buck-naked man and a equally nude comely lass in the same neck of the woods was a bit over the top for even Hearst. After seven days in the wilds, the Dawn Woman quit and went home. So did the media. Knowles followed suit.

In 1917, Knowles moved to Washington state's Long Beach Peninsula and devoted himself to his art, mainly illustrations celebrating the American West. He insisted to his dying day that he was the real deal. He passed away on Oct. 22, 1942.

As a footnote, when I interviewed Uncle Alfred back in 1988, I had not yet discovered the tale of the Nature Man and his 1914 excursion near the Oregon Caves. So I never asked my uncle if he knew about Joseph Knowles. But it is likely Alfred and Charles were familiar with the Nature Man since they were living in the Applegate Valley at the time, just a few mountains away from his near nude plunge in the wilds. Every newspaper in the West was reporting on his unclothed venture into the wild, at least in the beginning. There is no doubt folks in the picturesque valley were talking about the would-be Tarzan roaming about in the nearby mountains. Like other folks in the region, the brothers would have talked about what they would do if they had to survive in the wild. All they needed to put their speculations to the test was to have Uncle Sam call them up for military service to join the bloodbath in Europe.

TWELVE

Distant Drums
of War

U NLIKE THE 21ST CENTURY WARS WHICH allows aficionados to watch combatants being killed in nearly real time on a huge flat screen from the viewer's comfortable living rooms while munching from a bucket of buttery popcorn and gulping a large soda, World War I was a conflict whose grim news took a while to be served. Unless you received a telegram regretting to inform you of the loss of a family member, you read the latest news on the front of your local newspaper or in a letter from a loved one on the front. Unlike today's fast news thrown at us around the clock, this was slow journalism delivered at a pace where it could be thoughtfully chewed and digested.

Like most conflicts, the flames of WWI fire, after a long period of smoldering, were slow to spark. For years, the European powers that been bickering like siblings over long-forgotten slights. The war of words turned bloody on June 28, 1914. A nineteen-year-old Serbian nationalist named Gavrilo Princip, a member of a pro-independence group known as the "Black Hand," was waiting when the Archduke Franz Ferdinand of Austria-Hungary and his wife, Sophie, visited Sarajevo that day. One of several terrorists lying in wait, Princip pounced after the driver for the royal visitors took a wrong turn. The young assassin shot Sophie in the stomach and the heir apparent to the throne in the neck, causing wounds which would kill them both within minutes. Austria-Hungary, which had been trying to rein in Serbian attempts to become independent, immediately declared war on that small country. The dominoes leading to our planet's first global war began to topple. Germany declared war on France on Aug. 3, the day after signing a secret alliance pact with the Ottoman Empire, otherwise known as Turkey. When Germany invaded Belgium on Aug. 4, Great Britain declared war on Germany. Not to be outdone, Austria-Hungary invaded Russia. The guns of August, of which Barbara W. Tuchman wrote so well in her 1963 Pulitzer Prize-winning book by that name, were blazing away.

In bucolic southwest Oregon, life was unchanged, the Nature Man notwithstanding. After all, there were gold mines to work, crops to tend, cows to milk and timber to cut. These were rugged individualists who took pride in caring for themselves. The pioneer spirit still thrived in these river valleys. Let the Europeans with their funny names and strange languages deal with their own affairs. Oregonians felt smugly isolated from that distant debate across the ocean. Austria and Serbia could quarrel all they wanted. How in the world would it ever impact the Oregon woods?

Yet newspaper readers, in addition to poring over reports of a cow wandering down main street or a forest fire started by an unattended campfire, would have noticed that something major was afoot on the other side of the pond.

"Austria and Serbia May Go To War," observed a front-page headline in the July 1 edition of the *Daily Courier* in Grants Pass. Filed in Berlin, the wire service article noted there was a growing political rift between the two nations, a quarrel exacerbated by the assassination of Archduke Ferdinand. In one of the classic understatements of the century, the report concluded the archduke's death could cause further unrest in Europe.

Yet a book called *The Great illusion*, written by scholar Norman Angell shortly after the turn of the 19th Century, had proven on paper that war was impossible. The reason, Angell argued, was that nations around the globe had become so economically dependent on each other that all would suffer equally in war. Therefore, he reasoned, no more worries about having to send our sons off to battle. The future was overflowing with peace, he assured his readers.

In this case, the pen was definitely not mightier than the sword. Certainly the news that war had finally become unprofitable apparently did not reach the war profiteers who would get rich on the death and destruction that was WWI. By the end of the summer of 1914, the Allies—England, France, Russia, Belgium, Serbia, Montenegro and Japan—joined in battle with Germany, Austria-Hungary and the Ottoman Empire, a group known as the Central Powers. What has become the 20th Century's forgotten war had begun.

Although slow to ignite, the war gradually heated up with German soldiers—many wearing belt buckles inscribed with *"Gott Mit Uns"* (God with Us)—marching through Belgium and approaching Paris. Presumably, soldiers wearing other uniforms also had faith that God was on their side. With the Russian revolution spreading like a wildfire through that empire, Russian troops proved little use to the Allies. Bulgaria joined Germany's side, a move countered by Italy siding with the Allies.

When the USS *Lusitania* was sunk by a German submarine off the Irish coast on May 7, 1915, a growing number of Americans demanded the U.S. join the Allied cause. Albeit the *Lusitania* sailed under the British flag, there were 128 Americans among the 1,000 civilians who lost their lives when the ship sank beneath the waves.

Others pushed for peace. Industrialist Henry Ford, driven by the goal of getting the men out of the trenches by Christmas, assembled a hand-picked delegation which he took to Copenhagen late in 1915 in hopes of bringing peace to a hostile world. Among those chosen to attend the conference was LaMar Tooze of Salem, a junior at the University of Oregon where he was the student body president. Tooze would later serve as an Army officer in the war he hoped to stop, rising to the rank of major general before retiring from the military. After the famous industrialist failed to dissuade the warring factions from fighting and was severely criticized for his efforts, a run-down Ford motored back to Detroit to resume his own war against the horse and buggy.

Back in Oregon, life—and death—continued. To better understand what life was like a century ago, lets peek over the shoulders of readers poring over the *Daily Courier* out of Grants Pass or the *Mail Tribune* in Medford, the two daily papers which covered the geographic area where the anti-conscription uncles of mine hung out during these interesting times. Think what you will of newspapers, they were, despite their warts, the main conveyors of news a century ago. Radio was in its infancy and not yet assaulting listeners with angry rants by bloviating talk show hosts. Television had yet to fill our living rooms with reality-challenged reality shows. Granted, I'm a bit biased when it comes to printed news since my career was spent filling newspaper columns. Moreover, in the interest of full disclosure, it should be noted that I wrote for both the *Courier* and the *Trib* at different times and am fond of both. The *Trib* was the first paper in Oregon to receive a Pulitzer Prize, earning that high honor in 1934. This was a wee bit before my time, of course.

Medford and Grants Pass were—and are—prime examples of small-town America, microcosms of rural life across this great land of ours. While Europe was sliding into war, residents of southwestern Oregon had other matters in mind. Just south of the state line in far northern California, a dormant volcano was flexing its muscles. Mount Lassen, which rises to 10,457 feet in the Cascade Range, was emitting a smoky plume a mile high. Ash and light pumice rained down for miles around. The pungent odor of sulphur could be smelled twenty-two miles from the mountain, according to articles in both papers.

Farther south on March 9, 1916, a fellow named Pancho Villa led several hundred guerrillas north across the Mexican border into the border town of Columbus, New Mexico, killing seventeen U.S. citizens and burning the town center. Wire service reports indicated Villa was retaliating against a U.S. arms embargo to his country. President Wilson, who was reluctant to send troops to Europe, dispatched Gen. John "Black Jack" Pershing to Mexico on March 14 with more than 50,000 American troops to punish the revolutionary leader and prevent him from taking over that country's government. U.S. Marines were deployed to protect Mexico City. Villa wasn't captured but he would be assassinated in 1923.

Closer to home, the steamer *Santa Clara* ran aground off the coast near Coos Bay on the night of Nov. 2, 1915, drowning fifteen people. Among the dead was nine-year-old Delmar Bogue of Gold Hill in Jackson County.

The *Daily Courier* reported that businessman Roy Bush was robbed at gunpoint while crossing the Gilbert Creek bridge in Grants Pass on Nov. 11, 1915. A bandit wearing a handkerchief over his face stuck a gun in his victim's back and demanded money, the paper reported. The take? A whopping .35 cents.

But it wasn't all bad news. A campground was being established on the forks of Sucker and Cave creeks for tourists traveling to what would become the Oregon Caves National Monument in the mountains overlooking the Illinois Valley. Back then, the caves were known as the Marble Halls of Oregon, a grand moniker.

Three men hired by a movie company captured a live cougar on Grayback Mountain in southeastern Josephine County and displayed it in Grants Pass, the *Courier* reported on Feb. 26, 1916. They had apparently roped the adult female as though it was a tree-climbing steer. After being gawked at by locals, the poor feline was shipped off to Hollywood to be trotted out in a silent flick.

Over at the Bijou Theatre in Grants Pass, there was no cougar in the feature but the Keystone Kops were giving chase in *The Bowery Boys*. The silent spoof featured Roscoe "Fatty" Arbuckle, all 350 pounds of him, playing the role of a rotund housewife.

Mother Nature, with the help of an army of *Homo sapiens*, produced a bountiful crop of peaches, apples and grapes before the broadleaf maple leaves turned University of Oregon Duck yellow in the fall of 1915. Tokay grapes from the Grants Pass area were shipped out on six railroad cars bound for the Big Apple where growers were receiving up to $1.55 per crate. The locally-grown grapes were also displayed at the Panama-Pacific International Exposition in San Francisco before it closed on Dec. 4 that year.

Down on the farm, the Oregon-Utah Sugar Company announced it was seeking farmers interested in growing sugar beets on their Rogue Valley farmland. A sugar factory would be built in the valley, providing it could be assured that 5,000 acres of beets would be planted for at least five years, the company told the *Daily Courier*. With the acreage readily pledged by area farmers, the factory was built two years later in Grants Pass, sweetening local employment by 200 jobs.

There was talk of punching a railroad from Grants Pass through the mountains to Crescent City in the far northern corner of the California coast. By 1915, the California and Oregon Coast Railroad Co. had begun passenger service between Grants Pass and Wilderville, a tiny hamlet roughly a dozen miles south of the town spanning the Rogue River. Chief engineer selected for extending the track to the coast was George W. Boschke whose dream it was to build a coastal railroad route south to San Francisco. The railroad would enable passengers to make a round trip from the Bay Area, first going inland to Sacramento Valley and north to Grants Pass, then south along the coastal route, attracting tourists to the region, he explained. Although hailed as a genius for building a sea wall near Galveston, Texas, Boschke would never realize his dream of conquering the Oregon mountain wall to the coast. A corruption scandal caused the railroad company to go belly up and the land returned to federal ownership.

For the Oregon timber industry, the far off war in Europe was profitable, Angell's book denouncing the economics of warfare notwithstanding. In the fall of 1915, Great Britain ordered 100,000 board feet of Oregon spruce to build biplanes. The price was $98.76 per thousand board delivered of the light but strong spruce lumber. By 1917, Allied fighter pilots, sporting scarves and goggles in the open cockpits, would be flying nimble English-made Sopwith Camel biplanes, many of them built of Oregon spruce.

And it wasn't just Oregon trees that were being used in the war. Mineral from the very ground Oregonians stood on was being shipped overseas to make weapons of war. In Corvallis, E.K. Soper, head of the school of mines at Oregon Agricultural College, now Oregon State University, reported that the state's chromite, manganese, mercury and platinum mines were also profiting from the war. Platinum is sometimes found in placer gold mining.

"The state has never before produced these metals in such quantities as today," Soper stated in a *Tribune* article. "The opportunity is excellent for the discovery of new deposits of manganese, chromite and quicksilver [mercury]."

Although they had missed the gold rush of the 1850s, area miners were still kicking up their heels. The *Courier* reported that 1,221 ounces of gold was hauled into Grants Pass from the Illinois Valley under armed guard on April 3, 1917. The gold was brought by miner James Logan, one of the principals in the Simmons-Logan placer mine located near Waldo. The gold arrived in the form of seventeen bricks which were mined in a two-month period, Logan told the paper. At the time, gold was fetching $19 an ounce, compared to the more than $1,000 an ounce in 2016. The yellow treasure would be worth more than a million bucks. Not bad for two month's work.

In Grants Pass, the Stitch and Chatter Club, apparently a sewing society, was meeting weekly, presumably stitching and chattering away. It was also a time of the Chautauqua, a traveling cultural show of artists and lecturers. A large tent was erected on upper Sixth Street in Grants Pass to house the Chautauqua performers while Jackson County residents could attend the Chautauqua building in Ashland for their cultural fix. Although jeans or bib overalls topped by a flannel shirt were commonly worn by blue collar workers, most held a Sunday suit in reserve for Chautauqua.

For $20, the Wonder Clothes Store in Grants Pass promised to turn any young man into a natty dresser. "Here are smart, nobby single-breasted, double-breasted and English models for the young man, with all those details of finish dear to the young man's heart," its advertisement read.

Over in Medford, herb store owner Gim Chung offered cures for nearly every ailment, and perhaps for some that didn't exist. "Herb cure for earache, headache, catarrh, diphtheria, sore throat, lung trouble, kidney trouble, stomach trouble, heart trouble, chills and fevers, cramps, poor circulation, carbuncles, tumors, cures for all kinds of goiters," claimed his advertisement.

Early in 1917, McIntyre's Garage in Grants Pass offered for sale a rebuilt 1914 Ford touring car for $285. Shock absorbers included. Or you could buy a shiny new Maxwell for $635. The new vehicle purred along sipping a gallon of gas every twenty-two miles, the ad promised.

If you preferred four-legged transportation, there were daily classified ads for a one-horse power wagon with heavy single harness for $75. That didn't include the equine engine, of course.

Rent of a three-bedroom house along the banks of the beautiful Rogue River in Grants Pass was $4 a month. "Fine garden spot," according to the 1917 advertisement.

The river flowing past the little town was also supplying it with power, thanks to a hydropower plant operated by the Grants Pass Water, Light and Power Co. Medford also boasted of a privately-owned electrical power plant. But outlying communities in the Applegate and Illinois valleys had no electricity.

By 1917, Josephine County residents were the proud owners of a new marble county courthouse in Grants Pass. County commissioners decreed "no dancing, vaudeville shows or things of like character" soil the virgin building. Good times didn't jive with good government, they apparently figured.

Of course, not all was peaches and cream. Many feared domestic unrest would upset the apple cart. Indeed, the Industrial Workers of the World, known as "Wobblies," were violently active in the Pacific Northwest. Organized in 1905, the group preached radical rhetoric based largely on Marxist philosophy, one which condemned WWI as purely a capitalist venture. In addition to urging young men to refuse military draft, the Wobblies launched a war against the capitalists they opposed, attempting to unionize lumber, agriculture and marine workers.

Joining their philosophy was a group known as the Socialist Committee on War and Militarism. In St. Louis, the committee released a strong statement condemning the decision to go to battle with Germany. The group called for "unyielding opposition to all proposed legislation for military or industrial conscription."

Both uncles Alfred and Charlie were unabashedly anti-Marxist. As a child, listening to Uncle Charlie, I assumed the phrase "goddamned communists" was one word. In the interviews, Alfred repeatedly stressed their opposition was not based on politics. For him, the choice was based on his firm religious beliefs. But many others avoiding the draft in WWI would cite chapter and verse from Wobbly literature. Sympathizers felt the Wobblies were simply speaking for the common worker but those opposed to the movement disagreed. To them, IWW simply meant "I Won't Work."

Overseas, the war continued unabated. German leader Kaiser Wilhelm II announced early in 1916 that his country would launch unrestricted submarine warfare, a move that pushed American anger to the surface.

Yet President Woodrow Wilson would be re-elected to his second term in 1916 by constantly reminding Americans that he had kept them out of war. Point of fact, he had strived to keep the U.S. out of the conflict and had even attempted to mediate between the warring factions. But he was to meet with little success. The clashing countries began the longest and bloodiest battle of the war in northeast France. The ten-month-long battle of Verdun saw two million soldiers engaged. Before the last shot was fired in that bloody battle, one million lay dead. The bodies of soldiers were stacked like so much cordwood.

Speaking Jan. 29, 1916, in Pittsburg, Pa., a weary Wilson warned Americans of the potential for them to enter the war on the other side of the planet.

"The struggle abroad has now lasted a year and a half: the end is not yet in sight and all the time things are getting more and more difficult to handle," he said. "If all could see the dispatches I read every hour, they would know how difficult it has been to maintain peace.

"We are in the midst of a world we cannot alter, and therefore, as your responsible servant, I must tell you that the dangers are grave and constant," he added. "We are even dependent now upon the belligerents for the movement of our commerce. Where there is contact there is likely to be friction, and with nations engaged as many now are in a life and death struggle, they are likely to become stubbornly steadfast in their proposals and convictions."

Remember, this was less than a year after the *Lusitania* had been sent to the bottom by a German U-boat. Americans were still simmering over that incident. If it came to war, there was little question but that the Yanks would march alongside the Allies.

However, even before the United States officially took sides, a trickle of Americans had already joined the fray. Yet the Americans were not united in their support. Thirteen were reported killed while fighting for France on Oct. 5, 1915. But a few Yanks took up arms for the Kaiser before their Uncle Sam joined the Allied cause. Grants Pass resident Andrew Gigler received word on Jan. 30, 1916, that his brother, who had joined a Bavarian regiment, had been severely wounded in northern France. His brother, by then a prisoner-of-war in France, had suffered his wound at the hands of French forces the previous fall. Again, news was slow to make its way across the pond.

"He was accompanied by two of his comrades when he fell, and they assisted his as far as was possible in leaving the field of battle," the *Daily Courier* reported in its article on Gigler's brother. "They were obliged to desert him, however, to make their own escape.

"The censor cut out that portion of the letter that stated where and at what he was working, but the relatives were greatly relieved to know that he was in the land of the living and still able to work," the article concluded. "The letter stated that prisoners were kept on very short rations and were also much in need of woolens to keep them warm, showing the increasing cost of provisions in the belligerent countries."

Although it was already becoming obvious to some of our nation's pending participation in the war opposite Germany, the front-page article did not take the soldier to task for fighting on the side of the Kaiser. Rather, it simply reported the story.

But the paper was no longer an unbiased observer when the United States declared war on Germany on April 6, 1917. Even for peacemaker Wilson, the continuous death and destruction caused by the submarine warfare proved too much. In announcing the action to his nation, Wilson explained that it was an attempt to make the world "safe for democracy." The phrase quickly became the battle cry for the war's proponents.

It was, a young Winston Churchill observed, the first time the New World had come to the rescue of the Old World. An historical changing of the palace guard was taking place.

"Kaiser Runs Amuck," screamed the editorial headline that historic day in the *Daily Courier.* "War with Germany was not of America's making," the editor wrote. "For two years this nation has sought ways of peace even when the German government has applauded assaults upon American life and right and justice."

It further stated the fight was not against the German people but with the Kaiser, ignoring the fact it would be young Americans and their allies fighting German soldiers and their supporters in the bloody trenches. "The Kaiser has run amuck, and for the good of posterity kaiserism must be annihilated," the editorial concluded.

THIRTEEN

Choosing Peace

O N THE DAY THE UNITED STATES ENTERED World War I, a crew of
hardy young men was planting western yellow pine and Jeffrey
pine seedlings high on the eastern shoulder of Tallowbox Mountain
which rises to 5,023 feet above sea level over the Applegate Valley.

Among the stand of tree planters stood a sturdy twenty-four-year-old
who tipped the scales at a solid 180 pounds, giving his 5′9″ frame the
appearance of a stout oak trunk. In the idiom of the time and place, he
was tough enough to "rassle" a bear.

"We was working for the government, setting out little trees," recalled
Alfred Fattig whose willowy older brother was working alongside him.
"They were only about a foot tall. Guess they must be big enough for
saw logs now."

Indeed, there are some large pines currently growing on the steep
slopes of Tallowbox, some of whom may have been planted by the
brothers and their tree-planting brethren in the spring of 1917. Having
spent more than a decade slipping away to hunt and explore the local
mountains, Alfred felt at home on those steep slopes. Following the
footsteps of his father, he also found satisfaction in helping life spring
out of the soil.

Like others forming a rugged wall along the southern flank of the
picturesque valley, the mountain had been periodically blackened by

countless wild fires since time immemorial. Each summer down through the ages, fiery spears of electricity streak out of the anvil-shaped storm clouds, igniting forest fires in the region. Indians had also been torching the countryside for thousands of years to improve the hunting ground. When the miners first arrived in the 1850s, many cleared the land with fire in an effort to lay the soil bare in their relentless hunt for gold. Upon the tree planters' arrival, the mountain, battered by Mother Nature and mankind, had already been beaten up nearly as badly as some WWI battlefields.

Yet Tallowbox remains a looming silent sentinel over this land forged by upheaval and tempered by centuries of wind and rain. To the north and east, the Applegate River flows with waters which long provided indigenous people with trout and salmon.

Shortly after the turn of the 20th Century, pine lumber was in high demand throughout the nation. The U.S. Forest Service sought to prepare for the future market while at the same time helping to reforest barren patches of the mountain which was then part of the Crater National Forest. The area is now under the jurisdiction of the U.S. Bureau of Land Management.

Planting trees was hard work, requiring the planter to carry the seedlings up the steep mountain in a canvas bag, chop a hole in the rocky earth with a one-man grub hoe, then gently tamp in the dirt around each fragile seedling. Like an army advancing up the mountain, the men—there were no women planting trees in those days—stood some twenty feet apart as they climbed the steep slope, steeping to plant a seedling about every twenty paces. Their backs aching and arms hanging heavy, they charged slowly onward against the barren foe.

In an April 2, 1917 letter to the forest supervisor, forester F.E. Ames stressed the difficulty of replanting Tallowbox and the necessity of selecting a capable planting crew to ensure proper planting.

"Men who are unable to keep up with the crew, because of age or physical disability, should not be employed," Ames wrote. "In their efforts to keep in line they are practically forced to do inferior work. Only active, able-bodied men should be employed."

In addition to monetary pay, these hardy Johnny Appleseeds of 1917 were rewarded with a spectacular view from their mountain perch. For the Fattig brothers, they could also see their parents' farm just a few miles as the crow flies east of the mountain.

Shipped from the nearby Siskiyou National Forest on March 15 of that year, the pine seedlings were hauled to the end of the wagon road, then packed up to the 3,300-foot elevation on the mountain where their roots were temporarily covered with dirt until they were planted. Snow still covered the mountaintop.

Beginning on the day war was declared on Germany, planting continued through April 26. Although crews had intended to plant 1,200 trees per acre, the difficult terrain coupled with thick patches of madrone, mountain mahogany, canyon live oak and quinine brush restricted the planting to 1,000 seedlings an acre. All told, nearly 2,000 acres of conifers were scheduled to be planted in the region that year. Average cost of planting per acre was around $12.

Although Alfred's surmise that the pines they planted were mature after nearly eighty years, many of the tender seedlings never survived. Upon being planted, the seedlings faced 160 days without rain, followed by consecutive droughts in the summers of 1918 and 1919, according to Forest Service records. On some tracts, mortality was reportedly 100 percent. Winters would bring heavy snow to the high mountains but the blistering hot summers coupled with poor soil took its toll on the seedlings. Less than two months before the seedling planting began, Grants Pass received a record twenty-six inches of snow Feb. 20-24 of that year.

Yet some of those trees tucked carefully into the ground that historical spring no doubt stand today in silent testimony to the tree planters of long ago, providing an evergreen legacy. However, there are also clearcuts in the region which give the summer hillsides the appearance of an aging hound dog afflicted with mange.

But the chatter on the mountainside was not restricted to planting seedlings. Their nation had just gone to war and these were young men full of testosterone. Many talked of joining the military to battle the Kaiser. They'd make short work of the Huns, they promised each other.

When they came down from the mountain, both brothers registered for the draft as required by law. On May 18, 1917, the Selective Service Act was passed by Congress, authorizing President Wilson to temporarily increase the military ranks. In 1917 and 1918 approximately twenty-four million men registered for the draft in the United States. These included men born from Sept 11, 1872 to Sept 12, 1900.

There were three draft registrations during the war with the first held on June 5, 1917, for all men between the ages of twenty-one and thirty-one. Both Fattig brothers registered in the first round, despite their opposition to war. Alfred, then twenty-four, listed himself as a ranch hand while Charlie, twenty-six, described his work as a self-employed farmer. And both filled out question #12: Do you claim exemption from draft (specify grounds)? "I am opposed to war," Alfred replied. "Yes, I am opposed to war," Charlie echoed. Yet neither specified the grounds for their opposition such as religion, an oversight which may have nullified their exemption claims. After all, unless one is an arms merchant, most folks are opposed to war.

Meanwhile, if they were called to wear military uniforms, the brothers had other plans.

"Charlie, he was really the one who planned going to the mountains," Alfred said. "But he was an awful poor hand at going when it got to doing it. I was perfectly willing to go to the mountains. It was just as much my doing.

"That war," he added. "Just imagine human beings shooting each other down like they was dogs. It wasn't right."

Indeed, the younger brother did not back away from the responsibility, reiterating his reluctance to participate in war.

"We didn't wait for our draft papers," he stressed. "We went before they come. But we knew they were coming."

Keep that thought in mind as you consider the folksy tidbit which caught Medford area historian Ben Truwe's eye while poring over the Aug. 25, 1917, issue of the *Jacksonville Post* newspaper.

"Charles and Alford Fattig of Ruch transacted business in this city Monday forenoon," read the blurb which spelled the younger brother's first name wrong. It was in the paper's Local News section, which generally had a lot of two-liners reporting people's comings and goings in what would have passed for tweets roughly a century ago. The brothers were likely stocking up on supplies for a long retreat into the remote Oregon mountains that warm Monday morning in 1917.

As Alfred Fattig said in the interview, the draft summons certainly were coming, albeit later than the brothers anticipated. U.S. District Court records in the Seattle branch of the National Archives reflect that both brothers were ordered to report for the military draft on June 10, 1918. Upon failing to obey the conscription commands, they became wanted men. But the brothers had headed for the mountains more than a year earlier, believing their draft notices were eminent.

The *Jacksonville Post* ran another interesting blurb related to the Fattig brothers on June 29, 1918 which listed five local young men picked for the local military draft. "Hugh Combest of Buncom, George W. Wendt of this city, Edward Learned of Thompson Creek, Archie Rhoten of Applegate, Charles Fattig of Forest Creek, are called in the draft to leave for Ft. McDowell, July 5-9," the article stated, referring to an Army post in California. Of course, the Fattig brothers were long gone, although their parents would have been informed of the draft call.

Had the brothers answered the call to duty, they would have likely only been involved in the tail end of the war. But they had no way of knowing the war would end on Nov. 11 of that year. Moreover, it was the principle that was at stake, Alfred stressed. "We didn't want any part of that war," he reiterated.

Like two seasoned military strategists, they had planned their campaign down to the smallest items. They bought plenty of ammunition for their hunting rifles, enough to keep them supplied in meat indefinitely. They made crude but effective sleeping bags by sewing thick wool blankets inside canvas liners. A lightweight tent was sewn out of canvas to provide a rudimentary shelter from the storm. Extra clothing, fishing gear and plenty of salt was packed. Their wooden matches were dipped in wax, ensuring they would remain dry in the wettest weather. Noting he was hard on footwear, the younger brother estimates he brought half a dozen pair of shoes. He carried a straight razor for shaving but let his hair grow as wild as the buck brush along a mountainside. His locks would be cut in rustic style only when it got in his way. Fashion be damned. Models for *GQ* these latter-day mountain men were not.

Having recruited a pair of burros to haul their supplies, the brothers stashed some of their gear in well-hidden caches along the mountain trails they knew so well. They had their supplies, their survival skills honed from years of hunting and their anti-war convictions. They were locked and loaded to carry out their battle to resist war.

Bidding farewell to their parents and two siblings, all of whom were with them in spirit, they stepped out to begin their years-long resistance in late May of 1917. Heading for the deep woods, they wandered during the first year among the mountains of southwestern Oregon and the far northwest tip of California. They had no base camp, no place to call home. Frequently glancing over their shoulders, they watched their back trail for signs of pursuers.

To modify the famous line from poet Robert Frost, they took the trails least traveled. No area in the region was too remote for their boots. They ventured into the lower Rogue River canyon that writer Zane Grey would make famous in his 1929 novel *Rogue River Feud*. Like Grey when he first fished the lower Rogue in 1925, they fell in love with the roaring whitewater and the prehistoric beauty of the massive rock walls lining the river. But they found too many people drawn to the area, attracted by its fabulous fishing waters. They wandered onward, seeking deeper woods where few ventured.

They hiked south across the California state line to a remote area known as the Hole in the Ground along the north fork of the Smith River. They explored to the east, climbing high to a basin known as Youngs Valley, now part of the Siskiyou Wilderness in the southern tip of the Rogue River-Siskiyou National Forest in California. Crossing back into Oregon, they would hike through the mountains to drop down into the mining town of Waldo just north of the state line for supplies. If they had no furs they had trapped or gold they had panned from a stream to trade at the Waldo or Kerby general stores, they would hike farther along the Boundary Trail to Grayback Mountain and descend down into the Williams Creek drainage leading into the Applegate Valley. This was where they would be met by their parents riding a wagon loaded with supplies.

It was a lonely life, one that weighed heavily on the brothers. After all, America was engaged in a popular war, at least in the beginning, and they had embarked on an unpopular journey.

"We traveled—we didn't stay in one place," Alfred said, noting the exception was the Madstone cabin. "For the three years we was in those mountains, nobody came near us that we didn't want to meet."

Knowing they would be sought by authorities, they each adopted an alias. Alfred's *non de plume* was Albert Barnes; his brother assumed the handle of Charles Hooper.

As it happens, the *Daily Courier* reported on June 14, 1917, that an escaped robber from Grants Pass named J. Austin Hooper, 35, was killed by a sheriff in Greenville, Miss. after Hooper resisted arrest. It seems Hooper had escaped from the Grants Pass jail after disarming deputy sheriff Will Smith on Aug. 16, 1915. He was in jail on a charge of having robbed the Southern Pacific railroad station in that town as well as a bank in the town of Rogue River. These were but a few of numerous robberies he was suspected of committing along the West Coast, the paper noted.

But Alfred maintained it was a coincidence the surname adopted by his brother was the same as the escaped criminal. They didn't commit any crimes while on the dodge beyond evading the draft and illegally killing game to survive, he stressed. After his death, I learned that Alfred's alias was the same as the Jackson County sheriff from 1896 through 1898. I suspect he picked the name of a former sheriff of the county where his parents lived at the time as a bit of mountain man humor. As it happens, the sheriff was the grandfather of A. Donley Barnes who has already been mentioned in these pages.

Aliases aside, he was adamant they were not aligned with political groups opposed to the war in the form of socialists or Wobblies. He insisted it was the decision of two rural young men following the family's belief that killing is murder, even if it is legalized during a time of war.

"That is the reason we didn't go to war," he said. "That is the only reason we went into the Siskiyou Mountains. A lot of friends and neighbors was for us and against the war. They helped us in any way they could. But it was little help we accepted from them."

The brothers relied largely on their own survival skills honed during a youth spent in the outdoors. By the time he was a young teenager, Alfred knew how to field dress a deer and preserve the meat. With little more than a feathered hook and a piece of twine tied to a willow rod, he could coax a trout out of a stream. And he could quickly fashion a dry shelter out of fir boughs.

"You can live pretty well in the mountains if you know what you're about," he said. "I used to know Oregon like a book. I knew every range of mountains and most of the old mountain trails. I've been behind many a pack train in Oregon. The wilder it got, the better I liked it."

As he talked, his dark eyes sparkled. He became more animated, gesturing with his arms. You could sense he was walking those trails again or standing on a mountain peak, feeling the wind in his face as he took in the grandeur of the valleys below.

"I would like to make one last trip back there and that would be to the Madstone cabin," he said. "That was a wild place back in them days."

Actually, it is just as wild as it was a century ago, perhaps even more so. As mentioned early on, the region is now in the center of the Kalmiopsis Wilderness created by congress in the 1964 Wilderness Act. Aside from a few tiny islands of private in-holdings acquired through patented mining claims, there are no permanent legal human inhabitants in the wilderness he once knew. Save for fair weather visitors in the form of hikers, hunters, fishers and a few miners, the area is largely populated by bears, mountain lions and rattlesnakes. Alfred would still have loved it. For lack of a better term, the region has retained its wild tang. Once you taste the Madstone country, the flavor is lasting.

Undeniably, for someone wanting to sit out the ugly side of our democracy, say something like the nose-holding selection in the 2016 general election, the wilderness is still an ideal place to contemplate modern society from afar. However, the U.S. Forest Service is fussy about biped visitations in wilderness areas these days, requiring campers leave no trace and limit their stays. In other words, don't plan on setting up house in a rustic cabin.

Of course, the old man knew his days of hiking back into the wild country he loved were long gone. For him, it was a journey of the mind. He was retracing the dusty trails of his memory in search of images of the mountains he left behind.

"It's been an awful long time," he reiterated. "It don't come too clear."

Lingering still was the memory of their very first year on the dodge, a time spent roaming the mountains, hiding in vacated mining cabins or building makeshift shelters from the driving rain or softly falling snow. They wintered high in the Smith River drainage in northern California, the area known as the Hole in the Ground.

Bivouacked in an abandoned cabin with a small adjoining barn, the brothers prepared for their first winter on the run. Using hand scythes, they cut grass from the nearby meadow, storing it in a small primitive shelter built for the burros. Grain was also brought in from Waldo. They shot a large black bear, slicing some of the meat into bear bacon while making the rest into sausage.

"We mixed a yearling buck with the bear sausage to make it better and make it go further," Alfred said. "There was lots of fish in the river. We made it through that winter in good shape."

But spring found them eager to move on. Perhaps it was the fear of being found or simply a desire to explore pristine wilderness that drove them farther and farther into the mountains.

They were searching for a base of operations to better hide out from anyone the federal government might send after them. The ideal place would be so remote it would take days to reach civilization. It would have a nearby water source for both drinking and fishing. There would be ample game to provide fresh meat. And it would require a nearby forest to provide logs for the cabin.

If you were to stand in front of the Kerbyville Museum and look to the west across the Illinois River hidden by trees, you would see Tennessee Mountain rising to a point on the horizon. Beyond it lays the Josephine

Creek drainage where gold was discovered in 1851—some insist it was 1850—when Oregon was still a territory. Pouring into Josephine Creek is a lively little stream known as Canyon Creek. If you follow that stream due west to its source you will arrive at Canyon Peak, which rises to a little more than 4,900 feet above sea level. Standing on the top of the peak and still looking west past Hawks Rest, a mountain rising to some 4,000 feet, you can see the rugged upper Chetco River drainage running due north. The river is about sixteen air miles west of Kerby but a hiker will find it much farther since level ground is not permitted in this country. You walk up and down and around to get to your destination, never following a straight line. This was the place the brothers decided would be their principal hiding place.

Here a man could yell across a canyon and be answered only by his echo. Once frequented by lonely sourdoughs in quest of gold, the trails were already marked mainly by animal tracks when the brothers arrived. Save for a few crumbling cabins, there was little evidence of past human activity. On a cold fall morning, steaming piles of bear scat could be seen along the river as the bruins fished for a salmon for breakfast. Overhead, a red-tailed hawk could often be seen floating on a thermal, its piercing cries filling the canyons. Underfoot, an alert hiker may discover a beautiful blue-tailed skink under a rotting log. The reptile is harmless, feeding only on bugs. But you would want to avoid the reptile making that buzzing sound nearby. Rattlesnakes in Oregon may not be as large as their Texas cousins but they are just as venomous. Although they prefer to slither into a rock crevice or under a log when they encounter humans, they will strike out when startled or cornered. Best let them be.

For all its harshness, the upper Chetco River is ruggedly attractive country whose botanical beauty bursts forth in early summer. Wafting down the canyon is the natural perfume of azaleas, filling nostrils with a sweet scent and eyes with showy scenes of white, pink and lavender flowers hanging on the evergreen shrub. In the deep shade, dogwood trees bloom, their blossoms resembling large white buttons in the distance. Wild rose with small pink blossoms and yellow centers grow along the river bench. Under the shade of cedar trees grow trout lilies with their mottled leaves resembling the side of a fat trout. Beneath the darker umbrella of a madrone grove, delicate lady slipper orchids peek out, seeming too delicate to grow in this rugged land. Wild iris and cat's ear grow in abundance in the open. The white plumes of flowering bear grass wave like so many banners along the mountain sides. And within this rock garden is the rare *Kalmiopsis leachiana* for which the wilderness would get its name. Looking somewhat like a miniature rhododendron, its tiny pink flowers decorate the region in early June. In some areas of this remarkable wilderness there are also rare cobra lilies—*Darlingtonia californica*—which resemble a rearing cobra. They are often found in marshy areas with serpentine rock outcroppings in southwestern Oregon and the very northwestern tip of California. Their main food source is not from the ground but the insects which get trapped inside the sticky hollow hood. The poor bugs drop down the tube-like stalks where they drown, their decaying bodies forming a nitrogen-rich stew. Thus the plant creates its own source of fertilizer.

But this is no forest primeval of which Longfellow wrote. The Chetco River canyon offers a far more Spartan nature than the Acadians ever knew in Nova Scotia. Alfred had no Evangeline searching for him but, like Gabriel in the epic poem of that name, he was looking for a place to call home. Within the bosom of this wilderness Alfred found an environment indifferent to the politics of war. Here was where he elected to make his stand.

"I picked it because it was a good hunting and fishing place," Alfred said. "There was plenty of game. It was full of wild honey and lots of huckleberries, lots of deer and bear. There was lots of live oak loaded with acorns that stayed good all winter. Them deer and bear stayed fat on acorns. There was furs that brought a good price. There was gold, too. It was no trouble to make a living."

Nor was it any trouble avoiding people. Standing on the lonely ridge overlooking the Madstone cabin site, you are enveloped in solitude. The tall Jeffrey pine and shorter knobcone pine offer only silence. Save for the ghostly gusts of the wind swaying the conifer branches, the ridges are still as statues. Even the names of the geological features conjure up wild images: Hawks Rest, Vulcan Peak, Devils Backbone, Buckskin Peak, Eagle Mountain, Snaketooth Butte. This is no place for those accustomed to a hot bath and a soft bed. This is where you roll your own, push back your Stetson and breathe deeply of life, providing the tobacco smoke doesn't cause a hacking cough.

Few regions in the contiguous United States could have offered them a better command post for their retreat from the military draft. Even today, be prepared for an arduous thirty-mile round trip hike over precious little level ground to reach the site when hiking in from interior Oregon. It is only when the blue expanse of the sky is broken by the white contrail of a passing jet that today's visitor is reminded of the present. But a century ago there were no jets to disturb one's thoughts. At night, stretched out in their homemade sleeping bags, the brothers could watch a dazzling display of stars without being distracted by an occasional passing satellite. On those nights with a full moon, they would see the river canyon swathed in soft moonlight whose silence would only be broken by the occasional mournful cry of a coyote. Morning would bring the promising sunlight of another day in their beautifully rugged world of flourishing greenery amid the mountain rocks cut through by a wild river canyon. By the time the brothers discovered the region, most of the sourdoughs who had ventured far into the mountains in search of the mother lode had left for better prospects or had died hunting for the gleam of yellow, each firmly convinced with his dying breath that a big strike was just a shovelful of dirt away. Scattered throughout the mountains were still a handful of old miners, coarse men who preferred the call of the wild and the chuckle of a mountain stream to the tiresome conversation of their fellow man. We shall meet one such interesting character who befriended the brothers as we get further along, but first the brothers—Alfred and a friend did most of the work—had to build a cabin.

FOURTEEN

Erecting a Cabin

T HE SITE ALFRED SELECTED FOR THE CABIN is on a bench overlooking
the east side of the river which flows north at this point before
eventually turning west to empty into the Pacific Ocean. The bench is at
1,950 feet above sea level, an elevation which would bring wet snow
come winter but not so much they would not be able to hike out for supplies or flee from cabin fever. Within a stone's throw of the site is a deep
blue pool as clear as any swimming pool. The water is crystal clear, not
because of an infusion of chlorine and other chemicals, but because it is
filtered naturally by the rocks from whence it flows. The river water
would be used for drinking and, when they could no longer endure being
physically hygiene challenged, for bathing.

Having been on the lam for a year without a place to call home, Alfred
was eager to build a permanent shelter where he could rest for long
periods in a place he felt secure. It was early in the summer of 1918. Back
in the Applegate Valley, their parents had received the brothers's draft
notices in the mail and had notified them during a clandestine resupply
mission of the news. They knew they were wanted for evading military
conscription. No longer was it a topic of conjecture around the campfire.

But the brothers, who had wintered together, had temporarily parted
ways, a circumstance which periodically occurred during their exile from
society. They may have shared an objection to war but there were precious

few other beliefs they agreed upon. You will recall Alfred was not pleased to have a brother who was an infidel, although Uncle Charlie described himself in religious terms as a "damned atheist." I'm not sure if the pun was intended. The bottom line was their alliance was shaky at best. Like a troubled marriage, the partnership could only survive if they maintained their distance, parting occasionally. It isn't hard to imagine them sitting around a campfire at night, barking at each other instead of talking.

"Charlie and I weren't together when we started building that cabin," Alfred said. "He was off somewhere. I don't remember where. He came back up after we had pretty much finished the job."

During all my formative years, I had been told that uncles Alfred and Charlie had worked together to build the Madstone cabin. Yet Alfred informed us that his brother had little to do with the construction. Obviously, it would have been interesting to have the input of the older brother concerning the cabin's construction. As a contrarian, he would have likely had a different version of the story, albeit there is no reason to doubt Alfred's memory.

Although Alfred, who was handy with tools, said he built most of the cabin, he was assisted by a young man named Eldon Gregg, a friend from the Applegate Valley who apparently shared their views on the war. However, Alfred was quick to observe that his friend was not avoiding the draft. Rather, Gregg, who Alfred figured was about seventeen when the cabin was built, simply liked roaming the mountains. His was a carefree spirit as free as the water flowing down the river canyon.

Alfred described him as a lanky fellow with a hatchet face who was at home in the deep woods.

"He could handle a gun just like it was one of his arms," he said. "He had an old-time black powder rifle, 1873 model. There aren't many of those old guns around anymore. Eldon was wonderful in those hills and a good singer."

Alfred's floor plan for the mountain retreat was simple: there would be a single-room log cabin with a smokehouse a few feet away. The cabin's roof would be extended to the smokehouse, creating a sheltered area between the two structures which would be used to keep firewood dry. Remember, this was only some twenty-four miles from the coast as the crow flies. Torrential downpours were not uncommon. The site was also high enough to bring some snow come winter so the cabin would have to be snug, keeping out the bone-chilling cold carried on the biting winds whipping down the canyon. It also had to withstand the powerful curiosity of mischievous black bears looking for an easy snack when the brothers were away.

Alfred had selected the cabin site not only because of its proximity to the river: there was a stand of cedar trees on the river bench which would provide ideal logs for the cabin. The logs needed to be roughly a foot or slightly larger in diameter but could not be so large they could not be handled by two men. Within the stand were plenty of trees that pleased Alfred's critical eye.

Rolling up their sleeves and picking up their axes, the two young men turned to the stand of cedars.

"We built the cabin out of round peeled logs and red cedar at that," my uncle said. "They don't rot easy, last a long time."

Western red cedar, an extremely lightweight wood, is known for its straight-grained wood with its attractive reddish color. It also emits a pleasant fragrance long after the wood becomes part of a cabin or sawed into lumber. As he had observed, it resists decay, an important consideration in this region of heavy winter precipitation.

They worked with the same tools their forefathers had employed to build cabins. In addition to axes, they had a crosscut saw, known as a misery whip because of the backbreaking labor required to whip the teeth back and forth as it eats through the wood. They used a froe for splitting cedar shakes for the roof and a drawknife to peel the bark from the logs. But their most important tool was the knowledge they carried inside their heads, thanks to having helped raise barns and other structures back in the Applegate Valley.

For a power source they had their two burros which had helped pack their supplies back into the mountains. Shorn of their heavy packs, the beasts of burden were employed to drag the logs the short distance to the cabin.

"I tied rope to the pack saddles and they just snaked the logs right up there where we wanted them," Alfred said. "Now, you have to get acquainted with a burro or he ain't gonna do anything. You have to do it his way."

We were about to get a primer on working with a burro, something our uncle clearly knew of which he spoke.

"You just treat him nice and he'll work for you," he explained. "You don't be mean to them like some people do their horses. You treat them gentle. Firm, but gentle. A burro is little but they're strong, real strong for their size."

A few hundred feet upstream from the cabin sites the brothers discovered a small meadow. Although it contained more rocks than grass, the area, dubbed "Jack's Pasture" after one of the burros, would serve as a grazing area for the animals that had served them so faithfully.

"We took our burros and put them out there after they got done dragging them logs for us," he said. "They didn't wander very far. There wasn't any place for them to go."

With the logs laid out where they were handy, the men began forming a foundation for the cabin which would only have a single story. Truth be told, there wasn't much of a foundation, just rocks and gravelly dirt mixed together to form a level base on which to place the first layer of logs. They began with the larger logs at the bottom, followed by smaller logs as the walls grew. But they did not hastily grab the nearest log. They carefully chose each one so it would fit well with its woody neighbor. While it would not resemble a giant Lincoln Logs set, the cabin logs fit snugly together like masonry. Each log was carefully notched at each end to fit into the log onto which it was being placed. It was time-consuming work which took patience and planning. Working throughout the summer, the two would periodically take a break and take stock of their progress.

"Now, you can't hurry something like that," Alfred cautioned. "You gotta take it slow and sure. A log cabin ain't too hard to build if you approach it right."

Clay and moss was used to caulk the spaces between the logs. No cold winter wind was going to whistle through the cracks into this log fortress.

"The way we done it was to set the logs in as tight as we possibly could, then dig down in the earth to get clay," he said, noting they mined the clay from a site near the river. "You daub that clay in there real good. Seals it right up."

To bring much needed light into the log structure, they would install small glass windows salvaged from an old vacated cabin farther down the river. While the cabin with its dirt floor wouldn't have received the Good Housekeeping seal of approval, it was beginning to look like a home, rustic that it was.

The smokehouse was built about twelve feet from the main cabin with poles connecting the two structures. It was largely a stone fireplace with a small shed built around it. But there was no chimney. Instead, the smoke would diffuse slowly through the cracks in the shed. From a distance when salmon or venison was being cured, it must have looked like a shed about to burst into flames. Dried madrone, a hardwood known for burning slow and clean, was the wood they often employed for the job, mixing it with other wood to produce flavorful smoke. Pine was never used.

"I figured when I was building it that might be a fire trap, that smoke-house," Alfred mused. "But we always kept the smoking fire real low. You want smoke, not fire. You get better smoked meat that way anyway."

Capping the cabin and smokehouse were cedar shakes split to form a waterproof cover.

"You gotta get those shakes out of a big tree," he said. "Its got to be three feet through at least. It just takes patience to split 'em all."

Heat was provided by an old stove scavenged from another old cabin site. A stone foundation built beneath the stove stored heat which radiated out at night after the fire had died away.

"It's coming to me now," he said as he recalled where they found the stove. "I had found another cabin that had burnt down. The stove was still good enough to the use. I packed it over to the Madstone. It was a good many miles from there. I remember that."

No doubt packing a heavy iron stove over the steep, rugged terrain wouldn't be a trip easily forgotten.

"A man can carry a hundred pounds a short distance," he said. "Yes, a man is a mule when he gets used to being a mule. You just have to be toughened into it."

I had meant to ask him why the burros weren't employed to do the stove-packing job but his lunch was brought in at that point and we never got back to the subject. Perhaps the answer was that there are simply some things a burro refuses to do, no matter how much you cajole them. Packing a heavy wood stove may be high on that list.

While they were building the cabin, Alfred and his assistant periodically took a few days off to reconnoiter the area and look for any abandoned cabins which could be cannibalized for wood, rough hewed as it would likely be. It was permissible to take from a vacated cabin. Taking from a cabin still in use was stealing, something they did not condone. They may have been deemed scofflaws in the eyes of society but they had their principles.

It was kosher to enter an unoccupied but maintained cabin to escape a storm or while seeking a warm place to spend a snowy night, providing you treated the cabin with respect. Alfred and Gregg were in such dire straits when they happened upon a cabin on the Little Chetco River a half dozen miles northeast of the Madstone cabin during a ferocious summer thunderstorm. Flashes of light followed by thunderous roars filled the canyon. Rain came down in torrents.

The soaked men pounded on the door to the Emily cabin but no one was around. They opened the door and stepped out of the storm. Built by an Englishman named Emily around 1880, the cabin with its rock foundation had been owned by a succession of miners after Emily returned to his homeland, reputedly rich from the gold he found in the area.

"Me and the Gregg boy, we was two hungry guys, I'll tell you," Alfred said of their visitation. "We had walked a long ways without anything to eat. We took some jerked venison that had been left there."

Remember, this was during an era when cabin doors were seldom locked. Folks were expected to follow the unwritten code of the mountains. A hungry visitor could enter an unoccupied cabin to seek shelter or food as long as he ate only what was needed. After having eaten and rested, they would often leave a note expressing their appreciation. If possible, they would leave something in exchange for the uninvited hospitality.

The jerky was tough as sun-baked rawhide but helped quell their hunger pains, Alfred recalled. On the table was a plate which contained a small mound of white crystals. Being young and impulsive, Gregg wet a finger, stuck it in the pile and tasted the crystals. He announced it was sugar.

"Well, I tasted it and told him it was salt," Alfred said. "We both thought something was wrong with t'other."

More sampling determined that neither had gone around the bend with cabin fever. Turns out they were both right.

"What happened was someone had poured salt on one side of the pile and sugar on the other," Alfred said, laughing hard at the memory of someone's idea of mountain man humor.

To digress for a moment, when I hiked into the Madstone cabin site in the late 1980s with my older brother Jim and his son, Todd, the Emily cabin was still standing, although it had likely been rehabilitated since the sugar-salt debate. But the front door had been ripped off by a bear that had first stood on his hind legs and peered through a window to the left of the door. The hairy suspect left a muddy paw print on the window before he went to work dismantling the door. Sadly, the old cabin was burned by the half-million-acre Biscuit fire that swept through the region in July of 2002. The site is now one of the few patented mining claims in the national forest.

Back at the Madstone site in the summer of 1918, Charlie had returned shortly before the cabin was completed. He assisted with the remainder of the work but he wasn't much help when it came to heavy lifting. Something about a bad back, Alfred noted.

When the autumn winds began carrying the hint of the coming winter, Gregg would leave the wilderness to continue his wandering.

As he did frequently while talking about the past, Alfred stopped to ponder the distant years.

"I think he was shot and killed after that, so I heard later," he said of his young friend. "That was down in California. But I never did know for certain."

What he did know for certain was their rough-hewed hideaway was ready for occupancy, complete with a little pole and shingle outhouse. While some folks would look askance at the spread that included bunks whose mattresses were made of grass harvested from the meadow, Alfred was quick to observe that comfort is relative.

"It's a lot better than living out of doors in that country," he said, chuckling. "You get in a warm cabin, it's a mighty good feeling."

Strategically, it was also well placed. The cabin was only a two-day hike from Kerby with its general store where they could trade the fur they had trapped and the gold they panned.

"You could get to it without getting your feet wet by taking the trail up Josephine Creek," Alfred said as he mentally retraced his steps to the cabin. "You just follow along Canyon Creek to the peak, then stay on the left side of the ridge that goes down to river."

His mind did skip over a few miles of hard hiking over forgotten mountains and ridges but his directions are in the ballpark. Canyon Peak, which had a fire lookout atop it when I was a youngster, didn't have a name when the brothers were on the lam.

After a year of living out of doors, they were stoked about having a roof over their heads. Sitting warm and dry in a cabin with a hot cup of cowboy coffee in your hand while the rain is beating on the shake roof is comfort enough in the wilderness, he offered.

"Yes sir, it was a well-built cabin," he said. "We peeled the logs, made it real nice. It was a fine cabin, built like a cabin should be built.

"Back then, there weren't very many people who know'd about it," he added. "It was beautiful. I always thought it was the best looking cabin I'd ever seen. I feel bad that it's gone."

The cabin was still standing when the U.S. Forest Service used it as the base camp for fighting a wild fire in the Chetco River drainage in the summer of 1940. That fire did not reach the cabin, according to those who were there.

But it had already been destroyed by fire when the late Len Ramp, a well respected geologist who worked for more than thirty years for the Oregon Department of Geology and Mineral Industries, hiked into the site in 1954. Although Ramp was checking for chromite deposits in the upper Chetco River area, the avid hiker had a keen interest in regional history and made a point of checking out the site with the unusual name. There were few remote places in southwest Oregon he had not visited during his years working as a geologist.

"Madstone cabin burned a few years before I got there," Ramp told me in 1989. "A forest fire may have moved through there or someone may have burned it."

Noting all that remained then were the remnants of several burned cabin logs and a few rusting pans, he observed it wasn't unusual for an old cabin to burn down after a hiker or hunter seeking shelter started a warming fire and left it unattended.

"No one knows for sure what happened to the cabin," said Ramp who died in 2012 at age eighty-five. "I do know it is quite a hike in there."

MADSTONE

FIFTEEN

Life in Madstone Country

E AGER TO MOVE INTO THEIR NEW DIGS, the brothers quickly set up house and began to settling in. First on their agenda was making sure they would have a continuous supply of food. Grabbing their picks and shovels, they dug a small garden on the east side of the cabin where there was a little top soil over the rocky subsoil. After removing as many rocks as was practical, they planted turnips, cabbage and a few other vegetable seeds they had acquired during a resupply trip. Burro poop provided fertilizer.

The problem with establishing a garden in a wilderness, of course, is trying to keep wild creatures out of the vegetables in search of a free lunch. To guard against the detachment of deer posted in the area, the brothers erected a makeshift wooden fence of limbs and brush some six feet high. They felt confident no deer could breach their defenses.

"Well, we left there for a month or so," Alfred said. "When we got back we found we didn't have no garden. That high fence didn't even start to keep the deer out. Them deer, they just jumped the fence."

With their garden faring poorly, they turned to nature's nursery for wild vegetables. One favorite was miner's lettuce, also known as Indian lettuce, a leafy green plant which is rich in vitamin C. Since *Claytonia perfoliata* is ubiquitous throughout the region, they had a natural salad at their disposal wherever they went. Salad dressing was not on the menu, of course.

In the fall, they picked huckleberries which often hung thick from bushes high on the ridge. Small wild blackberries would be found down closer to streams in late summer. And spring brought wild strawberries which, while small, were packed with flavor.

They also gambled a bit by gathering a plant known as Queen Anne's lace—*Daucus carota*—which has a small root resembling a small carrot, giving it the alias of wild carrot. The problem is that poison hemlock—*Conium maculatum*—looks very much the same. Munching on a wild carrot is fine. Chowing down on poison hemlock can be life changing, something the philosopher Socrates could have attested to since he committed suicide by drinking a cup of poison hemlock.

Fattig family friend A. Donley Barnes, born a few blocks from the county courthouse in Grants Pass on March 1, 1905, recalled stories about the brothers surviving on venison, fish and Queen Anne's lace.

"It has a white flower about that big around," he told me in 1988, forming a circle with his thumb and forefinger. "But you got to be awful careful of it because it's exactly the same flower as hemlock, except there is a little purple spot in the center. That was supposed to represent a spot where the queen pricked her finger making embroidery."

The plants do have a taproot which is edible, although is it much shorter than a garden carrot, he said.

"I've never tried any," he said. "They resemble the hemlock so much that I didn't take any chances. Every once in a while you hear about some guy eating Queen Anne's lace and it turns out to be hemlock. That'll kill you."

Let his observations be words of caution to any reader out there who thinks he or she might like to snack on some Queen Anne's lace. You have been forewarned.

When the brothers were without coffee, a condition in which they often found themselves, they dried the leaves of the *yerba buena* plant, a native herb with a strong mint scent answering to the Latin name of *Clinopodium douglasii*. The Spanish name means "good herb." If you appreciate mint tea, it is a brisk morning drink which tends to clear the sinuses.

Shortly after moving into the Madstone cabin, the brothers found what they needed to sweeten their tea: a large fire-killed cedar with a dark porthole from which flowed in and out a seemingly endless squadron of honey bees. The bee tree was just up the river from the cabin. Early one morning before the airborne stingers had awakened to reveille, the brothers cut down the cedar. They immediately employed smoke to keep the attacking bees at bay. Swatting at an occasional sting, the honey bandits cut open the bee tree to harvest what Alfred estimated was some 200 pounds of honey the color of amber. From the honey rose the sweet fragrance of azalea and rhododendron blossoms. The honey was strained through cloth to rid the honey of wax and dead bees. Now they could sip sweetened mint tea or rare cup of coffee. Nor was the wax wasted. Using strands of twine, the brothers fashioned wax candles for the nights ahead.

While deer invading the small garden may have been a nuisance, they were welcome guests at the dinner table. In addition to being cut into steaks or made into a stew, the venison was also made into jerky. Salting it liberally, providing they had salt on hand, they cured it in their smoke-house. Often it was a piece of jerky which kept the brothers going during one of their frequent reconnaissance trips in the region.

"The older jerky gets, the harder it gets," Alfred said. "It gets so you can't eat it with your teeth. You have to pound it into dust."

When the jerky became too tough for the Oregon mountain men of the early 20th Century, they made their version of pemmican. The small pressed cake of shredded meat mixed with fat and dried berries were once a common fare of many North American Indians. After pounding the jerky soft, the brothers would add flour and berries to make a mixture which Alfred described as a thick gravy. "I thought it was tasty—Charlie, he didn't like it much," he said.

When they grew tired of venison, the brothers turned to bear meat. They purposefully waited to hunt bears in late summer or fall after the bruins had grown fat on berries and salmon.

"The smokehouse was where we made the bear bacon," Alfred said.

"Bear meat is a bit greasy and can be overpowering. But it made pretty good bacon once you got used to it."

During the fall, they would catch salmon swimming up the river to spawn. These were large Chinook salmon often tipping the scales at thirty pounds, had they any scales to weigh the lunkers. They could sometimes gaff salmon in the riffle below the pool near the cabin where the fish would gather to build spawning beds in the gravel. Steelhead trout, a migratory rainbow sometimes weighing as much as twenty pounds, often shadow the larger salmon, hoping to feed on the fresh roe released by a spawning hen. Strange though it may be, a female salmon is called a hen. The male? A buck. Just how those monikers came to be we'll save for another time since I don't have the foggiest. What I do know is that one large Chinook salmon, whose alias is rightfully the king salmon, provided a rich source of protein for the hungry brothers.

After all those years, Alfred still marveled at the annual run of salmon swimming upstream to spawn and die. After being spawned in a river or stream, the salmon fry—juveniles—eventually swim downstream to the ocean where they live until returning some four to five years later to the area where they were hatched. Sexually fulfilled, they die with a smile on their face, completing an ancient cycle of life.

"That fish is a strange thing," he said. "He gives up his life at a certain time. He has to, just to keep his kind going."

A salmon's death is not in vain. When its body decays in the river, it becomes important nutrient in the water, providing it didn't become food for a bear which became bacon for the brothers in the circle of life that was the upper Chetco River a century ago.

In the spring and summer, glistening rainbow and cutthroat trout filled the river. A careful angler dangling an artificial fly made of quail feathers or a grasshopper on a hook could often entice a trout to bite.

"I tell you, there ain't no fish that will beat them for flavor," Alfred said of trout caught fresh and shiny out of a mountain stream. "No sir, that fishing just couldn't be better. There ain't no fish that beats the mountain trout."

A cup of steaming yerba buena tea and some pan-fried trout was common breakfast fare at the cabin during the warmer months. Since the trout were often more than foot long, a couple would serve as a full meal.

If trout fishing was exceptionally good, the brothers would turn to the smokehouse to preserve the fish. After all, they had no refrigerator or freezer. Smoked food extended the shelf life of the food.

"Good as mountain trout are fresh, they are even better smoked," Alfred said. "Nothing better."

If the fish weren't biting, a meal could be made out of the gray squirrels barking at them from the tops of pine trees. A .22 caliber revolver was generally the weapon used to bag a squirrel since a large caliber weapon would blow the little animal to smithereens.

"After a while, I got to be a crack shot with that hand gun," he said. "I could pick those squirrels out of those trees pretty easy."

Although the brothers would eat squirrel in a pinch, they preferred anything but the skinny arboreal rodent. High on their wilderness shopping list were grouse and quail. The trick was to shoot them in the head to avoid ruining the breast meat where the bulk of the meat was found. Quail usually group in coveys but the larger grouse, about the size of a small chicken, are often solitary.

"You can hear them grouse a'hooting," he said, adding that he turned to a rifle when hunting grouse since they were often too far away for a pistol shot. "You just stand there in the trees, listening to their hooting until you locate them up in the trees."

But the brothers only hunted game when it was necessary for their survival. They did not shoot a buck simply because it was sporting a large set of antlers. Not only were they not interested in how large its rack, but they also knew that the meat of a younger deer was more tender and tastier. Not that they would pass up a large buck since it would provide ample meat, albeit tougher to chew.

When their larder was full, the Fattig brothers often made a point of venturing out to watch the wonders of nature. While deer were invariably interesting to study, the duo was also fascinated by everything from a deer mouse to a prowling black bear. They figured every creature filled a niche in Mother Nature's grand scheme.

But perhaps the most mysterious were the felines in the form of bobcats and cougars. Both were seldom seen but were out there in the woods, no doubt watching without being noticed. While bobcats are perhaps twice the size of one of our housecats, a large cougar can weigh in at over 200 pounds and stretch out to some ten feet if you include the long tail.

Because of its size and reputation, the mountain lion is usually the topic of hair-raising stories told around Oregon campfires at night. The tales usually involve a big cat creeping up on a man backed up to a cliff. Topping it off is the catamount's blood curdling scream as it leaps out of the darkness to land on its prey.

But Alfred scoffed at those stories, noting they were simply tales meant to entertain those who don't know their way around the woods. While I acknowledged his vast knowledge of the outdoors, I questioned his conclusion about silent cougars based on my scary experience as a runaway in Madstone country.

"Well, I never heard one make a noise," he said when I told him of my experience. "They are pretty quiet animals, quiet but smart. I stayed in country where their tracks are thick but I haven't seen many. And then it was just a glimpse. They know when anybody else is around."

So did the burros when a cougar came near the cabin, he said, noting they began braying excitedly when they caught scent of a cougar. A prowling bear would also set them off. An omnivore as well as an opportunist, a large bear would kill a burro if given a chance, he observed.

"There was a lot of bears around our cabin," he said. "You could listen at night and hear them growl at each other. The little cubs used to slap each other around at night and play rough. Sometimes the big bears would do the same. That was music to my ears."

More than once the brothers had to drive away a bear nosing around the nervous burros. Bruins were a much more common sight than people in the region. The brothers once discovered a bear wallow which Alfred described as a muddy place among a thicket of cedar trees. Standing on their hind legs, the bears left scratch marks on trees some ten feet off the ground, he said.

Occasionally, the brothers would meet one of the hairy fellows along

Jonas and Harriett Viola Fattig posed for a wedding photograph in 1889 in Beaver City, Nebraska. Smiling in front of a camera was not proper form back in the day.

Harriet Viola Fattig with daughters Laura (*standing*) and Bessie Bell early in 1904. Bessie died later that year. The photo was taken at F.L. Camps Studio, Ashland, Oregon.

Alfred Fattig in 1913, age 21, four years before
he evaded the WWI military draft.

Paul Fattig, Sr., the author's father and younger brother of Alfred
and Charlie, ca. 1912.

JOSEPH KNOWLES IN WILDERNESS GARB. PHOTOGRAPHED AT MEGAN-
TIC ON THE DAY HE CAME OUT OF THE WOODS, OCTOBER 4, 1913

A staged promotional photo of Joseph Knowles, aka "Nature
Man." The shot was taken in Maine a year before he ventured
into the wilds of southwest Oregon.

The actual madstone Alfred Fattig removed from a buck he shot in the Chetco River drainage in what is now the Kalmiopsis Wilderness. The stone was the inspiration for naming the brothers' wilderness refuge. Madstone Creek in the Kalmiopsis was also named for the madstone.

The entire student body at Uniontown School in the Applegate Valley in 1922. Paul Fattig, Sr. is the tall fellow in back.

The Fattig brothers would have found Kerby much like this when they hiked in from the Madstone cabin for supplies during their mountain days. This photo of Kerby was taken in the 1920s. Eight Dollar Mountain looms in the background.

Paul Fattig, Sr. poses proudly in his U.S. Forest Service uniform in the mid-1930s. As a ranger who periodically rode horses when out in the Siskiyou National Forest, he is wearing a pair of riding breeches called jodhpurs.

IS FIFTH IN UNION AR STAMPS

the states and terri-
elfth federal reserve
ale of War Savings
ads third among the
nion in the sale of
according to Theo-
San Francisco, direc-
ent war savings ur-
e Twelfth district.

here Wednesday on
from a vacation trip
ne park and the Cana-
held a brief conference
ingham and Robert E.
the thrift movement in

stment in Thrift and
mps and Treasury Cer-
19 amounted to $1,865,-
his state fifth place
of the union for that
e, "and nothing could
he prosperity of the
igures. Though condi-
the thrift movement
m last year we hope
success in leading the
g the homely ways of
. From January 1 to
gate value of Oregon's
thrift securities was

part of our work," said
in convincing those
Liberty bonds during
air interests are beat
g these securities and
government bonds at
rices. This effort has
troversy with promot-
oil well and mining
ve been reaping a rich
ing owners of govern-
ade them for compara-
hares of stock. These
a great deal to do with

MEDFORD BOY WHO DODGED DRAFT 3 YEARS GIVES UP

Alfred Fattig, draft dodger, is to
make his home in the Multnomah
county jail for the next nine months.
When his last visible means of support was about to vanish, Fattig surrendered himself Saturday to the sheriff of Jackson county, and Thursday
morning in the federal court pleaded
guilty to the charge and was sentenced
to serve nine months in the county jail.
He started out three years ago from
his father's home near Medford with
his brother Charles when they decided
they would not join the army on account of conscientious objections. The
two took 1000 rounds of ammunition,
sleeping bags and a large supply of
clothing and matches.

During the three years Alfred has
lived the life of a hermit in the woods,
existing on deer and bear meat, huckleberries and wild honey. Over a year
ago his brother became tired of the
life and returned to civilization to work.
Alfred does not know where Charles is.
Because he only had six shells left and
because his body was becoming so
weak on account of the lack of food
other than meat, Alfred decided he
would surrender and pay the penalty.
Fattig is unable to eat today because
his stomach is so weak it will not
stand solid food. Prisoners in the
county jail gave him the first real
haircut he has had for three years.
Fattig took along scissors and endeavored to cut his own hair whenever it
got long enough to bother him.

Fattig's hearing is impaired a little,
as he has been away from all noise.
Life became so lonely in the woods,
he said, that he even feared his own
voice. Fattig was raised in the Dunkard church and claims his religious
belief...
ficial...
broth...

SHIRKER WHO FLED GETS NINE MONTHS

Alfred Fattig

TRESSES SHORN AS GIRL SLEEPS

Grace Fairfax was proud of her
hair. It was dark brown wavy and
18 inches long. Before she went to
bed Tuesday night she braided it

Oregonian.

JULY 29, 1920   PRICE FIVE CENTS

LES' DAILY
ON SCHEDULE

K RAILES WALL
ARE HURT.

Open Ground and
neath to Flow,
cial Admits.

Cal, July 28 —(Spe-
21.s.M. today
was reported
in the tremblor, but
on one man was in-
fatally, and three
escaped death when
wall of a building
an at Seventh and
collapsed.
et was Harry Reid-
gnes. It is said that
shened by repeated

Cal., July 28 —A
shock was felt here
his morning,
which was light in
other recent ones,
its engineer to have
wells on property

the neighborhood of
in the "oil belt"
part of the city.
to be giving forth
ities of oil of high
her was reported as
ment dangerous for

public works au-
sound be developed
ity

VERBAL VOLLEYS ON MILK FIRED

Dairy League and Investi-gator Both Attacked.

KATZ RE-ELECTED PRESIDENT

Chief of Co-operative Body
Asks for Commission.

DISTRIBUTOR HAS QUERY

C. M. Gregory Asks Why Necessity
of "Hide-Bound" Contract of
8½ Years on Producers.

Re-election of Alma D. Katz as
president of the Oregon Dairymen's
Co-operative league, the firing of a
breach de of Lional C Mackay and the
milk investigated through a letter
addressed to Mayor Baker and a statement passed by C. M. Gregory, repre-
senting the Portland milk distribut-

GASOLINE RATIONING TO REMAIN EFFECTIVE

PRICE OF FUEL RANGES FROM
25½ TO 30 CENTS.

Shortage Expected to Continue
Throughout August—No Re-
lief in Sight.

According to announcement made
yesterday by officials of the Standard
Oil company, the existing rules of
supplying all commercial and industrial needs with gasoline to 100 per
cent capacity and of placing users to
20 per cent of their tank capacity will
be continued throughout August.
Emphasis is laid on the fact that commercial needs and industrial requirements are being met fully.

Developments of yesterday 'fen-
pisted of an increase in price from
15½ cents to 37 cents by the Union
Oil company.

The Standard, was selling at 30½
cents per gallon with no information
regarding any change. However,
Manager Hainly declared that the
price is controlled solely by supply
and demand, and so that it was impossible to make any statement as to
possibility of price changes.

The Shell company was pricing gasoline at 30 cents yesterday, Associated
at 37 cents and Standard at 15½ cents.
The Associated has adopted the method
of establishing its distribution by making an equal amount available each
day of its bi-weekly supply. When
that is gone no more is to be had until the following day). Consumers are

SLACKER LIVES 3 YEARS IN FOREST

Alfred Fattig Is Driven
Out by Solitude.

OREGON HERMIT SURRENDERS

Scruples Against Killing
Cause of Flight.

BROTHERS ARE SEPARATED

Medford Boys Support Life on
Game and Berries They
Gather in Woods.

Living on deer and bear meat, with
honey and huckleberries for three
years, and with only half a dozen
shells of ammunition remaining, Alfred Fattig, draft dodger, could stand
the solitude of the Siskiyou mountains no longer. He surrendered to
the sheriff of Jackson county

The end of the trail for Alfred Fattig. These articles detailing Alfred's surrender are from the *Oregon Journal* (top) and the *Oregonian* newspapers in Portland. Both are dated July 29, 1920.

Charlie Fattig *(left)* hold the reins of a pack horse at the Fattig farm in southern Oregon's Illinois Valley during the early 1930s. Looking on is family patriarch Jonas Fattig.

Charlie Fattig spent much of his time panning for gold in southwest Oregon after his encounter with Uncle Sam. This photo was taken in the early 1940s. The sidearm indicates he was ready for rattlesnakes or claim jumpers.

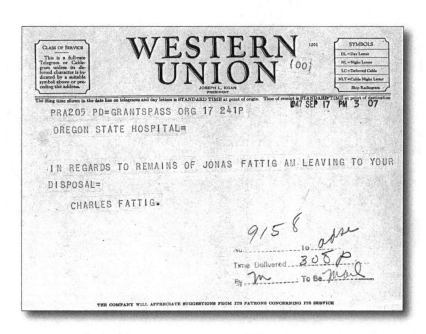

WESTERN UNION (00)

1201

JOSEPH L. EGAN
PRESIDENT

The filing time shown in the date line on telegrams and day letters is STANDARD TIME at point of origin. Time of receipt is STANDARD TIME at point of destination

047 SEP 17 PM 3 07

PRA205 PD=GRANTSPASS ORG 17 241P

OREGON STATE HOSPITAL=

IN REGARDS TO REMAINS OF JONAS FATTIG AM LEAVING TO YOUR

DISPOSAL=

CHARLES FATTIG.

9158

No. .... To ....

Time Delivered ... 3 0 5 P

By .... To Be ....

Upon learning of his father's death in September of 1947 in the Oregon State Hospital, Charlie Fattig displayed no feelings when answering the telegram from the hospital. The author and his wife obtained Jonas Fattig's cremated remains from the hospital nearly 60 years later and placed them next to the grave of Bessie Bell Fattig in the Hargadine Cemetery in Ashland, Oregon.

Charlie Fattig waits for a customer in front of the service station he purchased around 1947 a few miles south of Wonder, Oregon. Family lore is that he bought the business after selling the family patriarch's farm.

The water in the Chetco River that was within a stone's throw of the Madstone cabin site is crystal clear. Madstone Creek flows in from the west near this location. Bears are abundant in the Madstone country, a fact the author discovered upon venturing into the area while running away from home when he was 14.

In the early 1970s, George Fattig, the author's twin brother, checked out the fireplace built at their Waters Creek home by their father, Paul Fattig, Sr. An Army combat veteran in Vietnam, George let his hair out upon completing his tour of duty.

Save for the stone fireplace, the ramshackle Fattig house along Waters Creek near Wonder, Oregon, did not fare well after the family moved "uptown" to Kerby.

In the late 1980s, the author hiked into the Madstone cabin site with Rene Casteran, wilderness ranger for the Siskiyou National Forest. The cabin had burned down decades earlier.

Charles Fattig, the author's brother who served two Army tours in Vietnam, was the first sibling to visit the cabin site where their uncles hid out during WWI. During his arduous hike in the fall of 1981, Charles took only photographs, leaving relics that included square nails, old cartridges, frying pans and a well-worn shovel.

The Fattig brothers (*clockwise from top*): Paul, Sr. (age 40), Charlie (age 70), and Alfred (age 97).

a narrow trail. There was the day when the younger brother came around a bend in a trail to find two black bears ambling nonchalantly toward him. He simply stepped aside a safe distance to let them pass.

"They was as black as tar, both of 'em," he said. "They just went on by. Me, I didn't have a gun."

In another incident involving a close encounter with a bruin, the brothers were hiking out together for supplies. The encounter occurred just as they were walking through a heavily forested area where the light was dim.

"Me and my brother, we had just passed a big tree about six-foot through when I heard his gun crack," Alfred said, noting he nearly jumped out of his skin. "A big bear rolled out right by me. Why, I could have jabbed him with my finger. He straightened out dead on the ground. My brother had shot him right behind the ear."

That anecdote was the first I had ever heard of Uncle Charlie killing an animal, let alone carrying a weapon. He was decidedly not the kind of fellow you would associate with hunting. There was no doubt he had the requisite skill. But he never expressed interest in hunting during the few years I knew him.

Alfred, on the other hand, seemed born to hunt. Even as a nonagenarian, he looked like he could pick up his old Winchester .40-65, the rifle he used to plug the buck with the madstone, and hit the hunting trail.

"It had a good feel to it, like it was part of your hand," he said. "It had a long barrel that looked like a crow bar. It shot a shell as big as my finger. I had to hold it over my knees to shoot it or lay it across a tree branch. I was using that rifle when others were using them high-powered guns that would shoot a lot farther. But I done plenty good enough with the old .40-65."

When he wasn't hunting for food, there was always plenty to do around the cabin. Chores included everything from cutting firewood to repairing his threadbare clothing washed in tumbling river water and hung over brush to dry. After his clothes became too tattered to mend with needle and thread, he followed steps taken by mountain men of old.

"Well, I made some buckskin britches," he said. "I took the hair off with ashes, oak ashes. You let them soak in them ashes with water overnight. That hair'll slip right off."

But after slipping on his new pants, he discovered he had little envy for Jim Bridger and his ilk when it came to their mode of dress.

"I tell you, after I wore them for a while, why, I felt awfully sorry for the old timers," he said. "They were the darnedest things to wear, especially when it rained. Real cold. No, I didn't like them a'tall."

In addition to being cold, the buckskin chafed his skin, he recalled.

"I didn't wear them very long," he acknowledged. "No sir, I got rid of them as soon as I could."

Whether dressed in buckskin or store-bought clothes, the two continued to explore the region, keeping to remote areas where human footprints were seldom seen.

"The wilder it got, the better I liked it," Alfred stressed, repeating a refrain we heard often from him. "It sure didn't get much wilder than back there in that Madstone country."

Hiking west across the river and scrambling up out of a steep canyon, they found a small lake on the north shoulder of a jagged mountain. The lake is now called Vulcan Lake; the mountain known as Vulcan Peak. The peak rises to 4,655 feet above sea level about three air miles west of the cabin site.

"It didn't have a name when I was there," he said. "I was going to give it a name but never got around to it. The lake was about a day's trip, walking over there and back. Awful rough country through there."

Other hunting forays found him hiking randomly for the sheer joy of exploration. One such excursion took him downstream to a large bend in the river, then up a small stream flowing out of mountains he had not yet checked out. Filled with wanderlust, he continued hiking, intent on finding its source.

"Some places there, it was boulder after boulder the size of houses," he said. "Well, there was an old cabin up there. It was a peculiar built cabin, not like any cabin I ever saw before. It was just a bunch of slats. Couldn't hardly call it a house."

He figured it must have been a cabin built by a miner back in the 19th Century.

"Supposed to be a lot of gold up there," he said of remote sites in the upper Chetco River drainage. "If there was, it's still there. That's mighty rough country."

Sometimes he would hike south, a trek that took him over the rocky ridges to a mountainous plateau where he could look down into the Smith River drainage that flowed into California's extreme northwest corner.

"During the war, we was all over that country," he said. "We was from the top of the Siskiyou Mountains at the head of the Applegate through to the coast. It wasn't nothing for us to go north along the coast range as far as the Rogue River."

Caches hidden at strategic points along the way kept them supplied.

"We filled five-gallon cans with supplies, food and what not," he explained. "We hid them under logs and behind rocks. We'd get 'em when we needed them. We was pretty well stocked up."

Those hidden caches, restocked by supplies bought with cash raised by trapping and gold panning, coupled with smoked venison and salmon, enabled the two to survive well.

It was during the winter months when the fur-bearing animals were wearing their best furs that the brothers would trap. While his older brother preferred to trap mink along waterways, Alfred went after wary pine martin in the higher mountains.

"Now a martin is easy trapped if you know how," he said. "But if you don't know how, you might as well leave him alone. He's a slick thinker."

The trick, he said, is to lean a pole against a tree and nail a piece of meat above the snow.

"You put that trap down underneath," he said. "But you don't cover that trap. You just let it be."

With furs in demand and plenty of animals to trap, the two did well with their trap lines. They received as much as $20 each for martin, a substantial sum back in those days, he said.

"Why we was making money hand over fist," he said. "We shipped a lot of furs from Waldo when we was in the mountains. We done good. Of course, we was disguised and used our other names. We wasn't brothers. We was partners. Nobody knew the difference."

Furs certainly did provide a source of revenue for many local residents during that era. *The Daily Courier* reported on Nov. 8, 1918 that local resident Clyde Davidson brought the pelts of five coyotes, nine skunks and three lynx to Grants Pass that day. He received $64 for both the furs and the varmints, the paper noted. The lynx referred to in the article may have been bobcat since the few lynx which inhabited the region would have been found only in the highest mountains of southern Oregon. Our dad had talked about lynx being in the region when he was young but they were exceedingly rare even then.

Although the furs brought a good price in those lean years, the brothers lived a Spartan life. They had few comforts. Out of fear they may be recognized, they couldn't go into a town and check into a hotel. Eating in an uptown restaurant was out of the question, providing they could have spruced themselves up enough to be allowed in a fine establishment.

But they would go out on the town, such as it was. Heading north from their cabin, they linked up with the historic Rogue River Trail, a well-worn path largely used by miners toiling for gold in the region. The forty-mile trail runs along the north bank of the river, connecting the mining community of Galice to the lower reaches. To anyone meeting them on the trail, the brothers were just another pair of grizzled miners seeking solitude and the mother lode.

"We met a lot of people looking for gold the same as we was and a lot of people trapping like we was," he said. "Most of them wasn't too interested in talking about themselves."

Trail etiquette permitted small talk but one never pressed another about his past. One simply greeted strangers, chatted about the trail or the weather, then moved on. Although Alfred didn't recall any of the folks they met along the way, he never forgot the path-hugging cliffs along the narrow river canyon.

"That trail, I had to get back next to the wall to get around some of those places, just crawl around it," he said, referring to the narrow section known as the Devil's Backbone in Mule Creek Canyon.

The trail snakes along a sheer rock wall over the river which boils below like a cauldron. Falling over the precipice would definitely be a life altering experience.

"It was like going through a tunnel," he said. "There was rocks above and below. Awful rough country."

It wasn't until 1915, just two years before the brothers turned to the mountains to avoid the draft, that pioneer river runner Glen Wooldridge of Grants Pass ran the river from that community down through the canyon to the ocean. The journey to the coast was made in a small boat the nineteen-year-old Wooldridge built at home. By 1917, he had taken his first paying customers down the river, becoming the first to guide dudes through the rugged stretch. Wooldridge was also the first in the region to build the drift boats now popular on whitewater throughout the northwest. He later conquered other heretofore unnavigable rivers in Canada and Alaska.

While down the Rogue, the brothers were not river runners. They took advantage of an old Indian who charged folks twenty-five cents to be taken across the river in his row boat, Alfred said.

"We crossed the Rogue a couple of times in that row boat of his," he said. "I never liked crossing that river."

Farther upstream, the brothers took advantage of Sanderson's foot bridge, a swinging bridge held together by rope, lumber and Yankee ingenuity about a mile upstream from Rainie Falls. Built in 1907, the bridge was destroyed by a flood in 1927.

Once they crossed to the north side of the river, the brothers would drop in for supplies and a hearty meal at the Billings ranch, a green bench near the mouth of Mule Creek. Established in 1903 by George Washington Billings, the ranch included a trading post, post office and boarding house, making it a popular gathering place for those seeking a brief reprieve from the mountain solitude. Adjacent to the creek was an old barn dubbed the "Tabernacle." Upstairs was the site of Saturday night dances and other celebrations. Mules and horses were lodged downstairs, munching contentedly as the building fairly shook with mountain folk kicking up their heels as they frolicked late into the night.

Come Sunday morning, the old building lived up to its name. A fire and brimstone sermon would begin, serving to remind hung-over miners to repent their wicked ways. No longer the destination of miners looking for a good time, the old ranch is now open to the public as a museum. It was purchased by the U.S. Bureau of Land Management in 1970 under the National Wild and Scenic River program. When the program was launched by Congress in 1968, the lower Rogue was among the rivers set aside for preservation. Summer whitewater lovers running the lower river canyon now stop at the old Billings ranch to walk up to the picturesque two-story white ranch house with red trim which is on the National Register of Historic Places. I suspect Alfred would have been tickled to see it preserved.

While he always liked visiting the Billings ranch, it was a beautiful mountain valley hard against the California state line that still captivated him as he approached the century mark. Youngs Valley is beauty personified with a clear mountain stream flowing through green meadows sided by timbered ridges. It was named after pioneer Elliott Young who died in Kerby in 1918 during the flu epidemic.

"That's the most beautiful place in the world," Alfred said. He was no longer sitting on his bed in the Texas nursing home. He was walking in that green valley where deer grazed and nearby mountain lakes were brimming with trout. But "nearby" is relative in the rugged region. It was a long, arduous hike from the valley to the Devil's Punch Bowl, Sanger Lake, Bolan Lake or the Tannen lakes. But in his memory, the lakes were just over the rise.

"Youngs Valley is a wonderful place," he reiterated.

When cabin fever overwhelmed them and they took leave of the Madstone country to wander the region, they could always count on finding a vacant cabin in which to spend a night or two. The old structures represented the dreams of miners expecting to discover golden riches but found only hunger and hard labor with few pay days. After resting in an abandoned cabin, the brothers would move on down the trail, all the while keeping an eye out for anyone who might recognize them.

They would eventually return to the upper Chetco River and their cabin where they felt safe from the long arm of the law. They never became paranoid, Alfred insisted. But he allowed they were mighty alert to anyone who didn't fit the description of a typical down and out miner.

"They got in our territory once," he said of authorities looking for two draft-dodging brothers. "I found tracks of men who weren't mountain men. You could tell the difference by their footprints. I found tracks that was all smooth. Mountain men all had hob nails in their boots them days."

The hobnails helped give them traction somewhat like the caulk boots loggers began wearing in later years, he explained.

"You take a slick pair of boots, you'd break your neck trying to climb them high mountains," he said. "Too steep and too slick."

There came the day when he spotted several men hurrying along behind them on a mountain trail about a dozen miles from their Madstone base. The strangers were too well dressed to be miners, he recalled.

"They was right behind us in broad daylight," he said. "But I was sure they'd never overtake us. And they never even came close. I learned afterwards that they was up there trying to find us."

Was he ever concerned they would eventually be caught?

"I knowed we wouldn't," he said. "Now that there is telling you something."

It told us our uncles were at home in the woods, capable of disappearing into the forest at the first hint of any threat to their freedom. No one was going to chase them down. It was also obvious to us that they were Oregon mountain goats in their youth, proficient at bounding up a steep mountainside to make good their escape when necessary.

When Alfred looked back on their cabin in the wilderness, he didn't dwell on the lean times or the lonesome feelings that sometimes welled up.

"Some people that just can't live back there—gets too lonely for them," he said. "But it wasn't that way for me. I liked it fine back there. Yes, the farther back I could get, the better I felt."

MADSTONE

SIXTEEN

Jumping into
the Fray

W HILE THE FATTIG BROTHERS WERE HIDING OUT in the remote mountains to avoid the WWI military draft, the lion's share of young
Oregon men their age were volunteering to serve. From Portland to Port
Orford, volunteers for all the military branches stepped forward. The Army
National Guard unit based in Portland became the first in the nation to
mobilize. But few areas could compare with Josephine County when it
came to volunteering. Four sons from one Josephine County family enlisted
two days after war was declared, the *Daily Courier* reported.

"The four sons of Con Fenner of Slate Creek left last night for Portland,
all of them having enlisted in the Army," the paper noted on April 9,
1917, of the Fenner place which was not far from my childhood home in
Wonder. "The boys were William, Charles, Allen and Ralph, the youngest
being compelled to gain his parents' consent, which was willingly given.
This also broke up a dance to have been held as there were only seven
young men on Slate Creek, and six of those have now enlisted."

What's more, the Fenners invested heavily in Liberty Bonds, going as
far as to sell their surplus cattle to purchase bonds which would help
supply their sons with ammunition, the article noted.

The Fenners were only the beginning of the local military exodus. The next day after the Fenner story was reported, an overwhelmed U.S. Army recruiter in Grants Pass urgently telegraphed his brethren in the regional office in Portland for assistance, the paper noted. It seems that forty-two young men had stormed his office and demanded to be sworn in. One of those joining that day was a young man named Joseph Borough who would become the first Grants Pass native to die in service to his country during the war, albeit would be before reaching the front lines.

But even the Fenner family patriotism paled next to the sons of J.W. Scarberry of Murphy. Before the war was over, six stout Scarberry youths would join the military ranks. The seventh son, still in high school, vowed to join as soon as he turned eighteen years old.

"The father of these sons is proud of the fact that he has so many sons in the service and he would be with them did not age bar him," according to the *Daily Courier.*

Seemingly against the odds, all the Fenner and the Scarberry young men would survive the war.

The young men donning military uniforms apparently inspired those who were already settled down in life. Grants Pass police judge H.H. Basler enrolled in the naval reserves. The unit was activated nine days after he enlisted and the newly-minted ensign, who would receive $140 a month, shipped out. Not to be outdone, Jackson County Sheriff Ralph G. Jennings promptly exchanged his badge for an olive drab Army uniform and marched off to war.

It wasn't just men stepping forward. Uldawalla Basler, eighteen, enlisted in the Navy, joining her father the police judge as well as two brothers already in uniform. The charter member of the girl's honor guard in Grants Pass wasn't worried about what others thought of a young woman enlisting.

"Why shouldn't I enlist?" she asked in a *Daily Courier* article. "My grandfather Basler was a volunteer soldier and fought to preserve the union of the states in the 1860s. My father resigned his position and gave up his home and enrolled for service as soon as it was known that war was inevitable. At the same time my two brothers gave up their college life and voluntarily entered the service of their country. I guess I can postpone my university course until we win this war and the boys come home."

Until the boys and girls come home, that is. Her enlistment left only mother Basler guarding the home front.

More recruits were on their way. President Wilson signed the selective service bill on May 18, 1917, an action that had directly impacted the lives of Alfred and Charlie Fattig as we have seen. The legislation called for drafting the National Guard into the regular Army, procuring 500,000 able-bodied men age twenty-one to thirty to serve in the Army.

"Signing of the bill will automatically put into effect a perfected war machine, evolved by master minds in the war department," explained the page-one wire service article in the *Daily Courier* that day. A reader today would be hard put to find journalists using similar language to describe the agency now known as the Defense Department. Although some exemptions would be allowed, all men in that age group must register for the draft, the article concluded.

Reaction to the draft was swift in rural Oregon. The same day it was announced, seven percent of the population—eleven young men—in the coastal community of Port Orford in Curry County enlisted in the U.S. Army. "With the departure of 11 men for the Army today, the last men of conscription age left the town," the *Daily Courier* observed of the tiny coastal community.

Not all were locking step with the new draft order. A dozen people opposing conscription were arrested during a May 19 protest in Abilene, Texas. What's more, an armed uprising against the draft was squelched near Dallas the same day, a wire service article reported. "German money is believed to be financing the uprising," it noted.

Three women were arrested in New York City on June 17 following an anti-conscription riot at city hall. More than 300 women participated in the incident.

"The police broke up the gathering into small groups but were fought fiercely, the women using hat pins, their teeth and anything they could lay their hands on," related the article in the Medford paper. "The police finally commandeered a lot of automobiles and bundled the struggling women into them, carting the leaders to headquarters."

Former President Theodore Roosevelt, no shrinking violet when it came to war, joined the fray against those who would not fight, claiming that conscientious objectors were German agents. "If a man does not wish to take life, but does wish to serve his country, let him serve on board a mine sweeper or in some other position where the danger is to his own life," suggested the bully politician speaking in Minneapolis, Minnesota.

By late 1917, the adjutant general for the Oregon National Guard estimated there were thirty draft dodgers in the state. A $50 reward was offered for information leading to the arrest of each slacker. "If it appears that the delinquency was willful, they will be prosecuted before a court martial as deserters," officials warned, hinting that the sentence would be lighter if the shirkers voluntarily turned themselves into authorities. Through their parents or other contacts, the Fattig brothers likely learned their punishment would be lighter if they turned themselves in. However, at this stage, they were far from ready to face the music.

Many draft dodgers were caught. John E. Dillard of Brookings was nabbed in North Dakota early in October, 1917, a wire story reported, noting, "There is no getting away from Uncle Sam." Dillard was charged with desertion.

Deputy U.S. Marshal F.B. Tichenor arrested three draft evaders in Josephine County early in 1918, including R.B. West who had been hiding out in the Oak Flat area of the Illinois River about a dozen miles west of the Illinois Valley. West, who had been working as a miner along the river, was arrested when he arrived in Selma for supplies.

Yet there were a few young men excused for not answering the military call. Fate Wilson, a central Oregon sheepherder who was arrested when he came down from the hills late in 1917, had an iron-clad excuse. He informed sheepish authorities that he was unaware the United States had gone to war, having spent the previous twenty months in the mountains with his woolly charges. To demonstrate his patriotism, the young sheepherder invested his $2,000 in savings in Liberty Bonds and promptly joined the Navy, despite having never before seen a ship or the ocean.

The U.S. Attorney General drafted U.S. Postal Service employees as a domestic army to report any disloyal acts or utterances. "The department of justice is desirous of being informed as to suspicious characters, disloyal and treasonable acts and utterances, and anything which might be important during the existence of the present state of war," the *Daily Courier* announced on May 17, 1917, the same day the military draft was announced. Postmasters and all persons connected with the postal service should "keep on the lookout for individuals and the acts referred to above," it stated. As if to place their stamp of approval on the decree, Oregonians held a massive patriotic parade in Medford that day. It is not hard to imagine George Orwell gathering fodder for his *1984* book during this period. The dystopian novel about the Big Brother's surveillance state was published in 1949.

Nor were local schools safe from overzealous patriots early in WWI. In Medford, the history book, *Dawn of American History in Europe*, was taken from students at the request of parents who insisted the text was pro-German, the *Tribune* reported. Several enraged parents had wanted the books collected and burned but were pacified by their banishment.

In Jacksonville, local resident John Perl got in hot water for allegedly making pro-Germany remarks, according to the *Jacksonville Post* in its edition on Nov. 17, 1917.

"John Perl was given a hearing before District Attorney Roberts on Friday," the article reported. "He was accused of having declared that he was part German; that he gloried in German achievements; that the German atrocities in Belgium and elsewhere were justified and that he hoped Germany would win.

"At the examination Perl declared that if he had made such remarks he was only joking and kidding; that his father fought in the civil war and that he was a loyal citizen," it concluded. "Mr. Perl was warned to guard his future utterances for his own safety."

One of the most ludicrous steps to test patriotism was taken in mid-March of 1918 in Castle Rock, Washington. Suspecting some residents of being disloyal, a citizen's committee decided that all local residents must pass in review of the American flag and salute. Anyone who did not snap to would be dunked in the nearby river.

"The mayor issued a proclamation calling upon all residents to appear on the streets at 2 p.m. and give evidence of their patriotism," the wire service story reported. "The stores were closed. The schools were dismissed and the pupils joined in the demonstration. The mayor led the parade, followed by a band playing patriotic music."

Given the fact the weather was chilly, it should have come as no surprise that 100 percent of those tested for patriotism passed with flying colors. Even socialists balked at taking a March dip in a frigid northwest river.

Perhaps one of the most repressive laws in the nation's history was created during the war. The Sedition Act of 1918 made it a federal crime for Americans to utter a disloyal statement about their country. Never mind the law was extremely vague and arguably unconstitutional.

The long arm of the law was quick to arrest those who spoke out against the United States. In Medford, two "sensational seditious utterance arrests" were made in one day, the *Tribune* reported on Oct. 3, 1918.

"Both of the prisoners are of German descent, and on one of them after he was taken to the federal building yesterday forenoon, a loaded .38 caliber revolver and a small bag of cartridges were found," it noted.

The prisoners, both in their thirties, were Marvin Jackson Vedder, described as a "floating laborer and socialist" who was armed with the pistol, and Rolph Bieberstadt, a ranch hand living in the Rogue Valley. Both were jailed.

Several Josephine County residents were arrested for un-American utterances. Wolf Creek farmer A.W. Zollner was jailed in Grants Pass for having made unpatriotic statements concerning President Wilson, the American Red Cross and the reasons for which the nation entered the war, the *Daily Courier* noted. When a deputy U.S. Attorney wrote to him to ask if informants had accurately quoted him, Zollner angrily reiterated his earlier statements with vigor, the paper added.

In the Illinois Valley, Takilma resident Charles Gibbons was charged with "too much pro-German talk," the *Courier* reported on Jan. 23, 1918. Gibbons was accustomed to talking, having served as the barber in Takilma.

Henry Bacher, a thirty-year resident of Grants Pass, was also charged with seditious utterances. A painter, he had apparently been speaking out against the war for a year before he was arrested in 1918.

Uncle Sam reached out to grab Wobblies with his judicial arm. In Chicago, a grand jury indicted William Haywood, national secretary of the IWW, and 150 other Wobblies for conspiracy against the government on the fall of 1917.

"It was reported that the evidence shows plots and a broad company to hamper all the government's war activities and shows financial connections with German authorities," read a wire story with a Washington, D.C. dateline. "It is understood that the evidence gathered reveals the existence of the most far-reaching conspiracy ever unearthed, including the burning of crops, resisting the Army draft and fomenting labor troubles."

Some of the most damning evidence was a letter to Haywood from IWW activist James Rowan in Seattle. "We have the good will of the German people and we feel they will sympathize with our cause," Rowan wrote. "We intend to carry our points if we have to stop every industry on the Pacific coast. It is not we who declared war. We have not consented to the working men giving up their liberty by being drafted."

It didn't help their case when 6,000 feet of dynamite fuse was found in their Seattle headquarters. The Wobblies were all charged with seditious conspiracy.

This occurred right after the IWW was coming off one of its greatest triumphs, a successful lumber camp strike which nearly paralyzed the region's lumber industry in the summer of 1917. During the strike, Wobblies were blamed for sabotaging logging equipment and sawmills. But when the strike ended, they had won an eight-hour work day and improved conditions at logging camps.

While the Wobblies had their supporters, the controversial group had far more enemies. In St. Maries, Idaho, sixty-five Wobblies held in the town's jail were given only one meal a day—bread and water—following a disturbance in a logging camp.

"All employees of logging camps in this vicinity are being examined by soldiers as to their attitude toward the war and the doctrine of the IWW," read a wire story on March 20, 1918. "All failing to give satisfactory answers will be brought in and held." No, it wasn't a shining moment for justice.

But the Wobblies receiving short rations in Idaho could consider themselves fortunate. In Tulsa, Oklahoma, angry black-robed men calling themselves "Knights of Liberty" freed seventeen Wobblies held by the police, then proceeded to beat them unmercifully.

"The whereabouts of the 17 half-naked, severely beaten members of the IWW seized from policemen, flogged with a cat-o-nine-tails, tarred and feathered here last night by a band of 60 black-robed and hooded Knights of Liberty is unknown," revealed the wire story on Nov. 11, 1917.

For those who like grisly details, the reporter added a bit more. "'In the name of the outraged women and children of Belgium,' uttered the man in charge of the ceremony as he applied hot pitch to the bleeding backs,'" the article concluded.

The wounded Wobblies were apparently taken to the edge of town in the dark of night where they fled into the brush. The whereabouts of the police during this disturbance was not recorded.

Not to be outdone, angry residents in Collinsville, Illinois, lynched Robert Praeger for making disloyal statements. Born in Germany, Praeger, accused of making the statements to a group of miners, was apprehended by a group calling itself the Loyalist Committee, according to the April 8, 1918 article. He was forced to parade barefoot through the city streets, periodically kissing the American flag. Local police rescued him from the mob and whisked him into the city hall where they hid him in the basement. But the mob, estimated at 950, swarmed city hall and dragged Praeger from his hiding place. The victim, who had denied he was disloyal, prayed in German before being hung from a tree about a mile south of town, the article stated.

The incident could have occurred in southwest Oregon. A Gold Hill rancher blamed a suspicious fire which burned two acres of wheat and roughly two tons of grain on a "Hun," although the article in the *Tribune* did not indicate how the rancher knew the culprit was German. An angry group of vigilantes who searched for the suspect did not catch their quarry.

Indeed, it was a brutal time in American history, a period when justice—and injustice—was meted out by faceless mobs. In Estill Springs, Tennessee, Jim McTherron, a black man, was burned at the stake by a crowd on Feb. 13, 1918. Accused of killing two white men, a confession had been forced from him by application of red-hot irons, the wire story stated. It failed to observe that most people would readily confess to anything while being seared by glowing metal. "Another Negro Is Burned At Stake," shrugged the headline.

But Wobblies were the principal targets in the north. When a Klamath Falls box factory and flour mill erupted in flames in the fall of 1917, Wobblies were the prime suspects.

"A few weeks ago Klamath County was the scene of IWW activity and several fires destroyed property at that time," reported an article in the Oct. 9, 1917 Grants Pass paper. "IWW members were jailed, the street patrolled by armed men and every stranger coming into the city was obligated to state his business."

It was yet to be proven that Wobblies set the blazes whose losses were estimated at $150,000, the paper did caution. However, Carl Sweigin, an IWW activist arrested during the Klamath Falls fires, became the first German-American deprived of his American citizenship during the war when he was charged with "fraud in his naturalization proceedings," the paper reported a year later. The U.S. Department of Justice in Washington, D.C. had ordered that Sweigin be jailed.

A Wobbly was arrested in Grants Pass by Sheriff George Lewis on Nov. 24, 1917, on a charge of making treasonable utterances. Activist Archie Gerrells, who had arrived via the stage out of Crescent City, California, had apparently aired his political feeling en route. Fellow passengers turned him into authorities upon reaching the river town.

In January 1918, Oregon Governor James Withycombe deployed the Oregon National Guard to stand guard over shipyards and railroad years in the Portland area. Authorities had been warned that IWW activists along with pro-German sympathizers had been plotting to sabotage factories along the West Coast.

Wobblies weren't the only domestic political targets during the war.

In Cleveland, American socialist leader Eugene V. Debs, a five-time presidential candidate, was sentenced to ten years in prison for referring to the war as the supreme curse of capitalism. After serving three years behind bars, he was pardoned by President Warren Harding.

Debs had plenty of supporters across the nation. In fact, when the future Oregon state Senate President E.D. "Debs" Potts was born in 1908 in Buzzard Roost, a one-time mining hamlet in Shasta County, California, where his parents stopped en route to Oregon, his father named him after the socialist leader. Potts, who was born with a "gift for gab," was elected mayor of Grants Pass in 1958. The Democrat was elected to the state senate in 1960, serving until 1984. Fellow senators elected him senate president twice at a time when the state constitution dictated the senate president served as the governor when the elected governor traveled out of state. As a result, the man named after a socialist served as the acting Oregon governor for 196 days. Although he was a Democrat, his politics were decidedly more conservative than his namesake. Yet Potts, who died in 2003 at age ninety-five, was known for working with folks from both sides of the political aisle.

Oregon's most famous socialist was arguably John Reed, born Oct. 22, 1887, to a wealthy Portland family. Shortly after graduating from Harvard University in 1910, Reed began writing for the *Oregonian* but apparently grew bored. He became a political activist and in 1913 joined the staff of *The Masses*, a Socialist newspaper. When he wasn't writing, Reed, one of the founders of the Communist Party of the United States, was frequently being arrested for organizing and leading labor strikes. During WWI, he was sent to Europe to cover the battles for *Metropolitan* magazine. It was there he became a close friend of Vladimir Lenin, the Russian revolutionary philosopher and leader. Reed had a front row seat to the 1917 Bolshevik revolution. Based on that experience, he wrote the 1919 book, *Ten Days that Shook the World.* Back in the U.S., Reed became the leader of the Communist Labor Party in 1919 when it split from the U.S. Communist Party. But Reed was indicted for treason, and fled to Russia where he died of typhus in 1920.

A lesser known Oregon socialist was a fellow named B.F. Ramp, a

1918 party candidate for governor. When Ramp, who then lived on a ranch a few miles east of Roseburg in southern Oregon, did not buy any Liberty Bonds, a four-member delegation of the group known as the Court of Loyalty was deployed to apply pressure on the avowed socialist. Upon interviewing him, the committee immediately fired off a telegram to Dr. R.E. Steiner, head of the Liberty Loan Committee in Salem.

"Committee called on Ramp today," the telegram read. "He refused to buy bonds, saying he was not able, and had to borrow money, so he had none he could lend the government. When asked if he owned any bonds, replied, 'No.'"

A meeting of 100 people met in Salem to consider what should be done with Ramp and others who refused to purchase bonds.

"A local citizen who is in a position to have some knowledge of the matter expresses the belief that Mr. Ramp is the owner of property in this state to the approximate value of $60,000," the *Daily Courier* reported. "Hence he should be a heavy purchaser of Liberty Bonds."

The story, noting Ramp had a son in jail for making seditious utterances, also contained a not-so-veiled veiled threat to others who had not purchased bonds. "The Salem committee is evidently determined to round up all slackers in this line," it observed.

Ramp did not fare well in the general election. Incumbent Governor James Withycombe, a Republican first elected in 1914, won re-election with 81,067 votes while Democrat Walter Pierce, a state senator, garnered a respectable 65,440 votes. Ramp placed a distant third with 6,480 votes. But the loss didn't stop him from running for other public offices in the years ahead, including congress.

As it happens, when I was a student at the University of Oregon in the mid-1970s, I chanced to meet an old man on campus who must have been in his late eighties or early nineties. He was selling newspapers near the student union, a popular hangout. Brushing aside his shock of white hair, he was adamant I buy the paper he was thrusting at me. "Sorry, no money," I told him. However, as a journalism major interested in all newspapers, I was curious about the paper he was hawking. "It's only fifty cents," he said. At the time, I was going to school on the G.I. Bill and had not yet found a part-time job so money was tight. I repeated that I didn't have a dime. "Then just take one—it'll open your eyes," he said, handing me a paper. It turned out it was the English-language *Pravda*, the official newspaper of the Communist Party in the then Soviet Union. And the elderly gentleman? None other than Floyd Ramp, B.F. Ramp's son and one of the founders of the U.S. Communist Party. Hailing from Roseburg, he had been sentenced to two years in prison for conspiracy to obstruct the military draft of 1917. He apparently never lost his zest for socialism during the 101 years he lived.

Coincidentally, Len Ramp, the well-regarded geologist mentioned at the tail end of Chapter 14, was the son of Floyd Ramp. The senior Ramp had named his son "Lenin" after the Communist leader, but the younger Ramp was not a fellow traveler down that political road. Like my siblings and I who did not follow our uncles' lead when it came to serving in the military, Len Ramp did not share his paternal ancestor's politics.

During WWI, some former pacifists came around to support the war effort. A prominent one was Dr. William T. Foster, president of Reed College in Portland.

Speaking in Grants Pass shortly after returning from his role as an inspector of the American Red Cross on the front lines in France, Foster said he had changed his mind, becoming a strong advocate of the war. Having witnessed the suffering in France, he decried those who would not support the war.

"When I was in the trenches north of Reims, I found French soldiers twice wounded in action, twice discharged from hospitals and again at the front where they were facing cold, hunger, monotony, disease and shell fire 24 hours a day," he said.

Noting they were receiving the equivalent of five cents a day for their sacrifice, Foster said he was troubled by the fact that, upon returning back to the states, he found men on strike because they were receiving only $6 a day.

"If our people had any conception of the struggle in which our nation is engaged and of the sacrifices and heroism of the French soldiers who are holding the trenches of democracy, without a thought of striking and without pay enough to keep their wives and babies from cold and starvation, we would not tolerate in America a single able-bodied man who refused to work," he said.

The Josephine County Council of Defense agreed, and warned those who were guilty of not whole-heartedly supporting government and the war effort.

"Nothing but 100 percent, unadulterated, red-blooded Americanism will be tolerated," it declared April 21, 1918. "If any man or woman in the community is not making himself useful in these strenuous war times, measures will be taken to see that they give their best efforts or move to some other parts."

As it wore on, the war was clearly draining the local labor force. Local sugar beet growers and other farmers placed advertisements in area news-papers for women and youngsters to help harvest the crops during the war.

In late summer of 1917, the Oregon militia was mustered to help harvest the apple crop. But that work force was also being called away to the front. The Oregon National Guard unit headquartered in Ashland was mobilized in the summer of 1918. A huge crowd gathered on July 29 to cheer them off to war. The same tracks that had carried Alfred Fattig to southern Oregon were now being used to send soldiers to the East Coast where they would board a troop ship bound for war.

In an attempt to demonstrate the war was being won, the powers that be also used the trains to bring in war booty. Some 2,000 people gathered in Grants Pass during the Indian summer of 1918 to see a train pulling two box cars full of captured German guns and related materials. Buglers aboard the train heralded its coming. The proud patriots excitedly climbed aboard to inspect German helmets, uniforms, machine guns, even what was described as German whiz bang projectiles. Like an elephant dead on its knees, a battered howitzer was also displayed, its protective armor scarred and torn. There was no doubt about it: the American boys were giving the Huns hell.

MADSTONE

SEVENTEEN

Battle Cries
Still Rang

S URVIVORS OF WWI WERE ELDERLY FOLKS when I began research in the late 1980s into my uncles' Madstone years. It was already a distant time from the wildfires in the form of the first worldwide war that raged around the globe, fanned by the efficient war machines created by the industrialized age. Many who left Oregon to fight in the war never returned. Some young men were killed in a cold, mud-filled trench. Others simply didn't return to their relatively sleepy Oregon towns after the thrill of celebrating liberty in nocturnal Paris.

But even after some seventy years there were still a few around of sound mind and body. Those still standing in the thinning ranks of WWI veterans were proud men who said they were merely answering their country's call. To a man, no one belittled the choice made by Alfred and Charlie Fattig. Perhaps it was because they hailed from a time when the body politic was not full of hate as it often seems in our age. Or, having seen war at its bloody worst, may have felt some empathy for those opposed to killing each other over politics.

In southwestern Oregon, the keepers of the doughboy flame were members of the World War I Barracks No. 27, formed in Grants Pass in 1952. Sadly, no one answers muster now. Those who helped win the war did not survive the battle with Father Time. Originally stepping out with fifty-six members, there were only a little more than a dozen remaining when I met them. In place of the rifles they once carried they held canes. Their hair had retreated from their heads or had faded to white.

While some of the veterans were no longer up to chatting about the war, there was the remarkable Clair Heppenstall, born Aug. 30, 1895, and drafted in Grants Pass early in the spring of 1918. The former infantryman had fought in several battles, including in the bloodbath that was the Argonne Forest. He was ninety-three when he sat down to talk to me about the war. He recalled having heard about two draft-dodging brothers who hid out in the southern Oregon mountains but he offered no comment regarding their actions.

Like most veterans who survive combat, Heppenstall was not a braggart. Rather, he spoke quietly as he recalled the brutality of the war.

"I still think of it as though it was yesterday," he said as he began his walk down the road that led to his combat in WWI. "I saw some horrible things."

At the time, Rogue Valley farmers were already dressing down their field for spring planting. Bright yellow daffodils were blooming like so many war ribbons across the Rogue Valley's chest. The snow line was beginning its annual retreat back up the local mountains. Formations of Canada geese were flying overhead, eager to launch their summer offensive on the Far North.

A short man barely five feet tall, Heppenstall was working as a mechanic in the Rogue Valley. With his draft call, he bid farewell to Doris, his intended whom he later married in 1920, boarded a train with four other Rogue Valley draftees bound for war. The peaceful valley was left behind in a plume of smoke as the engine climbed north through the mountains.

Following basic training at Washington state's Camp Lewis, now Fort Lewis, the newly-minted doughboys hopped aboard a troop train steaming to the East Coast where they would take a ship to the European theater.

"When we went across the States in the train, everybody was out there to meet us," Heppenstall said. "I tell you, the whole country in them days just wanted to get the thing done. It seemed like everybody, the men, was in it. I didn't know anybody but was for it."

In South Dakota, a young girl ran up to the train to hand Heppenstall a pocket knife and shouted for him to write. That knife would later play a role in saving a soldier's life on the battlefield.

Arriving in Europe, Heppenstall spent several long weeks in the infamous trenches, anxiously waiting for the action ahead. While writing letters to his loved one back in Grants Pass during the war, he recalled humming a new tune called "Oh, How I Hate to Get Up in the Morning." The song was penned by a young songwriter named Irving Berlin who had the good-natured grumblings of soldiers stumbling out of their bunks for morning reveille. Berlin was inducted into the Army in 1917 but was not deployed overseas.

Down in their trenches, Heppenstall and his fellow soldiers oiled their U.S. Model 1917 rifles, commonly known as the 1917 Enfield. Patterned after the Springfield Model 1903, the rifle has a bolt action which chambers the .30-06 cartridge whose bullet carries a substantial wallop. As many German soldiers could attest, the rifle was both accurate and deadly.

Although life was tedious in the trenches, there were moments of sheer terror when an enemy sniper fired a round from another trench a hundred yards away. A few unlucky soldiers, Allied and German alike, popped up their heads at the wrong time to become long-forgotten battlefield casualties.

But on Sept. 26, 1918, the tedium was gone like a wisp of smoke, followed by high anxiety which hung over them like a black cloud. That was the day Private Heppenstall's company advanced into the Argonne Forest, a heavily wooded hilly region in eastern France. The deadly Meuse-Argonne Offensive to roust the Germans had begun. The forty-seven-day battle, which ended on Armistice Day, was the largest independent American offensive during the war. Stretching along the Western Front, the assault included nine American Expeditionary Force divisions, including four green divisions which were untested in war. They were about to be tested. Big time. By battle's end, 26,277 Americans were killed and 95,786 wounded. More than 2,300 American soldiers were falling each day of the battle. Horrific doesn't even start to describe the carnage.

"We had 190 men in my company," Heppenstall said. "When we came out eight days later, we had ninety-four."

Cut down by bullets, shells, diarrhea and battle fatigue, the solders' mental images of glory fed by the cheering Stateside crowds quickly surrendered to the blood-soaked reality of crawling along the muddy forest floor. Those crisp olive-drab uniforms that once impressed the folks back home were now filthy, reeking of sweat and caked with blood and dirt.

The shells screaming in overhead did not distinguish between the courageous or the cowardly, Christian or Catholic. During those rare moments when there was a lull in the battle, cries of the wounded filled the woods. Too often, the cries of pain died only when death triumphed. Battlefield acquaintances perished before Heppenstall learned their first names.

For him, the Rogue Valley now seemed as distant as the war once appeared from the peaceful banks of the Rogue River flowing through the valley. Death lurked behind every tree in what seemed to him as a ghost forest filled with moans of the wounded and drifting clouds of smoke from bursting shells.

As the Allied troops fought their way deeper into the woods, the German machine gunners retreated to their fortified bunkers.

"Everything in the Argonne was prepared for the enemy," Heppenstall said of the dug-in fortifications the doughboys encountered. "They had been there so long. But it didn't really take much to get them out. All you had to do was throw a hand grenade down there. They came out then, their hands in the air and hollering, 'Comrade.'"

Yet several Americans were killed when they attempted to knock out two machine gun nests the first day of the battle. Among them was Lt. Lloyd Cochran, a well-liked young officer from Ballard, Washington. His hometown now has an American Legion post bearing his name.

"He was a fine man, one of the boys," Heppenstall said. "We hated to lose him."

While Heppenstall's squad took prisoners that day, the squad capturing the German unit which had killed Cochran took no prisoners.

"They left them there," Heppenstall said, clearly referring to punishment meted out on the battlefield.

Heppenstall and two other soldiers began marching their eighteen German prisoners to the rear. The POWs were all members of the elite Hessian guard, men specifically picked for their large size to serve as an honor guard for the Kaiser. By this time, the war was going badly for the emperor and all able-bodied men were thrown into battle, including his honor guard.

En route, the group was hit by heavy shell fire. One shell landed nearly on top of them, knocking Heppenstall into a trench. Piercing pain shot up his left leg when he tried to stand up. His badly sprained ankle swelled up like a balloon attached to a water faucet. When Heppenstall reached up out of the trench for assistance, a big prisoner stepped forward and grabbed his hand, pulling him effortlessly to the top. For a brief moment, two enemy soldiers—a diminutive American from a small town in Oregon and a towering German—shared a personal truce in the middle of a war.

But duty called. Limping badly, Heppenstall pushed on to deliver the prisoners.

Three days later, still favoring his swollen ankle, Heppenstall was back with his unit, edging forward down a hill. As they approached a small stand of trees, a machine gun roared to life, strafing the hill side.

"Down into a trench I go," Heppenstall said. "Down they go in their trench, dug in. In my trench, it was full of dead and wounded Germans. I didn't feel very safe. I'm alone, see."

Isolated and in growing darkness, he took stock of his predicament. The nearby trench was full of German soldiers. Heppenstall's unit had fallen back. Crawling forward, Heppenstall came upon a dead German officer whose belt held a Lugar pistol and a pair of field glasses. He grabbed the belt and crawled on. Reaching a point where the trench was partially caved in, he was able to crawl out. Under the cloak of darkness, he made his way back to unit.

Heppenstall stopped talking to reach under a nearby coffee table to withdraw a pair of field glasses. In places where a German officer's fingers once gripped it as he peered across battlefield lines, perhaps directing artillery barrages, the lightweight black field glasses were worn to bare metal.

"The pistol was stolen from me when I was in the hospital," Heppenstall offered. Upon reaching his unit, he was ordered to report to a first-aid station to have his swollen ankle examined. From there, he was sent to a military hospital in France where he spent the next five days. Exhausted, he slept heavily for a full day. When he awoke, the Lugar pistol he had slipped under his pillow was gone. He never determined whether it was pilfered or taken away because of safety concerns.

But the soldier from Grants Pass didn't lose any sleep over the missing souvenir. After all, he was alive.

"I had a bed by a window," he said. "Every morning a big flatbed wagon went by with four horses and a French man driving and an Indian bugler walking behind it. That wagon was loaded two tiers high with coffins. They made two more loads each day."

As he waited for his ankle to mend, the war marched on without him.

"They emptied ambulances at that hospital all day and all night long," he said.

Heppenstall wasn't the only Grants Pass soldier to have fought in the Argonne Forest. In a Nov. 8, 1918 letter to his father in Grants Pass, Pvt. Ardell Bailey reported that he had survived the battle.

"Things have been quite interesting of late, as I have been quite busy chasing the Hun," he wrote in a letter printed in the *Daily Courier*. "I have been up front several times and have gone over the top with the boys on several sectors. I was in the Argonne Forest drive where things were quite hot. We captured lots of Huns and gained much territory."

Although Bailey reported that he was unscathed thus far in the war, he offered a complaint that soldiers have been grousing about since time immemorial.

"It is hard to get our chow up to us through shell fire," he wrote. As a result, the troops were forced to eat cold meals in the form of hard tack and what he called "bully beef." The latter refers to tinned beef which the doughboys found wanting.

After being discharged from the hospital, Heppenstall, although still hobbling, rejoined his company which had moved on to fight in Belgium. He found a different warfare than that waged in the Argonne offensive, which was still waging. In Belgium, the enemy hid in farm houses and behind hay stacks. Knocking a few tiles off a roof top, German soldiers would snipe at the advancing Allied forces with deadly accuracy, Heppenstall said.

"They'd also get behind the hay stacks, dig a pit and put in two machine guns," he said. "They'd shoot through the hay stack about a foot off the ground."

Allied soldiers were mowed down like so many rows of corn before a combine.

It was in Belgium where Heppenstall encountered mustard gas, a poisonous concoction known for its blistering and related disabling effects that often leads to death. Attacking the mucous membranes in the respiratory tract, the colorless vapor destroys lung tissue. It also inflames the membranes covering the inside of the eyelid and the front of the eyeball, temporarily blinding the victim.

Soldiers with gas masks quickly donned them at the first sign of poisonous gas. Those without masks dropped to the ground, coughing and choking. Many would die from its lingering complications.

"It would lay in the grass just like a heavy fog," Heppenstall said. "You'd go through it and it would get on your clothes and skin. It burned like scalding water."

As the weather changed, the soldiers faced a new enemy on another front: bitter cold re-enforced by hunger.

Battle rations were normally two hard biscuits and a small tin of what Heppenstall dubbed "monkey meat," another name for what Bailey referred to as bully beef. Although it was officially labeled corned beef, the soldiers figured it was actually horse meat, Heppenstall said. But food was food.

Indeed, Heppenstall remembers one long four-day period when the tough meat would have been eaten with no complaints. Left without rations, his company ate from a field of turnips growing on a farmer's field.

"I've never eaten a turnip since," he said.

The weary doughboys often slept in shell holes, curling up in their heavy wool overcoats known as horse blankets. One night, three weary soldiers crawled into a shell crater near where Heppenstall was sleeping. The trio never woke from their troubled sleep. In the dark of night, a shell made a direct hit. Lightning may not strike the same place twice but shells sometimes do.

"It blew their heads and upper bodies off," he said, shaking his head at the memory.

Despite the shells, lingering cold, hunger and lice, the Allies steadily advanced. Come nightfall, they pitched camp on ground the Germans had held that morning.

Yet the retreating enemy continued to pound away with its deadly cannon and mortar shells. Heppenstall recalled when a shell landed near a man leading a pack mule carrying explosives. The unfortunate animal was blown apart in the resulting explosion.

"It hit that mule a dead ringer," Heppenstall said. "Blew him all to pieces, all over the guy holding him. The soldier walked off in a kind of a stupor, still holding that bridle."

For a moment, he laughed loudly at the ludicrous image of the dazed soldier with the bloody bridle who still wanders within his memory. No doubt the absurd incident had also brought black humor relief to the battle-weary soldiers. These weren't people who enjoyed seeing an animal killed, but merely young soldiers yearning for a furlough from the horrors of war.

"They was lobbing them shells over the hill with real good accuracy," he remembered.

Later, when Heppenstall and other soldiers were going to chow, a shell exploded near the men, severing a soldier's arm. Using a piece of twine and the knife given to him by the young girl in South Dakota, Heppenstall hastily made a tourniquet to stop the bleeding. The knife he had carried to war went with the wounded soldier who hailed from southern California.

Eight months earlier, Heppenstall's tranquil life in southwest Oregon had been forever changed by war. Like his other brothers-in-arms who survived combat, he would never be the same.

"Looking back, we did what we had to do," he said. "I wonder, if we hadn't done it, what the outcome would have been."

He was silent for a moment as he once again mulled over memories of war. Even after all the years, he could still see the countless corpses and hear the dying crying out.

"After all, it was a failure," he said. "The results were not worth what it cost."

But his conclusion was not shared by Raymond Allen, another member of World War I Barracks No. 27 in Grants Pass. Born June 29, 1897, the retired minister joined the U.S. Navy in Bremerton, Washington, at the age of twenty-one, serving nearly three years. His military job was important, although not one most folks would equate with heroism. He was a cook. But anyone who has worn a military uniform knows those who cook the chow can either help build esprit de corps or send it plunging into the dumps. Their jobs are vital to the welfare of the unit.

During the war, Allen served aboard the USS *New Orleans,* a third-class cruiser charged with guarding ship convoys crossing the Atlantic Ocean during the war. Nine times he crossed the Atlantic aboard the *New Orleans* as it dodged roving packs of German U-boats preying on ships sporting flags supporting the Allies. A coal-burning ship, its armament included six-inch and three-inch guns.

"We got shot at a couple of times but I'm here," Allen said of his close encounters with German U-boats lurking in the dark depths during the Great War.

While Allen brushed aside any danger he was in during the war, he knew full well anyone aboard ship during that period was in harm's way. He could tell you about the troop transport SS *Tuscania* which sank after being torpedoed off the coast of Scotland on the evening of Feb.5, 1918. Army Pvt. Riley F. Murray, born in 1874 in the then-mining community of Galice along the Rogue River, was aboard the *Tuscania*. He was among thirteen Oregon men who perished when the ship went down that day, the *Daily Courier* reported. Carrying 2,013 American troops and a crew of 384, she was struck by a torpedo fired by a German submarine shortly before 6:00 p.m. *Tuscania's* lifeboats were launched by 7:00 p.m. and other ships in the convoy deployed their lifeboats but the German sub still lurked in the vicinity. All told, 230 men were lost when the Tuscania sank at 10:00 p.m., including Murray. Beyond the age of most soldiers when he enlisted, Murray, forty-four, had worked at the Southern Pacific Railroad roundhouse in Grants Pass. He left a wife and two children.

Under federal government insurance in WWI, the family of each American serviceman killed in the war would receive $4,300 in compensation, Allen observed. Although it was a significant sum in those hungry years, it did little to appease grieving families, he added.

Allen was a patriot's patriot when it came to talking about the war. As it happened, I interviewed him on Nov. 11, 1988, the 70th anniversary of the armistice. He was standing under a flag pole outside his Grants Pass home. The stars and stripes waved overhead.

"That flag—a lot of people don't know it but we wouldn't have had the flag if it weren't for World War I veterans," said Allen, his voice thundering as though he was still on the pulpit and wanting to make sure the folks in the back pews heard him well. They would have, that I can assure you. His voice still boomed like one of the big guns on his ship.

Like other veterans of the war, Allen's body no longer snapped to at his command. His eyesight was failing; his hearing following suit. But his pride remained at full alert.

"I had a mother and two kid brothers—those were the ones I was fighting for," he said. "Then I would think how it would be to multiply that by hundreds of thousands across this nation."

He was convinced there was no alternative but to take on the Kaiser and his armies. Plenty of Americans supported it, he added.

"Oh brother, they were all ready to enlist," he said of folks he knew in the northwest. "The ladies were out selling war bonds. The whole outfit was behind us."

But those rallying around the flag weren't merely rural residents, he stressed, recalling the times his ship steamed into New York harbor.

"In New York City, the wealthy people really went out for us," he said. "There was no entertainment that we weren't entitled to go to. Anything, from the Metropolitan Opera on down, we were free to go."

During the war, his ship also sailed to Siberia where it docked at Vladivostok. Its mission was to guard American troops stationed in the city, he explained.

"We had over 3,000 soldiers guarding the railroad against the Bolsheviks," he said. "They needed some backup."

Apparently even the deep freeze of Siberia did little to cool Russia's internal struggle during those turbulent times. The retired minister swore he saw Joseph Stalin several times in the city where the eventual Russian dictator sometimes attended dances. The mustachioed fellow Allen saw very well could have been the man who would later be responsible for slaughtering millions during World War II. After being arrested for the sixth time for subversive activities, Stalin was exiled to Siberia. Later he would rise to the head of that country's communist party and heads would roll.

After the First World War, Allen would become a minister and spent two decades in the Bowery section of lower Manhattan. When I met him, he was still cooking, serving up a hot lunch of rice and chicken for the "boys" who served with him during the war.

"Yeah, I'm still the cook," he beamed, noting the chow was much like the fare he had served aboard ship. But fewer aging doughboys were mustering for the monthly luncheon, he lamented.

"I just buried my old shipmate," he said, referring to L.F. DeBroux of the tiny town of Rogue River. "I don't know if I knew his first name. I just called him 'Frenchie.'"

Leon Ferdinand DeBroux died Aug. 11, 1988 at the age of eighty-nine, seven decades after he served in the war.

One of the members of World War I Barracks No. 27 was Earl Yocom who was born June 1, 1897, in a house about a mile north of Jacksonville. Drafted in the fall of 1918, he was deployed to Camp Kearney, Calif. where he trained to become an artilleryman.

"Yep, I was a gunner on a one-pounder," he said, obviously proud of his big gun. But the private never had a chance to send his one-pound shells whistling into the ranks of the German forces. The war ended as he prepared to head overseas.

Ironically, prior to being drafted, the rail-thin Yocom had tried to join the Army but had been rejected.

"They said I was too tall for my weight," he said with a chuckle. Before his back began to bend under the weight to time, he stood 6' 1" but barely tipped the scales at 130 pounds, he said.

"I wanted to get into aviation," he said. "At the time, I was working as a mechanic."

After spending about six months in the Army, he was deemed Army surplus and discharged as a private in February, 1919. He headed back to the Rogue Valley.

In the small world department, Yocom knew the Fattigs, including Alfred, when they lived in the Applegate Valley near his family's home. In fact, when his great aunt went blind and had no one to care for her, Jonas and Harriett Fattig—my paternal grandparents—took her in. Parenthetically, my grandmother's first name is alternately spelled with one "T." However, since there are two "T's" on her gravestone we'll go with that spelling for continuity's sake.

In any case, Yocom's great aunt lived with the Fattigs for several years, her great nephew recalled.

"They kept her there at their house," he said. "We'd go visit her quite often."

Times were hard. The Yocoms lived about six miles upstream on the Applegate River from the Fattig farm. Crops fared poorly in the Yocom's rocky soil, he said. To survive, he and his father cut firewood for a living. On a good day, they could cut two cords, selling each for a buck apiece.

"That place the Fattigs had, they could raise a little something there," he said. "They had some good land."

When he first met Alfred Fattig, the would-be draft dodger was briefly attending a one-room schoolhouse near Ruch known as "Logtown District No. 3." It was the spring of 1912. Alfred, who would have been nineteen in elementary school, had told me about going to school for a few months in an attempt to learn how to read and write. It wasn't unusual for young men in that era to drop in at a grade school to brush up on the two subjects, said Yocom who was fifteen when he met Alfred.

"Fact of the matter is we had double seats and he sat on the same seat with me there," Yocom said. "But he didn't stay in school very long, only about a month or two."

Yocom, who would master the eighth grade, had contemplated furthering his education but thought better of it.

"After I got out a year, they started two years of high school there at Ruch," said the retired mechanic. "By that time I was in a Ford garage in Medford, a'working. But I figure I done all right with an eighth grade education."

With his friend Alfred, Yocom shared a yearning to hunt and fish the wilds of the Applegate River drainage.

"Alfred? He was just an all-around good guy," he said. "He was a good man with a gun."

In 1915, Yocom bought—for the princely sum of $5—a .32 Winchester Special lever-action rifle from his friend. "That '94 Winchester was a fine-shooting gun," he said of the 1894 model. Deer hunters will know it as a good rifle for brush hunters, much like a .30-30 Winchester but with more of a wallop.

That same year they took a hunting trip up the Applegate River where they set up camp in an abandoned cabin.

"We hiked over the hills and got up there along towards evening," Yocom said. "I went down to a creek and caught a couple of fish. Caught them by hand, just reached in and grabbed them. We fried them up for supper."

They bagged two deer the following morning. However, they waited until evening to pack the meat home.

"About five o'clock in the evening we started out, seeing how it was out of season," Yocom said. As for poaching, he simply noted the hungry days leading up to the war found many families living off the land. Illegal or not, wild game was often the main fare on a family's table, he said.

"Ruch was mostly farming country," he said. "Folks had cattle, too. They'd feed them in winter and run them up in the mountains during the summer."

It was a time when nearby Jacksonville was still the county seat, he noted proudly.

"I remember when the streets of Jacksonville were mud in winter and dust in summer," Yocom said. "The old Model A's would angle back and forth so the tires wouldn't hit the water at the same time and get stuck."

The last time Yocom saw his old hunting partner was a few months before the brothers suddenly disappeared into the mountains.

"I heard they went some place but nobody much knew where," he said. He shrugged off suggestions by his fellow WWI-era veterans that blind patriotism permeated the local populace during the war.

"A lot of them didn't believe in the war," he said. "That was the best way to get out of it, just go back into the mountains."

Of course, we need to keep in mind he was talking about an old hunting and fishing buddy, a bond that no doubt still held even after seventy years. Yet after I pressed him he refused to judge those few who evaded the WWI draft.

"I never bothered anybody else about their business," he said. "What they did, that was their own affair. I guess the Fattig boys were just a little before their time. A lot of them did that in Vietnam."

EIGHTEEN

Hometown Heroes

Y OUTH LIVING IN RURAL TOWNS THROUGHOUT America have long
been low-hanging fruit for military recruiters. Young people want
to get away from what for them has become mundane, away from the
farm, away from the old folks at home who are driving them up the
walls. Even today, many young men and women eager to get out into
the world see the military as a ticket out of small-town America.

For many, it can be a rewarding experience, providing they aren't killed
or horribly mutilated in times of war, of course. When I joined the Marine
Corps in 1969, a strong desire to see the world was one of the reasons.
Other driving factors included immaturity and impulsiveness but we'll
ignore my character flaws for now. While I did not see the world as a
Marine, I met some fine folks, matured into a somewhat responsible young
man and went to college upon completing my hitch, thanks to the G.I. Bill.
Like most experiences, the military is what you make of it. Some recruits
insist on making miserable their lives and the lives of others who serve
alongside them. We called them non-hackers or, in the coarse language of
the Corps during that era, shitbirds. Just what comprised such a bird was
never clear in my mind but I never cared for that particular fowl.

Osborne de Varila was neither a non-hacker nor a feathered creature
covered with fecal matter. The gungho young soldier who joined the
Army in Grants Pass would become a major footnote in the annals of

World War I history. Born in Juneau in the then Alaskan Territory on Feb. 1, 1899, de Varila moved to Grants Pass with his family as a youngster. Like all young people who spent long summer days along the Rogue River in that era, he fished and swam in its cool waters while dreaming of one day traveling the world to see the sights. That day came when the United States declared war on Germany on April 6, 1917.

He was eighteen years old when he strode into the Army recruiter's office in Grants Pass and signed up a few days after war was declared. If he was like most youths volunteering for military duty, he was eager to earn fame and glory. He felt invincible. Others would be wounded but he just knew he would emerge unscathed. Sadly, while he would gain national renown, he would be dead in three years, a casualty of the mustard gas he inhaled during the war.

Corporal de Varila was definitely a good trooper who made the most of his enlistment. As a member of an artillery unit, he earned the distinction of firing the first shot by any American during the WWI. He pulled the lanyard tied to the breech of a French 75 field piece, firing a three-inch shrapnel shell at 6:10 a.m., Oct. 23, 1917. It was heralded as the first shot fired by any member of an American Expeditionary Force unit. After he was gassed the following March, he and thirteen other wounded young men were selected to return to the States to tell their stories of the war. Dubbed "Pershing's Veterans," the wounded soldiers were paraded about the country as cheerleaders for the war, starting on the East Coast. As for de Varila, any reason for a respite from the war and spend time in the States was just fine, thank you.

In a May 30, 1918 article in the *San Francisco Examiner*, de Varila, who was touring the nation as a member of Pershing's Veterans, spoke of the events leading up to that first shot. He was a member of Battery C of the Sixth field artillery which arrived at the front in France on Oct. 21, 1917. The following day his five-member gun crew was taken by their battery commander, Capt. I. R. McLendon, and a French colonel to reconnoiter the area where they were about to make history.

"That night word came from our headquarters that another regiment of American field artillery was trying to get their guns into position before we did," he told the reporter. "Our guns had only been brought up to a small village three-quarters of a mile back of our position, while the horses had been sent back to the base."

Captain McLendon called for volunteers to drag one gun into position by hand. In the dead of night, de Varila and other volunteers began edging the gun forward.

"It was raining cats and dogs, and the country we had to traverse, dragging the gun, was a mass of mushy mud, pitted with big shell holes and directly under the Germans' fire, which was only less heavy than the rain," said the corporal who obviously relished relating the historic event.

"No one could speak above a whisper nor show any lights as we stumbled through the darkness, dragging our gun into position," he continued. "It took us four hours to pull the gun the three-quarters of a mile to where we wanted it."

After camouflaging the artillery piece, the exhausted volunteers slept alongside it in the driving rain. McLendon gave the gun crew the firing data at 6:00 a.m. the next day. Ten minutes later, de Varila fired the first round, sending it shrieking into the German lines.

"That shrapnel was the first scream of the American eagle," he told the *Examiner*. "According to our forward observation officer, Uncle Sam's first present of hardware to the Kaiser landed plop in the middle of a German communication trench. A few minutes later we got the range of the kitchen and started to warm up Fritz' coffee for him."

German artillery crews returned the favor, firing back with six and eight-inch howitzers. But the American gunners—de Varila's unit was soon joined by other artillery as well as infantry—continued their barrage nonstop until the afternoon of Nov. 5, de Varila said. The German guns were silenced.

His exhausted artillery crew was sent back to the rear to rest. But the period of rest and relaxation was shortlived. In January, C Battery of the Sixth field artillery was deployed to the Toul sector, the first sector captured by American troops. It was there de Varila was gassed on March 22.

"It was mustard gas that got me, and all I can say is that I don't take mustard with my meat anymore," he quipped in the *Examiner.* "I didn't lose consciousness until I received first aid treatment three minutes later, when the oxygen entering my lungs evidently didn't agree with the mixture already inside."

For the next three weeks, the young man would battle to regain his health in an American base hospital. It was there he was selected to join Pershing's Veterans.

In addition to serving in the war and touring the nation, de Varila somehow found time to write a 254-page book, *The First Shot for Liberty.* According to patriotic war-time critics, the book, published in 1918, was written in "slangy, breezy English and permeated with sturdy American spirit." Given his young age and time constraints, it is likely the soldier, although very capable, was assisted in the effort. But he clearly had a flair for writing as he tells the story in detail about firing that historic first shot.

Published late in the summer of 1918 after de Varila was sent back to France, the book was clearly a cheer-leading effort to raise support for war bonds. Although marred by comments that would be deemed patently racist in today's world, it allows the reader to peek over the corporal's shoulder as he goes about his business. He even provides us a briefing on the French 75.

"The *poilu* call this piece the 'Little Frenchman' or 'Charlotte,' " he wrote, referring to the term of endearment for French infantrymen in WWI. "This gun is capable of firing 20 shots a minute of shrapnel or high explosive shells."

Let's jump to the point, alluded to in the *Examiner* article, in which the gun is finally dragged into position on a hill overlooking the German trenches.

"Every bone and muscle in my body howled with weariness, but I was happy—terribly happy—for I felt that I was near the crowning event of my career as a soldier of Uncle Sam, the firing of the first gun in the war for the United States," he wrote in the book. "It had taken us four hours to pull that gun over the marsh."

Exhausted, he and five other artillerymen slept along the French gun that night in the pouring rain, he added. But they rose early the next morning to make history.

"'Battery, attention!' called the battery commander in a cool, even voice," he wrote. "The momentous event was close at hand—the official opening of the war for Uncle Sam against Germany. I thrilled from head to toe, but my head was cool and my hand steady."

No question about it: the bright and brave lad from Grants Pass was more than ready.

"The gun was wheeled into position, its business end pointing toward Germany," he continued. "There was barely enough light for us to read the markings on the little piece. The battery commander gave the word to the sergeant and the sights were set. 'Use second pieces only,' rapped out the commander. A gunner cut the fuse of a shrapnel to meet the requirements of the order, and the shell was placed in the breech of the little '75' by a non-commissioned officer. 'Range 5,500 yards,' snapped the commander.

"I set the deflection and saw that the crosshair was on the target," he continued. "I was tingling from head to foot with the intensity of the moment. There was a brief pause, during which every mother's son of us were on our toes. 'Fire!' rasped out the commander. Filled with a thousand conflicting emotions, I pulled the lanyard of the little spitfire, and America's first shot of the war went screaming into German territory."

That night, an American infantry unit which he described as "helmeted and ready for battle," marched into their sector, he wrote. "The infantry beat us to France by nearly two months, but we of the artillery got into action more than twelve hours ahead of the doughboys," he hastened to add.

Indeed, he wanted credit to go where it rightfully belonged.

"I want all loyal Americans to paste it in their hats that it was C Battery, Sixth United States Field Artillery, that fired that shot, and that every member of the battery did their bit toward sending Uncle Sam's first calling card into the trenches of the Kaiser," he wrote.

The reader can almost feel the pulse of patriotism beating in the young soldier's heart as he writes.

"The savage departure of that projectile for the German lines was as sweet music to our ears," he wrote. "It was a shrieking battle-hymn without words. The warning scream of that eighteen pounds of shrapnel served formal notice on the Kaiser that the United States had started in on the job of exacting retribution for the sinking of the *Lusitania*, the rape of Belgium, and a thousand other outrages committed against civilization by Germany since she set out to rule the world by the sword."

All Americans within sound range whooped and hollered at their country's first salvo into enemy lines, he noted.

"As for me, I got the reaction when my hand left the lanyard," he observed. "I shut my eyes to stop the dizziness, but in a minute opened them again and tried to see through the mist into No Man's Land. I would have given a year's pay just then to have observed where the shell struck..."

He allowed the first round fired by American forces likely had no special meaning to the Germans crouched in their trenches that morning.

"It was just one blast in a chorus of blasts, for French guns were barking away at the Huns all along the line," he wrote. "If the Boches had grasped the significance of the shot they would probably have been a glum lot of creatures, and undoubtedly their beer would have gone bitter in their mouths."

His unit fired more shells throughout the morning, returning to its quarters in the village for chow, he added.

"The little gun that fired the first shot for world liberty was decked with fresh flowers in every village, and we of C Battery had to run a kissing gauntlet almost every step of the way," he observed. "I can tell you the French appreciated the significance of that first shot. They knew that it spelled freedom for them from the invading Hun."

While de Varila was clearly as gungho as any U.S. Marine in battle, he was clearly relieved when he was selected to join Pershing's Veterans to go Stateside and talk to the public about the war.

"I was picked to go because I had fired the first shot for Uncle Sam in the war," he wrote. "When I was told I was going back to the good old U.S.A. to boom the bonds, I couldn't believe it until I was actually aboard the transport and saw the coastline of France disappearing in the distance. Then I knew it was true and fairly hugged myself for joy."

Aboard ship, he and his soldier shipmates made up for lousy cuisine on the frontlines by gorging themselves on "chow that would have satisfied the palate of a millionaire," he wrote. When they weren't eating, they were treated to silent movies featuring the familiar faces of Douglas Fairbanks, Charley Chaplain and Mary Pickford.

"The trip back was an excursion for us warbattered men," he explained. "All of us had been gassed or wounded, and every man-jack was seasoned to our toes in modern trench warfare. Rigid training and the hardest of knocks had been our lot for many months, so that the life of luxury and ease on the transport was as balm to us."

Their troop ship reached New York harbor on April 28, 1918.

"Many of us could not restrain our tears when we sighted the coastline of good old Yankeedom," he wrote. "All of us had gone over to France prepared to die for our country, and never expected to see America again. Yet there it was looming on the horizon."

The WWI veterans were greeted by New York City Mayor John F. Hylan, paraded up Broadway, presented at the New York Stock Exchange and feted by the New York City Bankers' Association and the Harvard Club. Those were clearly heady times for the Grants Pass resident who was then deployed to Philadelphia with several other members of the group before heading west.

"I am happy that I played my little part in this big war by firing the first shot for liberty," he would write. "I think it was fitting that I should be sent to Philadelphia, the birthplace of liberty and the shrine of that wonderful old relic, the Liberty Bell. Every man-jack of us who came over is going back to put in more blows against the Hun. We feel it is our duty to do this, and besides the fascination of war has its grip upon us.

"The Hun peril is a real one, as every American will soon realize if they do not put their full weight into this war," he warned. "The Yank who fails to get into this war with both feet is losing the opportunity of his life. I will not rest content until I am fighting with my battery again over there in France on the front line. It is my burning desire to send over many more shots for liberty into Boche trenches."

However, in a letter to his mother back in Grants Pass, de Varila, who by then had returned to France but was on a break from the fighting, confided that he was in no hurry to return to the front. The letter lacked the bravado found in earlier interviews and in his book. Here was a man weary of death and destruction.

"I am back from the front now for a time but I am feeling scared yet," he wrote. "I am in good health, only water logged and very muddy. We had a pretty hard time for a while up there but it was a hundred percent better after we got settled down and got used to the work."

While he was concerned about the enemy, the damp conditions also discouraged him. He described it in a fashion only an Oregon webfoot would appreciate.

"The climate in the United States which resembles this climate is that of southern Oregon in February," he concluded. In other words, it was raining like hell.

Sadly, the young man with the once indomitable spirit would barely outlive the war. After being sent back to the front once again, he was gassed the second day he was in battle. He spent months in a hospital, returning as a tired and ill veteran to Grants Pass in October, 1919. With his mother accompanying him, he sought treatment in California where he had also spent time in his youth. He died in San Francisco on June 4, 1920. He was twenty-one.

Ironically, the first Grants Pass area soldier to die in service to his country never saw the front lines, although he, too, would be treated as a hero.

"City Honors Dead Soldier," announced the front-page headline in the *Daily Courier* on June 26, 1917. Remember, this was less than three months after we had entered the war. Memories of parades featuring young men in crisp uniforms marching off to war were still fresh.

"One of the largest funerals ever held in southern Oregon was the tribute paid this afternoon to Joseph Borough, the first Grants Pass boy to lose his life in the service of his country," the article declared.

The town's businesses, including the banks, closed that afternoon in honor of the dead soldier, the paper reported. "The Red Cross and Girls Honor Guard attended as bodies and the citizens generally paid fitting honor to the loyalty of the young patriot," it concluded.

An obituary the following day reported that Pvt. Joseph B. Borough, born in Wilderville in 1897 to J.B. and Esther Borough, had died June 19 in Texas where he was training. Although the cause of death was not listed, the article noted he had joined the Army's aviation corps on April 19 of that year. He was assigned to Co. B, First Corps based at Fort Sam Houston.

While well-meaning speakers at such memorials invariably insist the departed will never be forgotten, they are rarely remembered beyond a few years. Life continues unabated for the living. On the same page carrying Borough's obituary ran was a long story highlighting the ongoing twilight baseball battle between the Methodists and Presbyterians. The latter was winning the war on the diamond. The writer didn't hazard a guess who was winning the battle at the pulpit.

Several local soldiers were cited for courage in battle. Private Ferris Abbett of Grants Pass where his father was a minster was rightfully touted as a hero when he protected fellow American soldiers from an enemy hand grenade in the summer of 1918.

"Abbett was standing with a group of fellow soldiers when a German hand grenade alighted in their midst," the *Daily Courier* reported on July 31, 1918. "Abbett instantly cover the grenade with his steel helmet, then stood upon the helmet. A second afterward the bomb exploded, throwing Abbett into the air and severely injuring him, but probably saving the lives of a number of his comrades."

Neither the extent of Abbett's wounds nor his fate was reflected in the paper that day.

Sergeant Albert C. Presley, president of the 1916 Grants Pass High School graduating class, was cited for bravery while serving in the U.S. Army near Eclisfontaine, France on Sept. 18, 1918.

"Sgt. Presley, with a patrol of four other men, went out to reduce what was thought to be a sniping post," the citation read. "They discovered, upon arriving nearer, that it was a machine gun nest and attacked it with a series of short rushes. The attack resulted in the capture of 25 prisoners and two machine guns."

A month after the war ended, Presley would visit Mt. Kimmel in Belgium, a hill famous for being the site of a bloody battle in the waning days of the war. In a Dec. 22, 1918, letter to his parents in Grants Pass, he sent his impressions of the wasteland he had found. Everywhere he looked he saw death and destruction. Both sides had shelled the site, intent on removing the other and gaining the strategic position atop the hill. The battlefield reflected every horror of war, from the stench of dismembered bodies to shell holes that looked like "small Crater Lakes," Presley wrote. A nearby cathedral, previously beautiful with historic wood carvings, was now a shattered hulk, he noted.

"Nothing could live or endure the shelling that this ground was given," he wrote. "I don't believe there is a square foot that has not been turned over churned many times. There is hardly a yard of it that doesn't have some kind of equipment on it from cannon down to compass."

The sight obviously left a lasting impression on the young man. About him was devastation created by armed conflict.

"It seems to me that if all the men in the civilized world could take a look at that battlefield, it would mean no more war," he concluded.

Many young soldiers from rural Oregon had never before left the family farm, let alone watch a comrade die. The waiting glory they dreamed of as the troop trains pulled out, cheered on by flag-waving crowds, had given way to bloody, brutal reality in a muddy trench. They now knew the feeling of fear rising like bile from their stomach. The stench of bloating bodies clung to their clothes like smoke from a campfire.

Late in September of 1918, Pvt. Francis Speake who hailed from northern Josephine County posted a letter to A.S. Coutant in Grants Pass, informing his friend that he had been wounded in the hand. Like many letters home from local youths in uniform, it was published in the *Daily Courier*. The article indicated the soldier was a gold miner drafted in July of that year. Parenthetically, given the fact there was a prominent family of miners from that area named Speaker, it may be the paper left the "r" off the end of his surname but we will use the surname spelling used in the article.

The private, who was recovering in a hospital, was a member of Co. D, 109th Infantry.

"War sure is hell," he wrote, presumably with his good hand. "When you hear the bullets whizzing all about you and the big shells bursting over your head you have a queer feeling that one can hardly express."

Yet the young soldier considered himself fortunate to have emerged from battle with only a hand wound.

"Some of the boys were shot up awful bad," he wrote. "We were advancing on an open field with no protection at all, only when we lie flat on the ground. I had my gun shot out of my hand just before I was shot in the hand. After I was shot in the hand I thought it was time to keep my head down."

The lonely soldier longed for the green river valley of Oregon he knew so well and its rich fall bounty.

"Well, I hope the war will be over before long and I will be back to good old southern Oregon," he wrote. "I hope you have a good crop this year. I wish I was there to help eat some of the peaches and prunes."

Here was one soldier who, having seen gay Paree, was eager to be back on the farm.

Meanwhile, he was optimistic about the way the war would end.

"None of us have any doubt as to the outcome of the war," he concluded. "Besides, we all have the feeling that the folks back home are behind us as never before."

Corporal J. K. "Worth" Hamilton, writing to his parents in Grants Pass that month, also waxed longingly for his home state. Even the rain made him think of his native Oregon, even when he was in the rear watching a French vaudeville act. Whether it was bawdy he didn't inform his parents.

"Our mess sergeant is an Oregon boy and we have great times arguing with the other soldiers from the East in this outfit about the superiority of Oregon over the eastern states," he wrote, adding smugly, "We usually win out."

You know full well every soldier from the other forty-seven contiguous states—this was back when Alaska and Hawaii were still territories—were just as homesick for their home state which they knew was the best of the lot.

But there were a few who seemed enthralled with the war. In a letter to his parents printed in the *Daily Courier* on Aug.26, 1918, Pvt. Fred C. Norris of Portland excitedly related that he had been "over the top" twice, meaning he was among those charging up out of the trenches.

"The first time I went over was on my birthday and I never got a scratch," he wrote. "We advanced across an open wheat field with machine guns playing on us and big shrapnel shells bursting every place."

With their foot-and-a-half-long bayonets affixed to their 1917 Enfield rifles, his unit achieved their objective, he noted.

"The best part of it is that I got two myself," he bragged. "Kind of a birthday present. I had just jumped into a shell hole and found him there. We were both rather surprised but I was lucky enough to run him through before he had a chance to move."

Perhaps it all happened as he told the tale but it doesn't pass the sniff test when compared to stories told by countless other combat veterans. I have yet to meet one who glorified the gore of hand-to-hand combat to the death. However, it may be that Norris was suffering from what was then called shell shock, a mental fatigue we now know as post traumatic stress disorder. Then again, he may have been reading too many fanciful war novels.

But lets hear him out.

"I was so excited at the time that it didn't bother me a bit, but when I think about it now it makes me feel kind of queer," he allowed, demonstrating he still had a spark of humanity.

His other confirmed kill came when he shot a German soldier who had climbed out of a trench and charged him, he noted. However, the fortunes of war soon turned against him.

"The second time I went over I was knocked unconscious from a shell exploding near me," he wrote, adding that he was also struck in the foot by a machine gun bullet.

But he told his parents he was fine.

"You don't need to worry about me anymore now because I will be safe in a hospital," he assured them. Doubtless the letter did little to stop their worrying about his health, both physical as well as psychological.

They must have also been aware of the fact many soldiers who initially survived a battlefield wound did not survive the poor care received in many WWI-era hospitals.

While countless were wounded on the battlefield, some accident prone doughboys never made it to the front lines. When Pvt. Louis P. Miller of Grants Pass arrived in France, he lost a battle with a band saw, severing a toe. Infection set in, keeping him in the hospital for three months. Just how he cut off his toe was never explained in the letter his mother received on Nov. 3, 1918. What we do know is that a severed toe was the least of his worries. After informing his mom that he would be leaving a toe in France, the soldier got to the meat of his letter.

"I had a little accident and am now back in the base hospital with a few legs, arms, etc. broken," the letter continued. "Nothing serious or permanent, but I will be laid up some little time. I got tangled up in some machinery and broke my left arm twice and both legs. No compound fractures and no parts missing."

With that missive, oddly cheerful that it was, Pvt. Norris let his mom know he was sidelined from the action. With the war ending eight days after she received the letter, she must have been mightily relieved. But she had ample reason to be concerned should her son choose a career involving any kind of machinery.

In yet another hospital in France, Pvt. C.W. Courtney of Grants Pass could not write. His Oct. 20, 1918 letter home was written by a kindly YWCA volunteer, the *Daily Courier* reported. It was his fourth week in a hospital, the result of a shell landing nearly on top of him, he informed his parents.

"The doctor told me today that he thought I might be able to get up, possible four weeks more," the letter said. "My legs are improving wonderfully and are quite painful at times, but the doctor says it is because they are getting better."

His left knee cap had been blown off by the explosion, the letter explained. It appeared he had other wounds because he could not use his left arm or sit up.

"I asked the doctor if my left leg would be stiff," the letter noted. "He hummed a little bit and then said, 'Well, a little but you'd rather have that than none at all, wouldn't you?' "

Upon that, Courtney apparently cheered up.

"The nurse told me yesterday to have heart, that she thought I'd be home by Christmas," the letter stated. "I sure do hope that is true for I have a fear of the front line. I would be so nervous and scared that I'd be absolutely worthless.

"No one can ever imagine how horrible and how dreadful the modern warfare of today is," it continued. "There are so many different things to combat. The shell that wounded me was a double-explosive shell, exploding twice. It also contained gas. After being wounded I had the presence of mind and with one good hand put on my gas mask, thus saving me from being gassed."

In closing, Courtney urged his loved ones back in rural Oregon to go on with their lives.

"Please do not worry over me, instead just send up a prayer up to God," he said. "It will do me much more good and save you a whole lot."

Just three months before the war ended, pilot Newell Barber, the young son of Dr. Martin and Theresa Barber of Medford, was shot down on Aug. 11, 1918, along with a French aviator serving as a spotter over the trenches near the Belgium border, according to the front-page article in the *Medford Mail Tribune* on Sept. 7, 1920. Earlier reports had notified readers right after the local teenage hero had been killed, of course, but this was a lengthy report commemorating the dedication of the newly-renamed Newell Barber Field, the town's first public airstrip which had been established a few years earlier just south of town. A graduate of Medford Senior High School, the then seventeen-year-old had joined the Army Aviation Corps in the spring of 1917 and had been deployed to France with the 108th Aero Squadron. Their bodies were never recovered. The pilot was posthumously awarded the *Croix de Guerre* which, in French, means "cross of war." The highly-regarded medal was awarded to those who demonstrated courage in battle.

The article noted that one speaker at the celebration, which drew some 10,000 spectators, read a portion of the last letter Newell Barber sent home to his grieving parents. The brave lad had penned the following words: "If I should go, I want you to know that I go as a true American. I am not a slacker and I am not afraid."

Even by local standards where patriotism traditionally gets high marks, the celebration stood out, the article observed. Led by a band, the automobile parade from Medford to the airstrip was more than two miles long, it reported.

"Not an accident, not a hitch and not an unpleasant feature marred the big occasion, by which the name of Medford's high school aviator here who lost his life while flying over the German trenches in France is permanently perpetuated and honored," the paper reported. "It was a day of significance and bigness…It was a spontaneous outpouring in memory of one of Medford's heroes, and in honoring him everyone felt that they were honoring all the boys who parted with their lives during the war for their country."

While there is no doubt those cheering that day fully intended never to forget the young pilot, those wanting to see the area progress as a regional hub were less interested in preserving the memory of the military hero. A new and bigger airfield was created in the late 1920s at the north end of town, a change that had to inflict some emotional pain on the Barber family. Fast forward a century and a county-owned baseball park now stands where biplanes once landed on what had been Newell Barber Field.

As an aside, the local airport is now officially known as the Rogue Valley International-Medford Airport, a moniker which some find a bit pretentious. Many patriots among the local populace would prefer something like the Newell Barber Municipal Airport to keep alive the name of a brave young man who died in the war. Sadly, contrary to what the *Mail Tribune* reported in 1920, few military heroes are permanently honored. Progress does not stand still for sentiment. Regardless of the name, it is a fine regional airport and a pleasure to fly in and out of.

No doubt the first southern Oregon resident to enter the war was the remarkable Kenneth McKenzie Clark Neill, born in Scotland on Aug. 17, 1890. An independent fellow who had a passing resemblance to

Teddy Roosevelt as well as sharing his gusto for living large, Neill owned a 250-acre spread he bought in 1911 near the mouth of the Applegate River just a few miles south of Grants Pass. He fondly named it the Ardencraig Farm to honor his ancestral home in Scotland. He happened to be in Scotland attending an agricultural college when Europe exploded into war. Back in Oregon's Ardencraig in February of 1915, his pregnant wife, Ada Louise Neill, received a letter from her husband informing her that he had just joined the British Expeditionary Force as a second lieutenant. Apparently he felt duty bound to his native country and her Queen. Although he came home to Oregon on furlough at least once, he would continue to serve until Jan. 30, 1919 when he was released as a captain and returned to Oregon.

Throughout the war, Neill wrote faithfully to his wife in longhand letters kept by their descendants who still live in the Applegate Valley. In a letter from somewhere in France and posted with a one-cent stamp on April 5, 1917, he predicted that the United States was about to jump into the fray with both feet on the side of the Allies.

"I'm afraid the U.S. is into the war and that they (Germans) will poison your child or kill all our cows and horses," he wrote. "You have no idea what brutes they are. They have poisoned the water. They may try to blow up the dam across the Rogue River."

Apparently referring to domestic German saboteurs, the letter also indicated Neill hoped to join the American forces when they entered the war, a dream that never came to pass.

"The Americans ought to do us a bit of good, however, as I have heard they have captured all the interned German ships," he wrote. "And they may be able to show us some new stunts that will end the war.

"Germany has shown herself to be utterly ruthless in war and has just got to be punished," he continued. "You always say that England has not put up enough pep into the war but you just wait until we go through the Hindenburg Line."

Built as a German defensive position in the winter of 1916–1917, the line was along the Western Front from Arras to Laffaux in France.

German Field Marshal Paul von Hindenburg had routed the Russians in 1914 but, as chief commander of the Central Powers, he would see his troops overrun by the Allied forces just as Neill promised his wife.

But war was not always exciting. Consider Neill's letter to his wife on Dec., 28, 1917:

"No news today," he wrote. "We hear food is very hard to get in London, so hope the war will soon be over. I expect that Germany must be in a very bad way internally. Funny the Kaiser did not make a Xmas peace offer. His offers are always the same, greatly in favor of the Germans. However, you never know when the Austrians and the Turks will give in. The war seems to have stopped in Russia. There must be a terrible state of chaos there."

But Neill wasn't only worried about the war. While away, he was concerned about his Oregon farm.

"I hope the cows are doing well," he wrote. "It is freezing very hard here and is very bitter at night. It must be terrible for those thousands who have no cover over them at night."

He worried how Margaret, their wee daughter, was withstanding the winter chill. "How does M like the cold weather?" he asked. "Can she stand the heat well, or is she like me?"

Although Neill was gassed during the war, he would survive to return to his beloved Ardencraig in southwest Oregon where he died in 1946.

NINETEEN

Home Front Memories

T HE HEALTHY CRIES OF A NEWBORN COULD BE heard coming from a bedroom in an unpainted wood frame farm house in the heart of the Applegate Valley a few hours before sunrise on Valentine's Day in 1915. Oregonophiles will recognize Feb. 14 as the state's birthday anniversary first celebrated in 1859. Those cries were the first sounds of life uttered by Nanine Anderson Nichols, a baby girl born to Laura Fattig Anderson who, along with her husband John Anderson, was staying at the Jonas and Harriett Fattig farm nestled under the western shadow of Squires Peak. The infant was my first cousin whose maternal grandparents were my paternal grandparents. Her mother was my aunt and my father's older sister.

Satisfied that mother and infant were healthy, a tired Dr. Charles D. Sweeney closed his black bag and climbed aboard his buckboard for the long cold ride back to Medford that morning. Just a few hundred yards west of the wagon road, the swollen Applegate River flowed strong, fed by winter rain. Light snow dusted Squires Peak which rises to a 3,340-foot point above sea level. Heavier snow covered Tallowbox Mountain which tops 5,000 feet just west of the river. Down on the wagon road, Sweeney bounced along, trying to avoid the deep ruts filled with rain water.

"Mom said he came out in a buckboard to deliver me," Nanine observed in a 1989 interview. "A lot of people were still using a horse and buggy in those days."

Sweeney, who would switch to a motorized vehicle not long afterward, was a beloved doctor who paid house calls throughout the rural area, including occasionally stopping by the Fattig farm, she said. He was nearly ninety when he died in 1956.

"I still remember that old house where I often was as a child," she said. "Grandpa refused to paint it. He liked it that way."

A hard-working farmer, Jonas Fattig didn't cotton to wasting money on frivolous trifles like house paint, she said. In addition to maintaining his 120-acre homestead, he served as foreman of the large ranch near the mouth of the Little Applegate River. It was Mother Nature who painted the two-story Fattig farmhouse, using brushes of wind and rain to give the whip-sawed pine lumber a weathered gray coat.

Nor was it just paint that got grandpa's dander up. The Iowa native, accustomed to living in the treeless plains, could not abide trees growing near the house. Trees blocked his view, he told the family.

"He'd take an ax and cut down the trees," his granddaughter said. "I guess they made him feel closed in. I was very small but I still remember it. I can still see that house in my mind."

Through her eyes, and those of others who lived early in that century, we are offered a glimpse of the world inhabited by a young Alfred Fattig who also lived in the farmhouse along with his parents and his brothers.

The old wooden farm house, along with the barn, is long gone now, the victim of change. No doubt age also had a hand in its demise, without paint and all. But the memories of Nanine Nichols' childhood remained as solid as Squires Peak. As a young girl growing up in Medford, she would often visit her grandparents in the Applegate Valley.

Standing a lean six foot, Jonas Fattig was a staid man with a drooping mustache who didn't have a lot of time for small talk, she indicated. As the family patriarch, his was the countenance of the Old Testament, somber and solemn. Yet his granddaughter recalled he shed that dour cloak when he was called to play the fiddle at local community dances, filling the dance hall, often a local barn, with high-stepping, hand-clapping music.

"They would go to dances way up the Applegate and take us kids," she said. "But they wouldn't let us stay up late. We had to sleep in the cloak room."

Hailing from tiny Jamestown in northeast Kansas, our small but feisty grandmother always greeted her grandchildren with a broad smile and a bear hug, she said.

"Grandma was very nice," my cousin said. "But she had her religion. She felt that war of any kind was wrong, that killing was a sin."

Like her husband, Harriett was a faithful member of the Church of the Brethren whose members are called Dunkards, a name derived from the fact they prefer baptism by total immersion—dunking—rather than merely sprinkling a dash of holy water on the head. Originating in Germany early in the16th Century, its members were persecuted for their beliefs, causing some to flee to the New World, initially settling in Germantown, Pennsylvania. Like the Society of Friends—Quakers—as well as Mennonites and Hutterites, they are pacifists who follow a simple life while stressing obedience to Christ rather than creeds. Noting that Christ was not a veteran, few are keen on military service. Although there may have been a few members who slipped away to don a uniform, Dunkards did not participate in the Revolutionary War or the Civil War, even while supporting independence and abhorring slavery. They would treat World War I no differently.

Such was the moral message that Harriett Fattig drummed into her flock. Her hubby apparently followed suit, although not quite as zealously. You noticed he fiddled at local dances and sported a large mustache. A beard was encouraged but a mustache? That bordered on the heretic as did attending community dances where doubtlessly the demon alcohol would surface, causing unbiblical behavior.

While Jonas was a strict moral disciplinarian at home, it was the family matriarch who repeatedly sermonized the Dunkard gospel to their offspring, Nanine Nichols said.

"She preached to them since the day they were born that war was sinful," she stressed. "That was her religion. She clung to that until the day she died."

Of the three brothers, the one most receptive to it was Alfred, she said. Like the Rogue River, his religion ran deep and strong throughout his long life. But elder brother Charlie and kid brother Paul were repulsed by her religiosity, becoming what Alfred would call infidels. Yet they both seemed to adore their mother while clearly disliking— hating may be too strong a word here—their father. During the lengthy interview in Texas, Alfred repeatedly spoke glowingly of their father while saying very little about their mother. Still, the entire family shared a strong dislike for war. But my father served in the Merchant Marines during a portion of World War II, perhaps joining in part to help wash away any taint of having draft-dodging brothers.

While the brothers were embracing the pacifist approach to religion, other young men from rural areas like Oregon were following the advice of fundamental religious leaders who had reached conclusions diametrically opposed to that of Harriett Fattig and the Dunkards. Few were not moved to support the war after attending a lecture by William Jennings Bryan in a Chautauqua tent in Grants Pass on May 28, 1918. The passionate Christian fundamentalist and three-time Democrat Party presidential nominee may have supported neutrality at the outset of the war but was supportive of U.S. involvement during his 1918 spring visit to rural Oregon.

"No one left the tent yesterday noon that did not feel baptized with a shower of words and arguments that were irresistible in their logic and import from his portrayal of the duty man owes to government, man's duty to society and man's duty to God," gushed the weekly *Oregon Observer* newspaper in Grants Pass the next day.

Bryan would later participate in what is commonly known as the Scopes Monkey Trial in Dayton, Tennessee. The courtroom brawl during that hot July in 1925 was fired by the arrest of John T. Scopes, a local high school science teacher and coach who dared teach Darwinian evolution theory in violation of a Tennessee state law. A staunch Christian fundamentalist, Bryan stepped in to help the prosecution while legendary defense attorney Clarence Darrow argued for the defendant. In the end, Darrow made a monkey out of Bryan and his team but Scopes was convicted, no doubt thanks to the antievolutionary mindset in the local jury. Still, Scopes would be released on a technicality. Bryan would die of a heart attack in his sleep five days after the trial ended.

Although she was also a staunch Christian, one mother in the Applegate Valley was not swayed by Bryan's masterful oratory in which he declared God was on America's side during his Grants Pass visit. With her husband at her side, Harriett Fattig enthusiastically went on to help their two older sons evade the military draft.

She wasn't interested in technicalities. War was wrong in her eyes, plain and simple. She intended her sons would have no part of it.

Nanine Nichols could still faintly remember climbing aboard a wagon with her grandparents and her uncle Paul—my father who was a little older than her but still a boy at the time—and bouncing along the Applegate River.

"They told me we were going on picnics," she said.

They were certainly going on a camping trip which would result in picnic lunches. Pulled by a team of gentle horses named Babe and Cleo, the wagon would cross a wooden bridge spanning the river, then follow the south bank until reaching Williams Creek flowing out of the Williams Valley. At that point, they traveled south several miles to the foot of Grayback Mountain where they set up camp. A crackling fire would soon fill the camp with the aroma of cowboy coffee. Tethered nearby in a patch of grass by the creek, the horses were happily munching away. And the adults sat down to wait.

"We would camp there for several days," Nanine Nichols said. "They (Alfred and Charlie) must have come in the middle of the night. I don't remember seeing them during those trips. But I knew we were taking supplies to them."

Her recollection of those trips mirror an anecdote our father told of those wagon trips up the Williams Valley to rendezvous with two wanted men. The lone difference in the two tales was that he recalled seeing his brothers and being severely admonished not to say a word about it to anyone. Being nine years older than Nanine, his niece, he would have stayed up later for the nocturnal visits when his brothers stepped quietly out of the woods to pick up their supplies.

In any case, the "picnics" would continue every three or four months, weather permitting, until the spring of 1920, she said.

"Mom and I used to talk about those wagon trips to take food to Charlie and Alfred," she said. "That was so long ago. A lot of water has flowed under the bridge since then."

Another longtime southern Oregon resident whose life bridged that time span was Glenn Smith, an Applegate Valley resident born in Ruch on June 8, 1908. A pleasant fellow, Smith died in 1992 at age eighty-four.

As a youngster, he recalled seeing Jonas and Harriett Fattig riding past in their wagon following the gentle plodding of Babe and Cleo. He also remembered what they would often wear: she would be in a long plain dress while wearing a black bonnet while he wore a black hat with a wide rim, long-sleeved cambric shirt, Levi jeans (501s came out in 1915) and work boots. Toss in a pitch fork and they were Grant Wood's "American Gothic" aboard a farm wagon, Applegate Valley style. Indeed, these were country folk who lived a simple life with few frills.

"They were dirt poor but clean poor," said Smith who was in an assisted living facility in Medford during the 1989 interview. "Most people were poor out there then. He was a big, rawboned man. When it came to hard work, he had no peer. I remember he was as honest as the day is long."

He recalled an anecdote Applegate Valley residents once told of Jonas Fattig. The farmer was pitching hay in the barn loft when the tax assessor stopped in for the annual tax assessment.

"'Do you have anything different that needs to be added to the list this year?' the assessor yelled up to him," Smith said. "'No, same as last year,' your grandfather told him. Well, a few minutes later, he yelled down to the other workers, 'Is the tax fella still down there? I forgot to tell him about that new set of deer horns I got.'"

With that, Smith laughed at tale which he swore was true. In addition to being the Applegate Valley's Honest Abe, my grandfather was also a fine hunter, he said.

A retired insurance agent who farmed on the side, Smith said most folks in the Applegate country knew that Alfred and Charlie Fattig were hiding out to avoid the draft. But no one other than family knew their whereabouts, he said. Pausing for a moment, he corrected himself, adding there was at least one exception. A local district ranger in the local national forest, who had employed the two brothers to plant trees, knew where to find them, he allowed.

"He always said that since no one asked him, then he wasn't breaking the law by not telling," said Smith who declined to name the individual. Even after seven decades, the domestic wounds left by the war had not completely healed.

Like Nanine Nichols, Smith recalled that, while Jonas Fattig shared his wife's views on the war, she was the most outspoken in her opposition.

"It was through her conviction," he said of their decisions to avoid military service. "Back in those days, there wasn't really any such thing as a conscientious objector like there is now. Their mother just had a deep conviction."

Although he was a Navy veteran, serving after WWI and before the next world war, he did not weigh in on what he thought of their decision.

"The Fattig boys liked the outdoors," he said. "They loved the mountains and wanted to be free."

Don Barnes, the Fattig family friend who you first met in Chapter Two when he told us about his second-hand madstone, also attested to the fact the brothers loved the outdoors. A lifelong friend of my father, he knew the remote upper Chetco River country was a good hideaway from the authorities.

"Rough country, real rough country," he said. "No roads in there a'tall. Hell, even when I was in the sheriff's office we didn't have any roads in most of the mountain areas. We rode horses or walked the trails on foot. It would be hard to catch anyone back there."

Sporting a pencil thin mustache and a steady gaze, Barnes looked like he stepped right out of an old western movie, the kind in which the local sheriff was a straight shooter, both with his gun and his ethics. Point of fact, Don Barnes was. He served as the county sheriff from 1937 through 1943 and had a sterling reputation for honesty and integrity.

Speaking with the frankness for which he was known, he observed that Alfred and Charlie Fattig did not make a lot of friends when they elected to head for the hills during the war.

"The vast majority of the people were very much in favor of it," he stressed of the war. "Most every able bodied man in the country left and went to war. No question about it. Kaiser Bill was ridiculed. When he jumped on the United States, why, hells bells, it was war for certain."

He was referring to American ships being sent to the bottom by German U-boats. In addition, many local residents were the sons and daughters of immigrants from countries at war with Germany, he noted. Add the pride they had in their new country and they were ready to fight for both new country and the old country, he reasoned.

"They were very patriotic people in this area," he added. "The idea was, out here, that this darn upstart in Germany had no right interfering with the United States of America and they ought to reach out there and bat him over the head. That was the whole deal."

On the other hand, war was not something the generation who would be doing the fighting nor their parents had experienced, he said, adding the last major war to have rocked our country had been the Civil War which ended in 1865.

"Nobody knew much about it," he said of armies battling it out. But few young men entertained thoughts about not taking up arms for Uncle Sam, he reiterated. "Most in this area just volunteered and were gone," he said.

The vast majority of folks back home supported the boys at the front, he stressed, noting that public gathering places, from the courthouse to the schools, were festooned with posters supporting the war effort. The nation had called and Oregonians were standing up to be counted, he said.

"See, it's hard for people now to understand how it would be to live in a community like Grants Pass was at the time," he said. "About the only way to be in touch with the outside world was by railroad. Otherwise, you took a horse and buggy or you walked."

There was no interstate cutting across the state, no flights to San Francisco or Portland, he added.

Barnes was but a lad when he enviously watched young men in uniform gallantly hop aboard troop trains. The stars and stripes fluttered majestically when the troop trains rolled slowly through town. Sweethearts waved tearfully; proud fathers puffed out their chests. This was Main Street, U.S.A., a community that would have done Sinclair Lewis proud. Similar scenes were being acted out in nearly every town across the nation. Pride and patriotism surged as strong as the old steam engines puffing through the Rogue Valley.

True, change was in the air across the land. Horse power in the form of four-legged equines was being replaced by horsepower fueled by gasoline. But southwestern Oregon retained its old ways longer than most, thanks to its pioneer stock, Barnes said.

"Grants Pass was about the longest ways from anywhere there was," he said. "So there was this little community that was entirely self-sufficient. It lived off its own produce, its own people."

Throughout the region ran a proud independence, he said, noting that an Illinois Valley miner named George Max Esterly died because of his pride. Esterly, a once prominent miner whose mine closed during the war, was sixty-three when he died on Dec. 2, 1926.

"He died of malnutrition out at his mine because he wouldn't let anybody know he was hungry," Barnes said. "That's the kind of people they were. Why, you couldn't even give any of those guys anything if they were starving. They just wouldn't take it. They'd consider it an insult if you even offered it to them. They were individualists, real independent."

With a population of about 5,000 people during the war, Grants Pass was the largest community nearest the Madstone cabin, he said, adding that its population was close knit.

"They liked to have reasons to socialize," he said. "Of course, the war gave them that. They sold war stamps. Women made bandages which were picked up at the railroad station."

Grants Pass residents were even asked to throw in the towel for the war effort. Literally. An item in the Oct. 8, 1918, *Daily Courier* warned that the local linen harvest bound for French hospitals didn't pass muster. The call went for 125 hand towels and twenty bath towels.

"We must wake up to the importance of this call," remonstrated a Mrs. Griffin, the person cited by the article as being in charge of the linen detail. "You may give from your home supply and the towels do not need to be linen."

Barrels were even placed on street corners for gathering fruit pits used to make gas masks. Gathered from peaches, prunes, cherries, walnuts and apricots, the pits were employed to make carbon used in the masks. About seven pounds of pit were needed to produce enough carbon for one mask. "Do your bit by saving the pit!" became a familiar battle cry.

Even local deer hunters helped in the war effort by donating hides to be used in making aviation jackets. Properly tanned buckskin jackets were popular among the dapper pilots.

Most people followed war news through newspapers, Barnes said.

"And letters," he added. "When somebody would get a letter, why the whole neighborhood would come around." Those letters were later published in the local paper, he said.

To fully understand the era and the local folks when the U.S. entered the war, you had to walk the streets, attend social gatherings or visit a family on a rural farm in the Grants Pass, Jacksonville, Medford or Ashland areas, the principal towns in the area, he stressed.

"Nowadays, people look at things so differently," he said. "People who lived here then were either pioneers or sons and daughters of pioneers who had walked clear across the United States to get here. They were interested in what kind of man you were. They didn't give a damn what you did as long as you didn't bother them. But if you bothered them, why you were in trouble. They felt the same way about their country."

That does not mean they were ravenous mad dogs when it came to all wars, he cautioned.

"Hell, there was no question about being against war as war," he said. "They were merely against their enemies. That was the attitude."

While that statement may be construed as splitting hairs, his point was that folks back then didn't take too kindly to anything or anyone—domestic or foreign—trifling with their independence. Sinking U.S. ships was more than a trifle, he stressed.

When it came to individual decisions, most people he knew approached life with a live and let live policy, providing their decisions did not impose on others.

"They felt every man had a right to do as he pleased," he said. "My grandfather, walking down the streets of Grants Pass today, he wouldn't have ever stopped for a red light. He'd say, 'No Goddamn light is going to tell me how to walk down my street!' That's just the way he felt."

His grandfather was Albert S. Barnes, Sr., the Jackson County Sheriff from 1896 through 1898. The alert reader will recall that Albert Barnes was the name adopted by Alfred Fattig while he was on the dodge. A mere coincidence he used the same moniker as a sheriff whose name was still known far and wide when the Fattigs arrived in Jackson County? Not likely.

When war was declared, many young men left the region in crisp new uniforms, leaving a dearth in the work force, Don Barnes explained. Although only twelve when the nation entered the war, he was recruited to help fight local wild fires. Other youngsters his age, also joined the army of young firefighters along with hobos and drifters, he said.

"Those tramps, they weren't much good," he said of the hard work of stopping a fire. "But it is what they had to pick from. Most of them were too old to go to war and I was too young."

It was dangerous work for anyone, he said, recalling that one large fire in the summer of 1918 ignited a few miles west of Glendale in the Cow Creek drainage killed one firefighter. A blaze near the community of West Fork along Cow Creek killed one firefighter and seriously injured another, the *Daily Courier* reported on Aug. 13, 1918, confirming his memory of events.

Just before Uncle Sam entered the war, Barnes became fascinated by ham radio. For him, it was a space age device capable of connecting him with the world waiting beyond Grants Pass, thanks to scientific advances made by a fellow named Guglielmo Marconi. But the federal government intervened just as young Barnes and other Grants Pass residents were becoming interested in wireless.

"The War Department is now engaging in closing and dismantling all private amateur stations throughout the country and its possessions," the *Daily Courier* reported the day after the U.S. declared war on Germany.

"They were afraid the ham radios would be used to inform the enemy," Barnes explained. "They closed down every one of the ham radios."

Transatlantic transmitting had not yet been perfected but the War Department was concerned about information being fed to Stateside spies via the wireless, he explained. Parenthetically, the Department of War became the Department of Defense in 1949 after folks in Washington, D.C. decided it sounded less offensive.

While ham radio operations would resume after World War I ended, some local activities and projects never returned, Barnes said.

"A great many things were interrupted during the war that never became anything again," Barnes said.

For instance, an effort to punch a railroad from Grants Pass to Crescent City on the coast in far northwestern California never resumed, he said. The work had started before the war and some ten miles was completed when the war started, he said. His father—Albert S. Barnes, Jr.—was the one who came up with the idea, he said.

"It would have gone all the way through if it hadn't been for World War I," Don Barnes said. "That war stopped all such activity."

There was also a problem with financial hanky-panky by the railroad company working on the project which drew the attention of authorities but, as he obviously believed, perhaps it would have been completed had the war not intervened. One issue that is not debatable is that yet another Albert Barnes was in the local spotlight, giving someone on the lam the idea for an alias.

Although a few years younger than Barnes, Marvin Ramsey, born in the Illinois Valley on Nov. 16, 1912, also recalled the years the United States locked and loaded for war. Like Barnes, Ramsey stressed that nationalism permeated the region in that era.

"We was all so patriotic, you know," Ramsey said. "Hell, even us kids, we was buying defense stamps."

Although he didn't know the brothers at the time, he later came to know the elder brother while he was mining on Josephine Creek after the war. He related the tale Charlie Fattig told him about the day the authorities came after him to join the Army.

"Well, old Charlie got his notice to join the Army of the United States," he said. "He ignored that notice. So they sent the sheriff after him. That sheriff, he started up the lane to the Fattig house. Here was Charlie, building fence, digging post holes."

The sheriff sauntered over to the man he intended to arrest for draft evasion. After they exchanged pleasantries, the lawman got down to business, Ramsey said.

"He says, 'Guess you know why I'm here. I'm going to take you in,'" he recalled of the story. "Charlie asked him if he'd let him go up to the house to get some of his personal stuff."

The sheriff obliged, patiently waiting outside while the scofflaw disappeared inside the unpainted house, he said.

"Old Charlie went in the front door and out the back door," Ramsey said. "And he went right over to that Chetco River country."

Swearing the tale of how he escaped the clutches of the law was precisely as Charlie Fattig told it, Ramsey laughed heartily at the image of the lanky draft dodger sprinting out the back door, personal belongings in hand.

"The only one I ever knew who evaded the draft in that war was Charlie Fattig," he said, adding he wasn't acquainted with the younger brother. "Me, I'd go along with him now."

Ramsey served in the U.S. Army during World War II, fighting for control of Alaska's Aleutian Island chain against entrenched Japanese forces. Japanese forces had captured Attu and a neighboring island, Kiska, in June of 1942. U.S. and Canadian forces fought from May 11 to May 30 in 1943 to regain control of the islands. In the battle, roughly 1,000 American combatants died while more than 2,000 Japanese soldiers were killed.

"It wasn't a picnic," Ramsey said. "We suffered from exposure. We had to sit there and take it. It was awful."

It may have been May but the weather was bitterly cold, he recalled of the typical cold weather blowing through the end of the Aleutian Island chain that time of year.

"After going through that experience, if I could live my life over again, I would have done the same thing Charlie done, hid up there in them mountains," he insisted.

Before he marched off to WWII, Ramsey had himself gone to the Madstone cabin, although it was not because he was contemplating avoiding serving in the military. Rather, he was working for the U.S. Forest Service which was fighting a wild fire in the upper Chetco River drainage during the summer of 1940. As an employee of the then Siskiyou National Forest, Ramsey's job was to scout the fire, keeping the fire command apprised of the smoke-filled battle against the blaze. The fire incident command had established its field headquarters at Madstone cabin.

Ramsey, who kept a diary much of his life, noted that he left his home in Kerby before sunup on June 22, hiking double-time to cover the estimated twenty-mile distance by dark. Built of logs about a foot in diameter, Madstone cabin was as solid as it would have been when the logs were first laid, he said. The shake roof was fully intact, he added.

"The place was in good order," he said. "It hadn't deteriorated. Hell, it was still livable at the time. It was well put together, that's why."

However, he said the windows had been removed.

"Evidently, someone had raped that place and had taken the windows," he surmised. "Maybe someone built another cabin down river."

When I showed him the madstone that Alfred Fattig had discovered in the young buck, he rolled it slowly over in his fingers before commenting.

"Real interesting things, madstones," he said. "Only one time I ever seen a madstone before this one. My uncle shot a deer with a madstone in it. It wasn't attached to anything, just floating around down there."

As it happens, Ramsey also served in the Civilian Conservation Corps with my father in southern Oregon in the early 1930s. Intrigued, I asked him if he kept his diary during that period. If so, did he mention Dad? Sure enough, he had done both. In his diary, he referred to my father as "cousin sloppy," apparently because of his habit of throwing down his bedroll at night without regard to sprucing up a bit beforehand. No, I'm sure it wasn't the way my dad would have preferred to be remembered. But it still cracks me up when I think about it.

Longtime Kerby resident Glenn Young, born near Waldo in the Illinois Valley on Feb. 23, 1913, was also at the Madstone cabin during the 1940 wildfire, which he estimated burned several thousand acres. He also recalled the cabin surviving the fire and being in good shape at that point.

While he echoed sentiments that most folks supported the war during that period, he noted it was not universal. For instance, John Henry Edgar Wittrock initially refused to fly the stars and stripes in front of his Kerby general store to show his patriotism, Young said.

"They threatened to burn him out unless he got a flag," he said. Wittrock elected not to see his store go up in flames. It was to his store which the Fattig brothers often turned to trade their gold and furs while they were evading the draft.

"But most people felt that Germany started the war," he said. "Of course, there was the IWW—the Wobblies—who were stirring up trouble after the war started. The Wobblies were spiking logs going into sawmills and were causing trouble in the mines. They had a lot of explosions in the mines that the miners couldn't account for. Ranches were getting burned. They were leftists who were for Germany."

The Fattig brothers were fortunate, he said, noting that "slackards" were hung by vigilantes in some southern states.

"People forget that [President] Wilson was against going to war until they started sinking our ships," he said. "That got everybody angry."

It wasn't only the conflict overseas that brought death in those days, he said, noting that a flu epidemic claimed more than a dozen lives in Kerby during the war. Among the victims was his father Elliott Young who died on May 14, 1917. His sister Nellie, age ten, died of flu the following year. His father had worked at the Esterly Mine from about 1897 through 1913 before he started a freight business in Kerby.

"Their bowels would bake from the fever," Glenn Young said. "They ended up with pneumonia. That was what killed most of them. Some of them figured they were over it, then they'd go out and have a relapse. The relapse was worse than the first time. That got them."

He was a small child when his father passed away. His memory of him was troublesome.

"I remember being at the breakfast table, spilling some food and was playing in it," he said. "My dad slapped me and made me leave the table."

He thought about the incident for a bit. "I guess he was just correcting me," he added, speaking more to himself than his interviewer. Glenn Young died on Feb. 22, 1995, one day shy of his eighty-second birthday.

TWENTY

People of
the Chetco

W HILE OLDTIMERS IN THE LATE 1980s who knew of the Madstone
cabin builders' saga could spin wonderful tales of their ancestors
settling the region, let us not forget there were others living in the Chetco
River drainage for thousands of years before the Euro-Americans arrived.

They were the Chetco Indians, an Athabascan linguistic people who
lived principally along the lower river but made hunting and gathering
forays into the upper reaches of the drainage. Scientists who study such
things believe they arrived up to 3,000 years ago, having migrated south
from Athabascan settlements in what we now call Alaska. Down through
time the Chetcos had referred to themselves as the "Cheti" but the newly-
arrived settlers, not being fluent in Athabascan and finding the Chinook
jargon a poor substitute, changed the name to "Chetco." Since the
newcomers wrote the history books, the name stuck. No one seems to
know why they changed the name. Perhaps they thought Cheti sounded
too much like a car yet to be invented.

While there are historic accounts of the Chetco people, their culture
wasn't seriously studied until Joel V. Berreman, then a brilliant graduate
student of anthropology at the University of Oregon in Eugene where he
would become a well-regarded professor of sociology, visited the area

in 1935. For two consecutive summers, he led a dig into a shell mound in a village on Lone Ranch Creek about six miles north of where the town of Brookings is perched on the coastal bluffs. In addition to the shell mound, he and his team excavated twenty-three burial sites the first summer, followed by eleven the following year.

In 1944, Berreman published his scholarly work on the research under the weighty title, "Chetco Archaeology, A Report of the Lone Ranch Creek Shell Mound on the Gulf Coast of Southern Oregon." In the manuscript, he described the burials as "entirely pre-Caucasian, as not a single article of white man's culture, button, glass bead, or metal was found in any burial or surrounding shell layers." He further discussed how the remains were positioned in the graves and noted the craniums conformed to those of other skeletal remains found along the northern California and Oregon coasts. Having found no variations, he concluded the coastal tribes were of a common ancestry. Estimates of the Chetco populace vary but they were among the largest tribes along the Oregon coast.

To meander off point for a moment, it's fully understandable why scientists would want to study old burial sites to gain insight into the lives of those who came before. But you have to wonder how those scientists would react to having their forbears' remains dug up and examined by indigenous folks with impressive anthropological degrees curious about the lifestyle of those who invaded their homeland. A white-gloved finger poking around in Grandma Mildred's eye sockets could cause noticeable discomfort and fidgeting. Just a thought.

In any event, Berreman's peers concluded he did a stand-up research job, one that shed light on a remarkable people who once lived along the river. Judging from the charred cedar planks he unearthed, he noted they lived in plank houses, having perfected woodworking like other indigenous people along what is now the Oregon and Washington coast. He described what the Chetcos ate and how they lived off the land and the water.

For Elmer Jordan, a Chetco living off the land would have had a wonderful life.

"If a guy could just turn back to that time and see it with his own eyes how it was—now that would be something," he marveled during an interview in July of 1989. "They never had any income tax to pay. They never had rent to pay. They didn't have light bills. They would just come and go when they wanted. Their life was dictated by the weather and the grocery supply."

Born May 3, 1927, in a small house on the banks of the Chetco River within a short walk of the ocean where his ancient ancestors once walked, Jordan is a tribal elder and enrolled member of the Confederated Tribes of Siletz Indians. At this writing, he is the oldest remaining Chetco descendant still living in the tribal homeland. A retired logger standing over six feet, it is not hard to imagine him once scrambling up a mountainside or felling a tree twelve stories tall. Within him live the oral tales of a people who were first removed from their land, then overwhelmed by the constantly arriving incomers over the past two centuries.

"My people lived right by the ocean where the salmon runs was just lousy with fish in the river," said Jordan who caught a fifty-five-pound salmon in the Chetco River when he wore a younger man's clothes. "It surely was a good place to live. When they had the low tide, there was always plenty to eat. Every time the tide went out, the table was set."

Clams, mussels, even seaweed, were served up by the never-ending tides. In the fall, blackberries and acorns dangled along the river banks.

"Most of the grocery getting back in them days, to me, would have been fun," he said. "They had venison, elk and fish. They pretty much had it made until they was run out."

Well before the earth's civilized races were locked in the first savage global warfare on the other side of the planet, the Chetcos had already lost the struggle to retain their lifestyle of living off the land. Their first major battle was lost on paper they would never see in the form of the Land Claim Donation Act of 1850 which became law on September 27, 1850. Basically, it granted 320 acres of designated areas free of charge to every unmarried white male citizen eighteen or older and 640 acres to every married white couple. The caveat is they must have arrived in the Oregon Territory before December 1, 1850, although a provision in the act granted half that allotment to folks who arrived after 1850 but before Dec. 1, 1853. In addition, Indians of mixed blood were eligible. Sadly, black people were barred from applying for the free land. After all, the nation allegedly founded on freedom had yet to fight the war over slavery in an effort to make all its people free.

To gain ownership of the land, settlers had to live on the property and cultivate it for four years. To any fair observer, it would have been apparent that any donations made to the act were by the tribes themselves.

Like other indigenous people in the territory, the Chetco people were shoved aside in the rush for free land. In the spirit of full disclosure, it should be noted my paternal grandparents took advantage of a homestead act to settle in the Applegate Valley, albeit shortly after 1900 when the indigenous people had already been removed.

The Chetcos had about nine villages along the lower twelve miles of the river with the largest village where his family was from being near the mouth, Jordan said. In their native tongue, *Cheti* means "close to the mouth of the stream," according to tribal accounts. Since they were a horseless people, it stands to reason they would want to live near a food source.

While many historic accounts tell of brave citizen soldiers and Army troops defending Christian settlements, the Chetcos' oral chronicle relates a darker side of human nature. The Indian villages along the Chetco were destroyed, Jordan said.

"They burned the Indians out, shot half of them, murdered them after waiting for the men to go up river for venison," he said. "When they [Indian men] were up in the mountains, the soldiers went down and wiped out old women and children, burned their houses.

"The soldiers of the Army, they came and ran them all off," he continued. "They walked them up to the Siletz. They picked up a whole bunch of Indians off the Rogue River, too."

For a moment, his dark eyes burned bright with anger at the thought of his ancestors being forced from the land where they had lived for thousands of years.

"How would you feel if someone came along and shoved you off your homeland, then turned around and gave the land to someone else?" he asked, then answered the question. "I sure as hell feel resentment."

For him, it wasn't just a theoretical question. Among those marching north with her parents was a girl named Lucy who would become Jordan's great grandmother.

"When they came back, they had to buy the land they once had," Jordan said. "But they could only buy what was left over. That's a damn rotten deal as far as I'm concerned. Don't get me wrong. I'm not asking for nothing. I'd just as soon work for mine like everybody else."

The point, he stressed, is that no people should have been treated in such a manner. He was right. It was damn rotten.

His great grandmother was Lucy Dick, a short woman who cast a long shadow. When she died early in 1940, her obituary in the *Curry County Reporter* newspaper on Jan. 18 of that year reported she was believed to be the last full-blooded Chetco Indian in the county. The obituary noted she was born on the Chetco village at the mouth of the river between sometime from 1841 to 1847. However, Jordan insisted his great grandmother was born in the village in 1836 and lived to be 104 years old. What is certain is that she lived for roughly a century, give or take a few years, and she saw her world change drastically. In 1856, she and her family were forcefully moved some 160 miles north to the then newly-minted Siletz reservation with the rest of the tribe following the Rogue Indian War of 1855-56. She also kept alive the oral history of her people, a history she passed on to her children, grandchildren and her great grandchildren.

Although he was thirteen when she died, he remembered Lucy Dick as a frequent visitor to his childhood home along the lower Chetco.

"She used to come down and talk to Mom," he recalled. "They all talked Indian, just chat and chat. She'd give us kids heck if we did something wrong."

She spoke English as well as she did her native tongue, he said.

"She could go either way," he said. "I could understand some of it but I couldn't go at it good enough to hold a conversation."

Lucy Dick was a petite woman who stood only 4-foot-9 and wore number four shoes, he said, smiling at the memory of the tiny yet strong-willed woman. While in her late eighties and early nineties, she sometimes babysat young Elmer and his nine siblings. Any child who misbehaved was quick to receive his or her just reward, he said.

"Oh, she was tough with a switch, I'll tell you," he said, noting he discovered just how tough the day he let the chickens out of their pen as a prank. "She used a hazel switch. They lasted longer."

But it wasn't her hazel switch that left an indelible mark. It was her oral history of their culture which kept the story of their people alive, he said. The daughter of the tribal chief, she walked north with her parents in 1856 under the watchful eye of soldiers and members of the militia. While many of the tribal members were placed on boats and shipped north, she was among those walking all the way to the reservation, according to her great grandson. She told of seeing her father shot and killed, of her mother telling her crying daughter to keep walking and not look back, he said. Her father's brother, another tribal leader, was also killed, he added.

When they reached the Siletz Reservation, their lives changed forever. It was there his great grandmother was given her white name Lucy, he said, indicating her Indian name was tossed aside like trash into a garbage can.

But the tiny young lady was made of stern stuff. Determined to return one day to her homeland, she lived on as a member of the Confederated Tribes of the Siletz. It was there where she met and married Chetco Dick. Around 1870, the young couple and their daughter, Lydia, born on the reservation in 1868, received permission from the powers that be at the reservation to return to the Chetco River. Not long after they returned, her husband became ill and died. But his great grandmother stayed in their homeland, becoming known for her ability to nurse the sick and one to summon when help was needed to assist in the birth of a child, Jordan said. Her daughter Lydia—his grandmother—married Sam Van Pelt, the son of one of the first white settlers along the Chetco. Their daughter— Jordan's mother—May Magnolia Van Pelt, would marry Clinton Jordan and bear ten children. Elmer Jordan recalled the lean days after his father, who was drafted into WWI, died in the fall of 1937.

"After Dad died, we used to pick berries, peel chittam bark, anything we could to survive," he said, noting he was ten when his father died. "We'd send off to Montgomery Ward and buy plaid shirts, Levis and tennis shoes. We all wore patches."

Chittam bark, cut from the cascara buckthorn tree that grows throughout the Pacific Northwest, is used to make a mild laxative. Although the introduction of synthetics has reduced the demand for the bark, it continues to be used in a variety of medicinal products.

Although a bright fellow, Jordan was only able to attend school through the sixth grade. "After my dad died, we were so busy shifting for ourselves that there wasn't time for school," he said.

He and his siblings would pack driftwood up from the beach each evening to provide enough wood for their mother to heat their home and bake the following day. The mouth-watering aroma of freshly-baked biscuits greeted them each evening.

"She always baked sourdough biscuits," he said. "She never bought bread. Those sourdough biscuits got us through."

His great grandmother was also there to help the family through the hard times by continuing the tribal tradition of harvesting what Mother Nature had to offer.

"There was an old cabin up the river she used to visit," he said. "She'd take us grandkids, and my mom and her sister and brother."

Located about ten miles upriver, the cabin was used as a base camp during berry-picking time late each summer. "She'd take a whole bunch of jars up there in a gunnysack and can them berries," he said. "Then she'd pack them back."

In his mind, he could still see her walking along the old river trail during the dog days of August. He remembered the day when a grandson, little more than a toddler, wanted her to carry him.

"He kept a'pouting, then picked up a rock and threw it, hitting that sack and breaking a jar," he said. "She set her jars down and took his hide off right there."

Elmer Jordan's tall frame shook heartily as he laughed at the fond memory of the little woman who packed a powerful wallop. "After that, he was in the lead all the way," he said with a chuckle.

As a youngster, he spent many days hunting and fishing in the Chetco River drainage.

"When we were kids, we'd go up the river with a skiff and float back down," he said. "We'd spend three-four days in the summer. No hurry to come back down. Deer was thicker than heck. There wasn't another soul on the river. It was totally quiet."

At night, they would camp where the river had brought them that day. Tree boughs served as their mattress and their blankets; the river provided fresh trout for dinner.

"These guys go out now and unroll nice sleeping bags," he said. "When we were kids, we never had a sleeping bag and very seldom had a blanket. We just built a fire and laid down around the fire, freezing on one side and cooking on the other. We just kept turning around."

Among the tales told around the flickering campfire light were those of the Sasquatch, the legendary hairy giant reputed to dwell in the forests of the Pacific Northwest.

"My great uncle Tom Van Pel—he was my granddad's brother—was up on Mount Emily working at a mine one time and saw it," Jordan said. "He was going through brush when he heard it a'ripping above him and looked up there and saw a great big guy come trotting past."

The hairy creature was buck naked and stood about eight feet tall, so goes the story.

"The brush caught him [his uncle] around the shoulders and caught that thing around the waist," Jordan said of the height of the brush. "He [his great uncle] didn't want to stay around there."

Noticing the raised eyebrows of his listener, Jordan allowed his great uncle wasn't opposed to spinning a yarn now and then.

"Well, he might have been a tall tale teller," he said. "But he said he saw a big hairy man, real tall."

The incident would have occurred just before the birth of the 20th Century when the mountain was known as Mount Emney, he said. The name was later changed by mapmakers who got it wrong, he added.

Elmer Jordan's father was an avid hunter who ventured high in the wilds of the upper Chetco River, including the area where the Madstone cabin once stood. His father carried an 1894 .30-30 Winchester with an octagon barrel.

"My dad went all through them mountains, all the way up and through to the Illinois Valley," he said. "He could take that old .30-30, jump a deer and let it get going good to give it a running break, then break its neck every time with one shot."

Yet the life his father knew, like the brothers who lived in the Madstone cabin, was far removed from the culture that his great grandmother had known. Like his father, members of the tribe would periodically follow the river far upstream, he observed. He recalled stories of his indigenous ancestors traveling all the way up to Babyfoot Creek which flows out of Babyfoot Lake whose basin was carved out by a glacier. The stream flows into the Chetco River about five miles downstream from the Madstone cabin site.

"They would split up into groups," he said. "Some would go fishing, others would go hunting. They may have been lazy ones in there. They were just people. But they would kill a whole bunch of deer and make jerky out of them on the river bar. They'd bring back sacks of jerky. That way the meat wouldn't spoil on them."

The oral history clashes with the report by Berreman who, based on finding few animal bones in the digs he conducted, concluded the Chetcos did not depend heavily on big game for their survival. Obviously, there would be no bones if the meat was brought back in the form of jerky.

Before guns were available, they used bows made of Pacific yew wood and arrows made of cedar renowned for its straight grains, Jordan said, adding that animal gut or strips of hide served as the bow string. Arrow heads were chipped out of flint, unless they could trade for obsidian from inland tribes.

"If they could get obsidian, they'd get the rock hot and drop cold water on it," he explained. "They'd flake a chunk off, then work it with a deer horn."

The result was a razor sharp weapon capable of killing the wild game found along the river corridor. However, the Indians also dug pits to trap elk.

"We used to find a lot of elk pits they had made," he said. "They'd dig holes and cover them up to catch elk."

There were also creatures out there they did not want to catch and did not typically hunt.

"They used to talk about running into a lot of cougars," he said.

"Those cougars would squall and holler. When those old cougars would holler, it would really set your hair on end. You'd never know when it was around. It could be just outside the fire light a little ways."

Although Jordan had heard stories of the Madstone cabin, he never visited the site.

"There were places up there where they'd leave the river because the gorge would get too rough and there were no trails," he said. "It really gorges up in that canyon. Not many people go up there."

TWENTY-ONE

Philosophy of a Draft Evader

LIKE THE NATIVE AMERICANS HE ADMIRED, Alfred Fattig was a keen observer of nature who appreciated stepping into the wilderness. As you have seen, he was not well educated but he spoke with a wisdom well beyond the few months he spent in the classroom. His education was self taught, led by his curiosity and his hunger for knowledge. While some reared in his era may have had little regard for Native American ways, he saw in them a rare intelligence.

"To me, there was always something interesting in the Indian side of the story," he said. "They told me how they hunted deer, how they tanned their hides, how they fished. The Great Spirit was their god. When I look back, it looks like we all had the same guide."

To gain the proper perspective into his world, one must consider his unique philosophy. It is an odd potpourri of fundamentalist religion, Indian wisdom and horse sense cultivated from the land on which he roamed. With such a fascinating mixture to guide him, he had little choice but to choose a different path to follow.

"Freedom is just using your own mind," he said in one of his simplistic aphorisms.

It was while he was in the mountains that he felt free, free to think and free to travel. Perhaps he was born out of time, and should have arrived a century earlier when mountain men were beginning to roam the West. Obviously, his first love was the wilderness.

"I never got lonely out there," he insisted. "I love the hills, the tree, the streams, all the things in those mountains."

When the clouds parted and the birds sang in the spring, Alfred said he felt as though he was in paradise. Life was good.

"It was heaven sleeping out in a big fir forest," he said. "There was a murmur in them big trees no matter how still the air was. I always told my brother the trees could sing."

We can only guess as to his big brother's gruff response. Chances are it was not complimentary. No matter. Alfred was in his element.

"I used to lay on my back and look up through the tops of them big trees and see the stars at night," he said. "It gave me a thrill just to do that. Them are the things worth living for."

Our younger draft-dodging uncle was a philosophical amalgamation of Billy Sunday, Jim Bridger and Henry David Thoreau. Like Sunday, his powerful religious convictions would make nonbelievers squirm. Like mountain man Bridger, he loved to roam the wild country. And, like Thoreau, he was equal parts an observer of nature and a dreamer. Thoreau spent a little over two years at his cabin on Walden Pond, roughly the same span Alfred Fattig stayed at the Madstone cabin on the Chetco River. True, Thoreau and Walden Pond has a bit more gravitas in philosophical and literary circles than Uncle Alfred and the wild river. Still, there is a thread there worth examining.

You can see that, in the vein of Thoreau, Alfred Fattig was a transcendentalist, although he likely would have rejected the label once he wrapped his brain around the definition. But he definitely looked to experiences in nature to try to understand reality. In the natural world, he saw the hand of divinity in everything, from a deer mouse on the forest floor to a towering conifer swaying in the wind. He was a transcendentalist in his own right, stressing the intuitive and spiritual above the empirical. At times, he was a bit of a romanticist who sometimes took leaps of faith when it came to judging the behavior of creatures he found in the wild.

While in the wilderness, he willingly plunged into the very depths of his soul as he searched for answers to life's difficult questions. There, walking along a narrow mountain trail winding among towering old-growth timber, surrounded by the bottomless silence of the forest primeval, he contemplated life, looking for the wisdom of the ages.

Conversely, he often appeared to be peering at the world through the eyes of a young boy, wide-eyed and naïve. Although his skin was wrinkled and his hair had turned white when I met him, inside lived the soul of a young man, one still trying to understand the earth where he had spent nearly a century.

His Walden's Pond was a wilderness full of wildlife and wonder. He clearly felt at home while cradled in the arms of those rugged mountains as he watched nature.

"When I was in the Madstone country I like to stay out in the woods alone at night and listen to the wild animals play," he said. "The little cubs would stand on their hind feet and box just like two men and bawl until they could be heard all over the woods. There were deer. You could hear them snort all around you.

"I just love animals and the wild one is a real treat," he continued. "I liked to get up early in the morning and watch them to see what I could learn. The bear would turn over rocks to get the worms and bugs when there wasn't any acorns to eat."

Again, Oregon's answer to Henry David Thoreau was no intellectual educated in the ivory halls. Rather, he simply followed his gut instincts led by his curiosity and wonderlust. By society's measure, he was ignorant, barely able to write his name. He had not studied democratic theory or read classic literature. Yet he was quick to observe his lack of formal education was no hindrance, that his was an open mind. In fact, at the time of his decision to not report for the military draft, his mind was a clean slate on which little had been written. If nothing else, it gave him the opportunity to develop his own unique philosophy.

In his natural history classes taught by Mother Nature, he was the only pupil. He quietly watched and wondered as he saw life and death playing out before him. He saw salmon spawning in the river each fall, giving their lives so their species could continue. He watched an osprey drop out of the sky into the river, then flap away with a flopping fish clutched in its talons, heading to a nearby nest atop an old snag where its gaped-mouth fledglings awaited. He observed a spotted fawn hiding in tall grass while its mother fed nearby in order to provide life-sustaining milk for its young. And he had watched twin bear cubs rolling around a large sow, playing like children let out to recess.

"Back when I was young, I could see nothing wrong with the world," he said. "I never let my thoughts get outside of those mountains. We couldn't even hear the train whistle where we lived there in the Applegate and them old-time steam whistles could be heard a good many miles."

Yet he heard the war drums beating in the distance, growing louder and louder in the spring of 1917. From his perspective he had two options: kill people to survive or kill animals to live. He decided to march into the wilderness instead of the battlefield. During his years in the mountains, he looked inward, trying to resolve his inner turmoil over his decision to avoid the military draft. Was he a coward? He didn't believe he was but it was a question that would hound him nonetheless. After all, other young men were marching off to war. But he knew deep down that he was right. His was a simple logic from which he refused to deviate.

"Killing people isn't right," he stressed. "War don't make a difference."

The old man who had come out of the mountains seven decades earlier reiterated that he had no political ax to grind with Uncle Sam. Nor was he a supporter of the socialist movement in the years leading up to World War I. Fact is, he was unaware during his draft resistance years that a socialist revolution was occurring in Russia, creating a communist empire that was only beginning to crumble in the late 1980s.

"I met some people who called themselves Wobblies," he acknowledged. "I don't know what they believed in. All of them I ever met was a low class of people. The ones I met was hardly ever sober."

He had little time for those who would abuse alcohol. "That just makes a person silly," he concluded.

Instead, he drank from the cup of the American Indian, turning from the reverent Dunkard church to the native chapel of the woods, presided over by the Great Spirit. Like the Indians who had lived in the mountains for centuries before him, he came to believe that an omniscient spiritual being inhabited the forest. Walking the mountain trails, he found that being within every facet of the forest, from the tall timber looming over the river to the feathery ferns peeking out from a mountain spring.

"People ask, 'Well, what does God look like?'" he said. "Who can tell you that? We don't know what he looks like. I don't think he's got any shape. He's just a mighty force. That higher power can be called God or the Great Spirit. It don't make a difference."

He stressed again the constant friction caused by his firm belief in this deity and his brother's atheistic views. While he pondered the great questions of the universe around the campfire, Charlie bitched about the smoke.

"He claimed there was no such thing as life after death," he said. "I figured he was wrong, that's all. I used to tell him the trees had life in them. When I slept out in the big forest of fir trees I could hear and feel the trees. I told him that God was everywhere, even in the trees. My brother said he had seen a bear in a tree but he hadn't ever seen God in a tree. I told you he was hard headed."

That philosophical difference would cause a rift between them as deep as the Chetco River canyon. During those long days in the lonely mountains when heavy rain or snow kept the two inside a shelter, forcing them to talk to each other, the topic often led to the argument that has been with humankind since we first began questioning our origins in the dawn of time. With the friction warmed by cabin fever, it created heated arguments between the brothers.

"That was pretty hard to explain to an unbeliever like him that God and the bear could both be in a tree at the same time," Alfred said. "There is no use trying to learn somebody like him anything. I didn't like being with him for that reason. He was an infidel, a hard-headed infidel."

I didn't ask but I suspect Charlie's questioning whether both bear and the Big One could fit in a tree was a bit like asking how many angels could dance on the head of a pin. At this point, Alfred had stopped talking and was looking at me, frowning. I had the uneasy feeling he was still thinking about my waffling on his question a few days earlier about whether my brother and I were infidels. His laser beam stare seemed to be sizzling on a spot between my eyes, giving me some insight into what the forked-horn buck with the madstone must have felt in his final moments.

"There is a lot of difference between God and a bear, and there is plenty of room for both in a tree," he said, adding, "I believe in God and there ain't nobody ever gonna talk me out of it. I know there is one. I know it just as surely as you're sitting there in that chair."

Continuing to squirm and looking for a way to move the conversation off of infidels, I quickly noted his religious convictions appeared to have moved out of the strict confines of the Dunkard church.

"Yes, that's what I'm telling you," he said. "I believe that God and nature are the same thing. Nature is the good side of life."

That brought to memory an incident which he swore—without using blasphemy—happened when he was a youngster on the plains in southwestern Nebraska near Beaver City where his parents were married. It was a little more than ninety years earlier when he was five years old, he said. He described the sod house his family lived in, including a worn path leading to the front door. A local farmer's family was visiting that day.

"All of us kids was around the back with some dry-land turtles, pouring water on their backs to make them fight," he recalled."Well, we run out of water. I had been carrying the water in a tin bucket."

Eager to keep the turtle cage fighting continuing—remember, this was before television or smart phones provided entertainment—little Alfred grabbed the tin bucket and ran toward the nearby well to fetch more water. Tripping headlong, he rammed his chin into the top of the bucket. Blood spurted from his mouth.

"I had my tongue stuck out when I tripped and bit clean through my tongue," he said. "I can still see myself as plain as it was that day. There was a puddle of blood between my feet. It wasn't dripping down. It was a stream of blood."

The frightened youngster literally turned into a fountain of youth, one fearing he was watching his life flow out of his mouth. At that moment, a man riding a springboard wagon pulled into the yard.

"I can still see him wrap his lines around the brake and jump out," Alfred said, referring to method of keeping the team and rig from turning into a runaway. "Well, that man came over and said, 'I can stop blood.' Then he just draped a hand on top of my head. That stream of blood stopped right there."

After seeming to have appeared as if on cue, the stranger then returned to his wagon, unwrapped the lines and left without giving his name, according to my uncle's tale. Although it is likely the blood simply stopped flowing because of the natural coagulation process, the incident left an indelible impression on a terrified child standing on the endless Nebraska prairie.

Apparently noticing my disbelief, Alfred stuck out his tongue to reveal what he said was an old scar shaped like an "X" near the center of his leathery tongue. There appeared to be such a scar, although I confess I did not look too closely.

"Yes sir, that gave me something to think about pretty early," he said. "I done a lot of thinking on it. To my way of thinking, there is more proof there is a God than there is proof that there ain't. There really ain't no proof against it."

****

It was while living a short distance from the banks of the Applegate River that Alfred Fattig became fascinated with the native culture. As a youth, he visited long abandoned Indian settlements near the river and talked to the few Indian elders still living in the area.

"Along that river was still then remains of the old-time Indian villages and their graves with a row of rocks around them," he recalled. "There was big bowls made out of rocks to pound up their dried deer meat with. I found lots of spear heads and arrowheads made out of flint. It all gave me something to think about and dream about."

A few old settlers he knew had fought with the Indians and told him stories of those battles. Chances are they embellished their version of history, stretching the truth to capture the imagination of the wide-eyed youth. Nonetheless, the Old West came alive for him when they told their yarns.

"I used to talk to them about the Indian wars and about traveling across the Rockies in a covered wagon," he said. "An old white man once showed me five bullet holes in his body that he got from the Indians right there on the Applegate River."

Although it was unclear to which historic battle the aging settler may have been referring, several miners were killed along the Applegate in August of 1853 when their group was attacked, according to historic records. The bottom line is the stories of the mountains and the natives who once walked the wilds stirred a youthful yearning.

But he was also aware how the Indian culture had begun to fade away with the arrival of the whites which brought both disease and modern weaponry, both of which decimated the indigenous population.

"They took to the white man's way because it was much easier," he said. "Even with the old muzzle-loading black powder guns, it was easier hunting than with a bow and arrow."

While it took skill to kill a deer with a muzzleloader, it took substantially more hunting talent to bag one with a bow, even one made of Pacific yew wood, he said. When lever-action Winchesters came along, it made hunting easier still, he added, noting that 20th Century rifles with telescopes largely took the sport out of hunting.

"Unless you don't know what you're doing a'tall, why, deer don't have a chance now," he groused of hunters packing large caliber rifles with a telescopic sight.

Yet, despite the disparity in the two cultures, he saw more similarities than differences.

"Them Indians weren't as savage as you might think," he said. "It was a wonderful thing, just sitting there imagining what it was like before we got there."

Shortly after his parents moved the family to the Applegate, he spent long hours talking to the few Indian elders remaining in the vicinity about the ways of the woods. He learned how to tan a deer skin and make a comfortable shelter out of bark.

"Nothing handier than a buckskin string when you have nothing to take its place," he said. "You could use it for a rope if you need to. A greenhorn that don't know how to live in the mountains can load himself down pretty easy with stuff he can get along without and then not have the stuff he needs."

Using only an ax, a person in the outdoors can easily erect a shelter, he said.

"You can build one with a little hatchet," he said. "They don't leak and they are more comfortable than you'd think. Now, that was a white man's house. But the red man had that beat. The old-time Indians built them out of bark without using a white man's ax. But they made them real nice and warm."

Yet he was quick to observe that life for Native Americans was not always comfortable, despite their ingenuity in using nature's sometimes lean breadbasket.

"From what Indians told me, there were lots of them that starved to death in hard winters," he said. "Wild animals killed some of them. They didn't have it easy all the time."

One difference between the two cultures was that native people accepted the natural cycle and lived in harmony with it, he said.

"I have often thought that them that goes back into the mountains and lives and dies there, why, they is just as well off as anyone else," he said.

After observing that modern medicine can prolong physical life well beyond the point in which the spirit is willing to put up with ill health, he expressed concern whether those developments have enhanced life.

"You know, the human race was all just savages not very long ago," he said. "I can sit here and think about a lot of things they didn't know about fifty years ago."

But some discoveries, including the advent of nuclear weapons a little less than half a century before the interview, didn't seem to him to advance civilization. "Those atomic bombs, that sure wasn't progress," he said.

For him, progress was not to be found in inventions. He looked to the old ways for answers. He developed faith in dreams as a guide into the future, perhaps under the influence of his enthusiasm for the Indian culture. Like some indigenous people, he believed dreams are nothing more than spiritual visions of the future.

"I was a dreamer who often had his dreams come true," he said. "Even as a child I felt I was being guided by a higher power. In the years to come I was often alone in body but not in spirit.

"I had many dreams come true," he continued. "I was a dreamer of true dreams. It didn't just happen when I was asleep. I could dream just as well when I was awake."

He scoffed at my suggestion he was merely daydreaming, something he would be likely to do during those lengthy days of watching the sun rise on the eastern mountains and set on the western ridges.

"There are times when I knew what was going to happen," he insisted. "When things turn out just like you seen it in a dream, well, that proves it to me. Now that Chetco was a great place for a daydreamer to live. If you are spiritual-minded, you are going to daydream like I'm saying. That kind of daydreamer, he is close to nature."

These were apparently dreams showing glimpses of the soul but what he felt were glimpses of the future. Make of it what you will but I thought it made him more interesting.

Although it was rare, his dreams during the day were sometimes interrupted by an occasional human being walking along a trail or panning for gold in a stream. Most were likeminded in spirit, drawn by the remote mountains for the freedom they offered, he said.

"They went there for all kinds of reasons," he said. "Some went where life was free. Some went because of the gold. Some of them went there to think."

Then there was the man and his wife he met in the lower Rogue River drainage.

"They said they went there to think," he said. "They said they were both writers and that when they got tired of writing, they would go fishing. Now that's about the best reason to go."

Unfortunately, Alfred did not remember the name of the couple. Zane Grey, arguably the most popular author of his day, did bring his salmon and steelhead fishing gear along with a pen to the lower Rogue during that period, first arriving in 1919. He became a familiar fisherman in the area, and built a rustic cabin on Winkle Bar in 1926. While I read many of his romantic westerns when I was a kid, finding many of them a bit syrupy, I was awed by his 1928 *Tales of Fresh Water Fishing.*

It's too bad the name of the writer did not stick in my uncle's mind but it could be the couple merely romanticized their river trip. Zane Grey was an honest-to-goodness writer but far too many folks falsely claim the title of that honored profession. I don't consider the scribbler of this book much of a writer, by the by. But you have to give him some credit for giving it the old college try.

Writers or not, the couple he met had sought out the area to find solace as well as some mighty fine fishing. Others would come for a short visit but stay for a lifetime, ostensibly searching for gold.

"If you talk to them you will find it is not always gold that took them there," he said. "I found one man that said the reason he went to the hills was so he could live honest."

The man figured that life in the mountains was wholly dependent on an individual, he explained. Others he chanced to meet were little more than hermits who did not care for crowds of people.

"A lot of them just wanted to be alone," he said. "They were hunting a happy place to live. All of them had a story to tell what drove them to the mountains."

Aside from the true recluse, most didn't stay long in the mountains after finding they didn't like to be alone, he noted.

"I never felt like I was alone," he offered. "I would go hunting and stay out in the woods by myself for three or four days."

When it was all quiet on the western front of Oregon, he reveled in the stillness.

"Silence is sometimes the greatest thing in our lives," he said. "It allows you to think things over."

You can only imagine what he would have thought of today's world in which people are constantly texting, trying in vain to stay connected around the clock. Even a television turned down low in the background was a distraction Uncle Alfred found vexing.

"We know so little about ourselves," he said. "If we knew more about ourselves it would help us learn more about other things. When I was in the mountains, I lived as though there was nobody else in the world and there wasn't, not in my world anyways."

Like Thoreau, he found plenty of interesting things to study in the wild. Filled with questions, he would watch animals, trying to find answers why they behave the way they do. Wildlife may not have had a Gregorian calendar to chart their lives, but he found animals followed a definite pattern. He observed that buck deer mate with does only during a short period each year.

"That time of year starts 'round Thanksgiving," he said. "No deer breaks the laws of nature. Other animals, even fish and birds, have the same laws they never break."

All other animals, that is, except humankind, he added. Humans multiply at will, following no plan, he would tell you.

"It seems that the human being is the only thing on earth that breaks God's laws," he said. "The wild animals are happy, living according to God's plan. Humans could learn from them."

It was sort of the reverse anthropomorphizing but he was clearly convinced of his convictions. What's more, he felt the collective action of some wild creatures such as bees working together could teach us all lessons.

"That honey bee, he can make bee bread and honey all out of the same flower," he said. "Can you do that?"

The mention of the busy honey bee prompted another recollection, causing him to pursue the flights of bees he had followed through Oregon forests. Never mind this was no pastime enjoyed by ancient Indians. Honey bees are not indigenous to North America but introduced by settlers when they began arriving in the New World. That fact didn't bother the old hunter.

"Hunting bees, that's one thing I really liked," he said. "You take some beeswax and burn it. If you ain't got no wax, you put some sugar in water and they'll come to pack it away. Of course, they'd rather have honey."

After preparing bait for honey bees, he'd sit down to wait to get a fix on the direction the bees would fly after getting their fill.

"If you are anywhere near a bee tree, why, first thing you know, you can see a string of bees going all one directions," he said, waving one hand over his head in a rising circle to indicate a bee taking flight.

"They'd go round and round like this until they get to the tree tops, then they'd take off," he said. "If you've got good enough eyes to see them, you just follow them. They go straight after they clear the trees.

"I found many a honey tree just like that," he continued. "I cut down one tree that had eleven feet of honey in it. It was clean, too. They clean that tree out before they put their honey in it."

After locating the tree, the next stop was to chop it down and cut open a side to locate the cache of honey. Mosquito netting over the face prevented bees from avenging themselves, although he could always expect several stings.

"We was never without honey when we was in the mountains," he said. "Honey out of bee trees from the low lands is not so good as mountain honey. It tastes different."

Presumably, honey took on greater importance to men hiding out in the mountains since they did not have access to sweetened food. It was the sugar of the wilderness, a sweetener that could be mixed with most anything to improve the flavor, he said.

"If you want to know what is good, it's huckleberries sweetened with wild honey," he said. "There is lots of good things in the mountains. Good, fresh air and clean, cold water. It's a good place to go to get away from the world and think. The scenery is beautiful and there is lots of wood for a campfire. You can't beat it."

He recalled one foray to a mountain lake one fall when the huckleberries hung like marbles from the bushes. The lake boiled with trout rising to insects. Near the lake the brothers found a bee tree.

"We dried a lot of berries and we dried a lot of fish," he said. "And we cut down that tree and got the honey. Them is the days I like to think about in the mountains."

Other than picking the berries, most folks today wouldn't be able to take advantage of nature's bounty, he acknowledged.

"I supposed I enjoyed things that other people wouldn't have anything to do with," he said. "Now, I like to go back in the mountains where nobody else had ever been. I like to stay there until I get acquainted with it."

He wondered aloud if the untamed country deep in the mountains was any wilder than that found in the populated regions where war has broken out with the frequency of changing seasons.

As a young man, he was filled with wanderlust. He had witnessed the beauty of seeing the morning mist rising on a high mountain lake, the sun painting pink a snow-covered peak in the evening and an alpine meadow thick with green grass.

He followed the urge to see what was over the next ridge or down in the valley below. In many ways, he had lived a century too late.

"Any country is beautiful the first time you see it," he said. "After that, you feel like moving on."

While he may have often talked about the thrill of the hunt, it was apparent that his thoughts on hunting have also moved on. He may have been proud of his ability to shoot straight and true but he no longer found honor in killing a wild animal.

"I wouldn't be worth a hoot in the mountains anymore," he said. "I couldn't kill anything. I think one life is just as valuable as another. Used to be that killing deer was all right. Well, it ain't right to me now and I don't want the job again. I don't want to never to have to go back in the mountains and kill deer. It wouldn't be a pleasure anymore."

But he acknowledged it was a pleasure when the heart of a younger man beat within his chest.

"Yes, I was a good hunter and a good shot," he said. "Many times I would see a deer a long ways off, then take sight on it with my rifle. I'd keep raising that barrel until I figured it was about right."

Using his Kalmiopsis windage, he would often bring down the deer.

"I've hit deer that looked like they was almost a mile away," he claimed. "You could just barely see what they was. I was always pretty steady with a gun."

With that, he proffered his right hand. "You don't see me shaking now, do you?" he asked. The withered hand was as steady as bedrock.

Recalling the first deer he ever killed, using his trusty .40-65 Winchester, he said his trigger finger didn't jerk like that of a neophyte hunter.

"When I pulled the trigger the black smoke rolled out of that old black powder gun and settled in my face until I couldn't see whether I had killed that deer or not," he said. "It seemed like a full minute before the smoke cleared. There laid my first deer."

He was seventeen and immensely proud of making his first venison kill. But the years in the mountains would change Alfred Fattig's philosophy.

"I thought then to be a good shot and a good hunter was a great thing," he said. "I don't see anything great about them things anymore."

He remembered the day his enthusiasm for killing animals died away. It was while he was evading the draft. He shot a young buck, stunning the animal but not killing it.

"I had just walked up to it and leaned my gun against a tree when that deer jumped up right quick," he said. "I grabbed him by one horn and 'rassled' with him until I was just about wore out."

Holding onto the deer with one hand, he fought to free his hunting knife tied onto his belt with a leather thong. With the knife finally freed, he plunged the long blade into the deer's chest, holding it there until the animal quit thrashing.

"I was all bloody and the deer was bloody," he said. "There was blood all over the ground. Everything was a bloody mess."

The irony of the situation dawned on him that day as he looked at the scene. True, this was no battlefield in France and the foe was a wild animal whose flesh he intended to eat. But, as he was wont to say, killing is killing. The fire in his belly for hunting flickered out that day. From that moment on, he squeezed the trigger reluctantly when firing a killing shot to survive. In essence, he had entered a battlefield of his own making.

"That deer is doing his best to save his life, then you are proud because you can shoot it down," he said. "That isn't right. But I kept it up for years. We was surviving."

Silence filled the room as he stopped talking to think about hunting to survive versus hunting for the sport of killing. He looked down at his hands, then at his two nephews.

"I have asked myself a lot of questions that I couldn't answer," he said. "I know a good story can be put up on either side of them arguments. I don't know the answer. I just know I wouldn't want to be killed and eaten."

Trapping an animal was even worse from his vantage point late in life. When the steel jaws snap shut over the leg of an animal, it causes them more pain than a well-placed bullet, he said.

"I had what they called good luck trapping martin," he observed of pine martin. "But it sure wasn't good luck for the martins. They was just looking for something to eat to save their lives when they was caught. They found my bait and lost their life. You know, in all my years I never found a martin alive in one of my traps. Nobody killed them in the trap. They must have worried themselves to death. I made them suffer."

Although really smart folks in white lab coats and carrying impressive graduate degrees would question whether animals can think in the fashion of humans, Uncle Alfred would have argued otherwise. He had his own evidence.

"Just get on a deer's track when there is about two feet of snow on the ground and track him all day," he said. "You will find out that he knows how to save himself all right. He will make circles and come up behind you and back track himself and jump sideways out of his tracks and light in close to a bush where you can't see his tracks. Another trick he plays he will make a circle and come within a few yards of his own tracks and watch you go by. He is spiritual minded just like some people.

"Now the bear is tricky, too," he added. "He is bold about it."

He recalled finding cabins after hungry bears had torn through walls after getting a whiff of bacon or syrup. Bruins were the kings of the wild kingdom he knew. To them, a cabin would seem to be a picnic box to open.

"When they get in a cabin, bears never leave anything right side up," he said. "A man told me about a bear going into his cabin one day when he was gone and got his bacon. Then he got a gallon can of syrup off the shelf, laid it down on the floor and mashed all the syrup out and licked it up. When he come home, that bear was sitting in the yard licking syrup off his paws."

Since the man didn't have a gun, he had to wait until the bear ambled off, he recalled with a laugh.

"I once shot a big black bear in the head and he put both his paws over his eyes and bawled like a baby," Alfred said. "That bothered me and got me to thinking about life and how animals hurt. It hurts them when you shoot them."

As he recalled the animals he had shot, he wondered aloud if he did the right thing. While it was almost always for food, including the bear meat he would mix with venison, he questioned whether it was warranted.

"Maybe I would be better off if I had never killed any of them," he said. "They show more intelligence about some things than people do. Every man that has taken a lesson from them is a lot better by it.

"I sometimes think about when you walk around on the ground you can kill ants," he noted. "You can't help it. But if I could avoid it, why, I would."

He paused again, thinking about his impact on the Oregon mountains so far from the Texas flat lands.

"I've always been a mountain man," he reiterated. "I like them mountains. I liked being on my own out there. You can live off the land, and live real good."

No doubt that is true, providing you have the presence of mind to take advantage of nature's gifts, but that philosophy would be sorely tested by the end of his sojourn in those rugged mountains. There is ample evidence that the three years he spent roaming the mountains was too much, even for the man of nature. The lean meals and lonely nights would eventually drive him from his mountain retreat.

TWENTY-TWO

Wilderness Prison

I NSIDE THEIR FORTRESS OF MOUNTAIN WALLS, the two brothers were entrenched like folks in the middle ages waiting behind the castle walls for a siege to end. The wild rivers served as their moats; the razor ridges as their battlements. The siege was brought by the federal government waiting out the draft evaders.

Here was a stronghold that even General John "Black Jack" Pershing, commander-in-chief of the American Expeditionary Force who would be welcomed by a rousing reception in Grants Pass early in 1920, could not have encircled with the two million soldiers at his command during the war. Efforts to remove the draft dodgers would have proved too difficult because of the vastness of the mountain wilderness. There was too much tough terrain, too many hiding places and too little knowledge of the mountains by law enforcement officers. The brothers were safely housed in a citadel that no army could storm.

Yet there was apparently little effort by the government to search out the two brothers beyond an occasional visit by a marshal to the family farm in the Applegate Valley. But officials were met with a stony silence as still as the darkest forest.

Thus it was a war of attrition, one which the brothers could not hope to win. The authorities would simply wait out the wanted brothers as they would most draft dodgers. Uncle Sam could afford to wait. Time was on the government's side.

While the mountains provided protection, they also served as prison walls for the brothers. Despite Alfred's love of nature, they often fought a battle to survive in the harsh world where the nearest store was at least a two-day hike. Hunting, fishing, trapping and occasionally gold panning, they eked out an existence during the lean times, constantly moving like a small military unit on maneuvers. Their camp sites were carefully selected to allow them several avenues of escape should unwanted company drop in bearing gifts in the form of handcuffs.

"The Madstone was my home and my home took in more than the cabin," he said. "The cabin was headquarters. But sometimes I didn't see the cabin for a long time. Any place in them mountains was home. I traveled that route between the Madstone and the head of the Applegate River a lot of times."

It was a route where he was often hungry. Food was particularly scarce during the winter months. Sundown would find the two brothers hunkered around a campfire, chewing on a hard piece of cold venison jerky while thinking about a hot meal and a soft bed.

There is no question our boys were often a little more than ripe. When Alfred was wearing his buckskin wardrobe, it isn't hard to imagine you did not want to be downwind. I would be remiss if I didn't note that he was a clean-cut fellow when we visited him in Texas. But he hadn't been camping out for a couple of years, wearing animal hide and gnawing on bear bones, although I'm told that some Texans have a hankering for such a lifestyle. As a veteran camper, I know if you have spent more than one night in the wilds, things can quickly get a little grimy, no matter how fastidious the camper. If you camp on the ground for a week, hygienic ways are no longer a major concern. When the camping weeks turn to months and the months to years, we are talking really gamey. Standing downwind of these two mountain dwellers would have made one whiff of the Nature Man seem like a freshly powdered baby just out of a bath. Come to think of it, I don't ever recall Uncle Charlie ever having bathed since his little cabin on Waters Creek was not equipped with running water. Then again, I wouldn't have known if he had. It is not something a nephew—or reader—wants to dwell on.

In any case, after two years on the run, Alfred and Charlie weren't talking much. They may have been blood brothers but each had little love for the other. The siblings had become companions out of a joint opposition to war but they had virtually nothing else in common. The contempt bred by their familiarity coupled with the stress of being constantly on the dodge caused ongoing friction. Civility was tossed out the cabin window. Even seventy years later, their personality clash remained apparent.

"My brother, he was pretty shaky," said the younger brother. "He wasn't much of a hunter. We would have starved to death in the mountains if I was as bad a hunter as he was."

But the irreconcilable differences between the two were largely set aside as they struggled to survive. Mother Nature proved to be a stern task master when it came to living off the land, particularly during the lean days of winter. Finding food was a full time job which took most of their time and energy.

Once, driven nearly mad by hunger one winter, the brothers ate meat that Alfred described as rancid. Coming from someone who clearly wasn't fussy when it came to his mountain victuals, the venison must have been downright nasty. Remember, they had no refrigeration, no freezer. But they didn't want to make all their venison into jerky so they frequently hung some meat in a nearby tree for a day or two if the weather permitted. On this day, they had returned from an unsuccessful hunting trip with no fresh meat. There were no wild carrots to munch on, no supplies from home. The river was running too high to fish. The only potential meal they had was the aging deer haunch they had hung high in a tree near the cabin days before the hunting trip. Alfred brought it down and gave it the sniff test. After all, there was no USDA expiration date to check for freshness. The meat was ripe. But it was the only dinner they had. So they cut off the least offensive portions and sliced two steaks which they fried on their woodstove.

Driven by hunger created by an all-day hunting trip without any food since the day before, they decided to risk it. If they could keep the food down, it passed the test. The meat apparently had not studied for the test. It failed miserably.

"It made me so sick," said Alfred who had volunteered to be the taste tester that day. "I throwed it all up. Before I ate that spoilt meat I thought being hungry was about the worst thing there is. But that spoilt meat, I don't believe there is anything worse."

As luck would have it, a deer walked by the cabin the next morning and joined them for breakfast. But Alfred said it was several days before he could keep anything down stronger than venison broth.

"I never ate anything again that I figured might have gone bad," he said. "I was sicker than a dog for days."

If the chance of meat going bad wasn't bad enough, the brothers could never count on eating the fresh meat they bagged until it was in the frying pan back in the cabin. Consider one winter hunt Alfred took when the cabin larder was as empty as his flat stomach. Walking along a ridge, he came upon a thick stand of ancient trees growing out of a large basin several hundred feet across. About two feet of snow covered the ground.

Alfred stood on one side of the basin, looking down a cliff about twenty-five feet high. Large boulders were strewn about the basin floor as though scattered by a giant hand. Leaning over the rim of the cliff, he saw a cave below him about six feet high and several feet wide. Leading into the mouth of the cave were giant bear tracks, he recalled, estimating the tracks were a foot long. For a black bear, that is a mighty big bruin. Although the tracks may have grown a mite in his mind over the years, there was no doubt the veteran hunter had seen some humongous bruin tracks.

Wary of the steep cliff, he did not climb down into the basin. No doubt the size of the bear tracks played a part in that wise decision. Instead, he continued hunting and killed a small deer a short distance away. After field dressing the deer, he covered the carcass with snow to keep the meat cool before continuing to scout out the area. In particular, he was looking for a place where he could build a log bear trap. He figured he and Charlie could return to the site and build the trap which they had success with in the past.

"When I come back to the deer it was gone and there was big bear tracks in the snow," Alfred said. "Well, I took after him. With him dragging that deer, it was easy to track him. I stayed on his trail for hours. I was a good walker then. But I never did get that deer back."

However, the brothers later went to the site together and built the bear trap, eventually catching a small bear, making up for the lost venison. But they never saw the large bruin with the big feet. Actually, maybe it was just a medium size bear with enormous feet.

It wasn't a chance meeting with a large furry animal flashing lengthy canines that gave him the heebie-jeebies. Rather, it was the rattlesnakes of summer that raised the hackles on the back of his neck. In fact, when he returned to the basin the following summer, he again balked at exploring it.

"I wasn't too keen to go down into that hole," he said of the basin. "It was a good place for a rattlesnake den. Every time I think of a rattlesnake it gives me the creeps. I would rather meet anything in the mountains than a rattlesnake."

While the western diamondback rattlers found in southwest Oregon aren't as large as their cousins in Texas, they are plenty dangerous, capable of a bite that would ruin your day. Alfred was never snake bit but he had several close encounters, including stepping on what he believed was a rattler near the Applegate River one summer night en route to making a clandestine visit to his parents' farmhouse while on the run in 1919. He was about two miles from the Fattig farm when it happened. Of course, this was before flashlights were available. He was walking along the road that sultry night when he stepped on something that squirmed. The hackles stood on end.

"It felt like stepping on someone's arm," he said. "I ran all the way to the house."

If there weren't bears or rattlesnakes to contend with in the mountains, there were plenty of other dangers that threatened the brothers. Slipping on a rock could mean a broken limb which they would have to set. An accident involving a gun could be deadly. Falling into a river swollen by rain or melting snow was dangerous. Like two Boy Scouts on an endless campout, the two had to be prepared.

Life on the trail often found them building a lean-to for shelter from the storm. It was a simple process, he said. First, he would make a bed out of fir boughs, then drive a pole into the ground at each end of the bed. The vertical poles, each with forks at the top, would then be used to cradle a horizontal pole, he added. He would then drape fir boughs across the horizontal pole until the boughs formed a slanted green wall on each side.

"That made a regular little house to crawl into," he said. "It kept a lot of the cold out."

But during the depth of winter, with the snow several feet deep and frozen as hard as concrete, the shelter retained only enough bodily warmth to sustain life. Daybreak would find the occupant shivering in a fetal position, praying for the moment when the sun's warming rays would break over the mountain.

"I went through heaven and hell," he said. "When the snow was frozen hard, it was no trouble to walk on. But the cold took all the joy out of life. Them skis or snowshoes didn't do much good in soft snow unless there was a trail broke already. When you are moving from place to place, there was no trail broke."

One trip found the draft evaders traveling south of the state line into California's giant redwood trees which grow close to the Pacific coast. After resupplying at Crescent City, they hiked back north into the redwood forest along the lower Smith River to camp.

"I believe that's the wettest place on earth," he said. "We could hardly keep a fire going long enough to cook a meal. We got out of there as soon as we could and went back up into Oregon."

It isn't the rainiest spot on the planet, but Gasquet, which judging from his description sounded like the area where they had camped, does receive an average ninety-five inches of rain each year. That is a lot of water. However, according to the National Oceanic and Atmospheric Administration, the wettest place in the United States and one of the wettest on the planet is Mount Waialeale on Kauai in Hawaii where an average 460 inches pours down annually. But the roughly eight feet of water drenching the lower Smith River drainage each year is nothing to sneeze at. Second thought, perhaps it is, particularly if you are shivering along the Smith River beside a smoldering camp fire.

Anyone who has camped in the rain without the benefit of a tent or other shelter can attest to the utter misery one feels. You can't find dry wood to keep the fire burning. The wet cold permeates everything in the coastal mountains. The cold creates a chill that clings like frost to your very bones.

It was that cold that drove Charlie Fattig close to the campfire one night as they hiked north toward the warmth and security of the Madstone cabin. Both brothers were exhausted. After chewing some jerky, each grabbed their blanket and promptly fell asleep even though the rain had turned to snow as they climbed higher into the mountains. But the younger brother awoke with a start on this particular night. A man's scream pierced the deep silence of the forest that was as dark as the bottom of a well. Sitting bolt upright, a groggy Alfred looked over to where his brother had been when he went to sleep. His brother was gone.

Just as he started to stand up, an agonizing scream once again shattered the night. He turned around and saw his brother writhing on the snow behind him. His jacket was on fire.

"By the time I got to him, his clothes on his back was all ablaze," Alfred said. "He was trying to find a soft place in the snow to put it out but the snow was all froze."

The young brother grabbed some snow that had been melted near the campfire and threw it on his brother's back, dousing the fire. Fortunately, the elder brother wasn't seriously burned. But he was in dire need of a new coat and another blanket.

Cold was the constant enemy on the winter trail. They once tried out a canvas shelter fashioned like an Indian teepee.

"It was as cold inside as it was outside, that place," Alfred said. "About the only place where we didn't get cold was in the Madstone cabin. That was real snug."

But they were not always at the cabin. The brothers periodically ventured forth on resupply missions or on exploration trips to keep from going stir crazy when the walls of the already small cabin began to close in.

To understand what they faced, let's join them on a winter excursion early in 1918 before the Madstone cabin was built. The brothers were on the move, traveling light. This journey took them into Youngs Valley in the remote mountains just south of the California state line. During the summer months, the valley offers an alpine-like setting with green grass carpeting the floor. Snow lingers on the surrounding mountain peaks into late summer. The valley was once used by Illinois Valley ranchers as grazing for their cattle come summer. The bovine found plenty of grass and water in the high country. A hungry cougar or a bear may have picked off an occasional calf but it was a considered part of doing business with Mother Nature in the high country.

But it was no walk in the park when the snow began to fly in the mountains late in the fall after the cattle were rounded up and herded back down to the ranches to munch on hay. On the north end of the valley, aptly named Polar Bear Mountain rises 6,281 feet above sea level. Yet the white-topped peak was indistinguishable from the other mountains above the mountain valley that cold season. A blustery storm had slammed in from the coast, dropping heavy snow in the mountains. Although he brothers were prepared to wait out a short storm, they were caught off guard by the deepening snow.

"That one winter, me and my brother was snowed in, right in the top of the Siskiyou Mountains," Alfred said.

They stumbled upon a cabin on the side of a mountain overlooking Youngs Valley. The structure had no chinking, allowing the winter winds to whistle between the logs. "Why, a rat could have run between them logs," Alfred recalled.

Light snow already covered the ground when the brothers arrived. With temperatures plummeting and ominous dark clouds blowing in from the coast, they decided to hole up in the cabin to wait out the storm. Bad move.

"It started to snow," he said. "We decided to wait until it quit snowing. That was where we made our mistake."

Floating softly to the ground, large snowflakes are beautiful to behold when you are looking at them through a double-pane window while sitting by a crackling fire in a cozy cabin, sipping a steaming cup of coffee or tea. That outdoor scene turns menacing when the cabin is cold with snow filtering in between the logs and your heat source is a smoldering campfire on the dirt floor.

The younger brother spent one day hunting in vain. There were plenty of tracks but he was unable to locate any deer. The snowfall increased.

"I told my brother the ways the air feels that there was going to be a heavy snow," Alfred said. "I thought we'd better get out of there the next day or we weren't going to get out a'tall. Well, sir, next morning there was three feet of fresh snow and it was still coming down. We had about three days of grub left if we ate light. We figured to wait one more day for the snow to settle."

But the snow continued. Three more days they waited, watching the large flakes flutter silently down like white butterflies.

"Like two fools, we stayed there until the snow piled up," Alfred said. "Why, it was just as deep as the door was tall."

With their meager supplies dwindling, they knew their best chance of survival was to reach Waldo, a community about a dozen miles north as the crow flies. There, they could trade in their furs for supplies. Providing they made it to the little settlement, that is.

"That snow was seven feet deep," Alfred said. "The door of the cabin opened out. We couldn't open it so we cut the top out of the door. We had to use wooden paddles we made to dig our way out."

Once outside, they found they could make no headway in the deep snow. With each step they sank up to their thighs. Thoughts of the Donner party must have passed through their minds. And neither brother had surplus fat to share with the other should it come to cannibalism.

"We made some skis, made them of cedar," he said. "They was about six feet long. Well, we got on our skis and made a few circles to test them. We skied right over the cabin. It was only a little rise in the snow."

Neither one of the brothers was an accomplished skier. Moreover, their equipment was not something you would find in your local ski shop. The crude boards were tied onto their boots with leather thongs made from deer hide. Ski poles were cut from willows. As a result, they floundered in the deep, powdery snow as they slowly made their way towards Waldo.

"Finally, we just throwed them away," he said. "They just got in the way."

For six days, they pushed ahead in the snow, sapping their strength. Ironically, their survival rested on their reaching civilization which they had been taking great pains to avoid.

"I broke trail every step of the way," Alfred said. "I don't know if my brother was lazy or sick. He couldn't make it, breaking that snow. He just played out right there on the trail."

With the older brother staggering along behind, hungry and tired, the younger brother plowed onward. Each step farther toward their destination further drained his energy.

"When night come, we built a fire up close to big trees where there wasn't much snow underneath," Alfred said. "Our fire was melting the snow up over our heads and that would drip down on us. No, sir, there wasn't nothing easy on that trip."

A rabbit sprang up in front of them on the fifth day but the brothers, shaking with cold and weak from hunger, were unable to hit it with the rifles. The would-be dinner scampered away into the underbrush.

It was the older brother who broke the trail on the final day. Alfred, having taken the lead for six days, awoke too weak to continue breaking trail. Cold and exhausted, they finally stumbled into Waldo where they joined several miners gathered around the pot-bellied stove in the Decker General Store in Waldo. Like the others, they waited out the storm.

"We nearly died getting to Waldo," he said.

While the following winter at Madstone cabin wasn't as challenging, it had its moments. Turns out being holed up in a snug cabin in the winter mountains can be very trying.

Remember the burros put out in Jack's Pasture for the winter? With the grain they had packed in, the brothers figured the animals would survive easily until spring. But they hadn't counted on the winter of 1919, which dumped heavy snows on the coastal mountains. By March, the grain was gone and the animals were growing thin.

The burros' feed had to be packed in from the Illinois Valley on trails winding through very rugged terrain, much of it covered by snow during the winter. The brothers waited, hoping for an early spring. But heavy snow fell on March 22nd that year, Alfred said, adding he recalled the date because they had kept a calendar in the cabin. It may have been Spartan inside but they kept track of the days.

"It wasn't long before the burros could not get anything to eat, only what we fed them," he said, noting they were cutting brush for them to browse on.

The snow continued falling until it was four feet deep outside the cabin on the 29th. Atop the ridges, the snow was deeper still.

"Of course, we couldn't get the burros through that much snow so there was only one thing to do," he concluded.

The brothers elected to strap on snowshoes and hike to Kerby where they would buy 150 pounds of grain. Remember, the burros had carried their grain when the brothers first took them into the Madstone country. Now, the draft evaders would be serving as draft animals for the burros.

The two hiked back to Kerby together, picked up a load of grain each and together made the hike to about the halfway point to the cabin. Once there, the older brother returned to Kerby to pick up some more grain while the younger brother hiked the rest of the way west to the cabin and fed the starving animals.

"We kept that up until we knew we had enough to make it clean through the winter," Alfred recalled. "I don't remember anymore how long it was we kept it up. My brother had cabins to stay in and not much snow. I had deep snow all the way and only our headquarters to sleep in."

Life was often hard even during those periods of pleasant weather. The problem was a steady diet of food that invariably meant consuming nothing but the flesh of wild animals, he said.

"People can't just live on meat," he said. "They got to get other food. A hunter could live if he could get enough food out of the store to keep from getting the scurvy."

Scurvy occurs when a person's diet lacks a sufficient amount of Vitamin C in his or her diet. Aside from berries in late summer, the brothers seldom ate foods containing high levels of Vitamin C. Symptoms of scurvy include bleeding gums and anemia. His elder brother was often ill when he was on the dodge, Alfred said.

"It was his stomach more than anything else," he said. "His teeth would also ache. He'd always have a tooth ache. He didn't have very good teeth."

The mountain life and poor eating habits had obviously taken a bite out of their dental hygiene. Toothbrushes weren't part of their required gear when survival was the prominent concern. A toothpick carved from a cedar branch was their only dental care. There came a point when the pain from a throbbing tooth drove Charlie to take medical matters into his own hands. Literally.

"Yeah, he pulled some out himself," Alfred said. "He got some string around them, worked them back and forth for a while, then just jerked them out."

The image of him pulling his own teeth causes most folks to wince but Alfred shrugged it off. No dentist was available, he offered. After sitting around the cabin for a few days nursing a swollen jaw, Charlie eventually regained his strength by sipping venison broth.

"He'd hurt for a while, that's for sure," Alfred said. "But he'd get over it after a bit."

TWENTY-THREE

A Friend in
the Wilderness

W HEN YOU ARE AVOIDING THE LONG ARM OF UNCLE SAM, you tend to
be a little distrusting of folks you meet along the way. Everyone
you encounter is a potential threat to your freedom. Along with a touch of
alienation after months of muttering to oneself, you become a mite paranoid.
Yet paranoia, providing the voices in your head don't start threatening
you, can be a healthy trait when you are on the lam. You are not just
skittish of strangers but even of acquaintances from back home who may
accidentally let it slip to the wrong person that you are in the vicinity. As
a result, Alfred said, when you see people heading your way along a
mountain trail, your first inclination is to slip quietly behind a tree and let
them pass.

Consider the day in late 1917 when the brothers were in the mountains
overlooking Williams, a hamlet in the Williams Creek drainage on the
southwestern end of the Applegate River Valley. They were en route to
a place where they would rendezvous with their parents in a prearranged
secret location as part of a periodic resupply mission. The brothers had
just sat down to rest when they spotted a short fellow heading their way.

"This man come along, following his trap line," Alfred said. "I
knowed him. But we just had to let him go by. He didn't see us a'tall."

In addition to being concerned about their own liberty, they knew they wouldn't be the only family members wanted by the feds if the word got out that their parents were aiding and abetting fugitives. Friend or not, they could not take the chance on chatting with a kindred spirit in the mountains. It was too close to home.

Alfred insisted the man was none other than Elijah Davidson, the fellow credited with discovering what would become known as the Oregon Caves. Although short of stature, he stood tall among the pantheon of southern Oregon mountain men in the late 19th and early 20th centuries. Presumably, local Indians would have known about the caves for eons but history, tilting towards those of European heritage, credits Davidson with the discovery. Acclaimed for his hunting prowess, he found the caverns in 1874 during a deer hunting trip with his dog Bruno. The son of Oregon pioneers, Davidson, born Jan. 22, 1849 in Monmouth, Illinois, had just bagged a buck deer with his muzzle-loading rifle. As a hunting dog is wont to do, Bruno began sniffing around and soon picked up the fresh scent of a wild beast. Bruno immediately raced off, hot on the heels of a bear which he pursued into a dark hole in the side of a mountain. Using matches to guide his way, Davidson pursued his pooch after hearing it yelping inside the cavern. When his last match went out, the hunter groped his way back to the surface by following a small stream which flows out of the cave. Bruno emerged shortly after, bearing only a few scratches. Davidson returned the next day to find a bear nosing around the carcass of the deer the hunter had hung up in the woods. The hunter fired one round into the bruin, adding bear meat to his venison larder.

"Elijah was a little bit of a man," Alfred said. "But he was a real good hunter. I used to stop and talk to him about hunting out in the Applegate before we took off. He would come into the post office in Ruch sometimes. I've often wondered why such a little man took up a thing like bear hunting."

Despite growing long of tooth, the diminutive Davidson never slowed down when it came to roaming the mountains to hunt, the *Daily Courier* newspaper in Grants Pass reported at the end December in 1915. He killed a seven-foot-long mountain lion in the shadow of Grayback

Mountain, the second cougar the cagey hunter had taken that winter in the area, the paper reported. He had also bagged two bears in the vicinity during the same period, it added. The hunter died in his cabin alongside Williams Creek in 1923 at the age of seventy-four.

But he had lived to see his discovery become famous: President William Howard Taft declared the caves a national monument on July 12, 1909. The small stream Davidson followed back to the entrance after running out of matches was dubbed the River Styx, named after the river that formed the border between Earth and Hades in Greek mythology. And you thought cavemen were dullards who had never read the classics.

After Davidson passed their hiding place, the Fattig brothers moved quickly to meet their parents, gather their supplies and fade back into the forest. While they trusted Davidson, they had to err on the side of caution. Again, they couldn't take a chance on word getting out they were periodically returning to the Applegate country.

In addition to meeting with family members on the sly to resupply and learn the latest war news, the brothers had a few mountain friends they confided in during their days on the run, although they certainly never had to worry about overloading their social calendar. There was one friend in particular they regularly visited throughout 1917 and for much of 1918. In turn, he reciprocated by paying a call at the Madstone site on occasion, offering advice on how to build the cabin. His name was Silas Simon "Si" McKee, a colorful old miner born Oct. 11, 1844 in Sullivan County, Missouri. This was not for tea and crumpets in the drawing room, mind you. If they were lucky, a plate of beans and cowboy coffee was on the menu. But their repast was more likely a hunk of venison jerky, chased by a cup of water. No doubt their guest would have made good use of his shirt sleeve to wipe the cup clean.

When our father talked about Si McKee, he spoke with a certain reverence about a man he admired for being tougher than horseshoes. Given the fact Dad named his first born male child after a famous mountain man, it's obvious he had high regard for those with the fortitude to live alone in the mountains. He also appreciated the fact Mr. McKee had befriended his older brothers at a time few folks were supportive of their draft-dodging ways. When our nation first entered WWI, Americans were frothing at the mouth with patriotism. It was only later, after Johnny was listed among the dead or came home sans an appendage and listless from shellshock, that grim reality began to erode the patriotic fervor. Cooler heads may not prevail in the emotional debate over going to war but calmer minds are often the ones to whom folks turn to clean up the ensuing mess.

Like the brothers, McKee had family back in the Applegate Valley. He also had a few scrapes with John Law over shooting deer out of season. Then there was his penchant for igniting a forest fire here and there to clear the land to make it easier to mine or run cattle, something that would lead to his eventual imprisonment, albeit short term. He most certainly wasn't the only one to skirt the law by taking food on the hoof or clearing land by fire when surviving on his own in the mountains. Mountain denizens in those days tended to look upon the laws of civilization as abstract concepts that were little more than suggestive guidelines as opposed to hard and fast rules. The distant mores of society don't hold much sway when you are starving and a steak strolls by in the form of a three-point buck. Out of season or not, venison is going to be on your menu.

There is a sense of freedom in being able to breathe deeply of fresh mountain air and drinking cold water from a spring bubbling out of a mountain. Your spirit soars in the mountains, providing you aren't cold and hungry or suffering from snakebite or a grievous bullet wound. Back then, someone who was a bit of a klutz wouldn't last long since amputating a digit with an ax or shooting off a toe could lead to a deadly infection. Summoning a doctor was not an option.

Alfred recalled first meeting Si McKee in 1909 when the future draft evader was seventeen years old. The two brothers had taken a summer hiking trip from the Applegate Valley over into the Smith River drainage. At the time, McKee, one of the last stage coach drivers who took passengers over the mountains from Grants Pass to Crescent City on the coast, was living in an abandoned stage stop along the Smith River where he had staked a couple of mining claims. After spending a little time working with McKee on his claims, the Fattigs hiked down to the coast, then north to the Rogue River where they took the trail up river to the Applegate River and back to the family farm. Unknown to them, they had just walked full circle—some 200 miles—around what I have come to refer as the Madstone country.

"We was afoot with packs on our backs," he recalled of the trip which would be a preview of their Madstone years.

The old miner was one of the few people who knew the location of the brothers' hideout during the war. But they knew they could trust him with their freedom.

"Sometimes he would come over to see me at Madstone," Alfred said. "He told me a lot about his life. I wondered about some of the stories that was told about him. He told me that he got a check from Uncle Sam for being in an Indian war."

He speculated that McKee had fought in the Modoc Indian War in 1872. During that brief war, the small band of Modoc Indians held off the U.S. Army in the rugged lava beds near the California-Oregon border. In the end, the Indian leaders, including a fellow named Captain Jack, would be hung following a trial at Fort Klamath near where Alfred had worked in the hay fields for the Klamath Indians in his youth.

On the surface, it seems incongruous that an old Indian war veteran and a young pacifist would befriend each other. But their shared disenchantment with society and love of the mountains apparently overcame any potential disagreements over war. Besides, there was their silent pact not to pry.

"In Si's younger days, he got pretty tough with anyone who tried to run over him," Alfred said. "But I don't believe he was an outlaw. He told us about riding the stage road and what a tough place it had been."

Evidence of those tough years could still be found along the old stage road in the form of lone graves, Alfred said. He was told some graves were those of highwaymen who were buried where they met their fate.

The McKee cabin the brothers visited is just south of Biscuit Hill and a few feet north of the McGrew Trail which once led miners back into those rugged mountains. The old miner also had rustic cabins down along Baldface and Diamond creeks, both tributaries to the Smith River.

You'll find his McGrew Trail cabin site on a Rogue River-Siskiyou National Forest map at 1,837 feet above sea level in eastern Curry County, which hugs the southwest corner of Oregon. To say it is a bit rocky is like saying Mars is a little stony. In fact, remove the vegetation and the area would look remarkably like photographs take of the red planet by the current Mars landers.

Alfred recalled the cabin near Biscuit Hill with fondness. The old miner had a claim in the drainage that he periodically worked, he noted.

There were plenty of odd dwellings to be found in the mountains, and none designed for their aesthetic appearance or to receive a nod of approval from Frank Lloyd Wright. These were simply shelters from storms or to keep the inhabitant out of the reach of a hungry mountain lion. But McKee's hut on the hill was unique in its own right, even for the strange structures inhabiting the Siskiyou Mountains. For instance, the chimney was built of scrap sheet metal which was girded by cedar shakes some five feet long, Alfred said, adding the cooking stove was simply a pile of rocks covered with a metal top from an old wood stove.

"He built the cabin himself, built it out of cedars to keep the fleas away," he said. "It had no windows. It didn't need any. The logs were far enough apart to let in plenty of light."

It stands to reason that if the logs were spaced widely enough to let in light, then it would have been a bit drafty. But McKee apparently kept his rustic fireplace stocked with logs come winter.

The cabin was an extension of McKee's colorful personality. The former stagecoach driver, Modoc War veteran and miner only had one good eye, according to Alfred.

"A gun blowed up on him," he said. "But he was one of the best shots I ever seen. I don't know how he done it, either, because it was his right eye that was put out."

McKee was right-handed, he explained, observing it would be difficult for most right-handed people to sight along a rifle barrel with their left eye. To achieve the act of contortion, you would have to scrunch over until you would line up the sights with your left eye while the rifle butt is firm against your right shoulder. I've tried shooting a rifle in that pretzel fashion but found it mighty awkward. It could be managed out of necessity, however.

While social niceties were largely dispensed with in the mountains, there is some decorum among those who dwell in the wild. We're not just talking about avoiding eating yellow snow. When approaching a cabin, shouting out a greeting loud and clear was always considered good manners, Alfred observed. After all, you don't want to surprise the occupant answering nature's call in the outhouse. You also don't want bullets whistling over your head fired by a miner a little paranoid that someone is out to steal his gold. Since there were no banks in the area, miners tended to hide their valuables out on the back forty.

"Si showed me what he called his 'cache,'" Alfred said. "He dug a hole in the ground and covered it over with a big flat rock." Actually, he was a bit more specific than that, but the secret is safe with them both.

Si McKee died in the fall of 1918 when he was seventy-four, apparently of natural causes. According to the tale I heard as a kid, one which Uncle Alfred confirmed, the miner had gone to Waldo to buy some grub and perhaps pound back a few at the local watering hole. Feeling a bit poorly and plagued by a cough, he climbed aboard his horse and headed to the cabin he had in the Diamond Creek drainage. He expired in the cabin and wasn't found until weeks later.

"He had been dead a long time before they found him," Alfred said. "Well, he was so near rotted out that they took the bed and all right out in the yard, dug a grave, chopped the (bed) slates loose and let him fall right down in the grave. Last time I was along there, why, the old bed was still standing there."

For a moment, he was lost in thought, thinking about the old miner who befriended them.

"He was a mighty fine old man," Alfred recalled. "He told me about all the mines he had found. He was a fine old guy. If things would have been different, I sure would have stayed with him. I guess him and me was pretty much alike."

Alfred was sitting on the edge of his bed as he spoke of his old friend who never judged him for being against making war on other humans.

"Yeah, old Si was quite a man," he said, then softly added, "a good man."

Glenn Smith, the fellow reared in the Applegate Valley who first popped up in Chapter Nineteen, was Si McKee's nephew. He expressed surprise that his uncle knew where the Fattig brothers were hiding during WWI.

"Si never divulged where they were," Smith told me in 1989. "He would come and stay with us for a few weeks at a time during those years. Nobody ever knew that he knew where they were."

Before the war, in 1912, a very young Glenn Smith accompanied his parents on a gold mining venture with McKee. After reaching the south-western extreme of the Illinois Valley, they journeyed to the foot of Oregon Mountain near the California state line. Leaving their wagon behind, they traveled past the old Bain Station stage stop to Diamond Creek where Si McKee assured them they would find gold. They didn't.

"We almost starved, and it took a year before we could get our ranch back," said Smith who chuckled at the experience.

"Yes, he was quite a character," he added. "He always wore a red bandana. About the only time he took a bath was when he fell in the creek."

Smith confirmed that McKee received a pension from an Indian war, although the nephew wasn't certain in which war his uncle had participated or to what extend he had fought.

"He used to come into Ruch to get his check," he said of the little hamlet in the Applegate Valley. "It was only $20 a month. But that was a hell of a lot of money then."

He also recalled that the old mountain man had died in his cabin, pre-sumably the one on Diamond Creek, and wasn't found until the body had badly deteriorated. Like Alfred, Glenn Smith said the remains were buried in the bedding.

"They had to shoot his dog—it had gone mad," he said, adding that Si's horse was also nearly dead when it was found. "They led his old mare into the cabin and shot it and burned the cabin."

If his remains didn't suffer enough indignities, some well meaning individual later placed an iron grave marker on the site but McKee's name was misspelled as "McGee." The old marker is now gone, reputedly residing in a museum in northern California. He deserved better. Although I haven't been to the site in years, a fire-twisted horse shoe, apparently originally draped over the fork of a hardwood tree, could be seen sticking out of the tree which had grown around it. Perhaps it was from the old miner's mare. The answer lies dead and buried in the red clay dirt, part of Oregon's forgotten legacy.

Smith didn't directly weigh in on whether he thought my uncles were right or wrong in avoiding the draft, although the fact he was a Navy veteran spoke volumes. Since he was nearly nine years old when the U.S. entered WWI, he recalled hearing about their draft-dodging ways as a child.

"People talked about it," he said. "Most didn't look favorably on it. Young men from our area were dying over there and the Fattig brothers were hiding out in the hills. But I didn't know Alfred or Charlie. I suppose they had their reasons."

****

In the interest of research, as well as *auld lang syne* and a desperate desire to escape my writing loft for a day, I went into the McKee cabin site near Biscuit Hill in early June of 2016. This would have been the place my uncles periodically visited. My guide was Cliff Phillips, a friend since the second grade at Kerby Elementary School. Picture a stocky Paul Bunyan and you have Cliff down pat. Unfortunately, he was battling cancer and was weakened a bit, making him only as tough as a bull when we ventured into the site. Back in high school, I recall him running downfield with the football when an opponent made the mistake of trying to tackle him. Cliff lowered his head and hit him head on, sending the poor fellow cart wheeling through the air in what appeared to be slow motion. Yes, we won the game, thank you.

A retired U.S. Forest Service employee, Cliff had been to the cabin site in earlier years. Without him, I would have never found it. The cabin site near Biscuit Hill included a large pile of red stones which appeared to have been part of a fireplace like the one Alfred described. There were also fragments of what appears to have been the heavy top of an old woodstove which must have been a bear to haul back there. The stove top may very well have been the one used to heat coffee when Alfred and Charlie Fattig paid a visit nearly a century earlier. There is no wood left of the cabin although several square nails can be seen in the red dirt where the structure once stood. Standing near the pile of stones is an incense cedar, its two-foot thick base blackened by fire.

We didn't find any flat rock covering a stash of Si McKee's nuggets. Nor did we look. Contrary to mining myth, miners who discovered the mother lode didn't continue to cling to life in a filthy cabin on a rocky mountainside. Many headed straight to town to consort with women of ill repute and to drink themselves silly.

"The Biscuit Fire came right through here," Cliff observed of the nearly half-million acre blaze sparked by lightning on July 12, 2002. "Before the fire burned through here, it was kind of a nice little spot with quite a few trees. There was some shade. It's pretty desolate looking now but back in those days when Si McKee was here it would have been a nice little timbered basin."

In addition to cedar, there were also knob cone pine trees in the vicinity which are serontinuous, meaning they require the heat from a wildfire to open their cones. However, like Goldilocks, knob cones don't like it too hot or the cones burn in the fire.

It was because of the chance to write about rare individuals like Si McKee that I became a journalist. He would have been a fascinating character to spend a few hours chatting with. Unfortunately, he died well before I was born. But I once had the good fortune to chat with such a fellow who must have been strikingly similar to Si McKee. His name was Bob Cutler, a tough eighty-three-year-old gold miner whose habitat was his twenty-acre mining claim on the rugged upper reaches of Josephine Creek west of Kerby in the Illinois Valley.

Although I had heard plenty about him during my Kerby childhood, including the fact he wasn't averse to distilling a little moonshine, I didn't meet him until early December 1979. I was a freshly scrubbed

University of Oregon graduate who had just been hired to write features and cover natural resources for the *Daily Courier* newspaper in Grants Pass. I wanted to have an article in hand when I started the following Monday, so I dropped in to see Kerby resident Abe Cutler who was Bob's kid brother. Although I only knew of Bob through his hard rock reputation as a rugged recluse, Abe, eighty-one, and his wife, Edna, were old family friends who lived near our home in Kerby. My sister, Delores, and I used to ride their white horse named Anselmo. If you are an avid reader, you will recognize the name Anselmo as the fellow who was the elderly guide to central character Robert Jordan in Hemingway's *For Whom the Bell Tolls.* Edna Cutler was a former teacher and an avid reader. Fine people, the Cutlers.

"He'll talk to you—if we grease the skids," Abe said of his brother. "We'll need some gin."

I took Abe to the local liquor store in Cave Junction where he purchased a quart of less-than-the-finer stuff. Apparently brother Bob was not persnickety about his booze.

"Give that to him—tell him it's from Abe," the younger brother instructed me. "He'll talk. What he tells you, you can take to the bank."

To reach Bob's one-room remote cabin, you parked on a rough dirt road just west of Kerby, then hiked about five miles into the mountains. Once you crested Tennessee Pass, you headed south along a road that would have scared the bejabbers out of a mountain goat as the narrow track hugged the steep slopes over Josephine Creek. Level ground in that country is unknown. Forced marches back in the Marine Corps had been far easier.

The march ended when I arrived at a foot bridge fashioned out of a log. Serving as a hand rail was a weathered rope stretched between two trees on each side of the stream. For those who took a misstep, unforgiving boulders waited some twenty feet below.

But it wasn't the bridge that made me nervous. It was the silent cabin on the other side where a wisp of smoke drifted out of a rusting chimney. I called out his name. Nothing. His two dogs started barking. One Cujo was frothing from the mouth at the mere thought he may get a chance to sink his fangs into some fresh flesh, apparently unaware that consuming a chunk of journalist would sour his stomach.

Walking gingerly, I stepped out on the log. Halfway across the log I recalled rumors that the old gentleman had been known to fire off a few rounds at strangers. Sucking in my gut, I hurried across, took off my pack, grabbed the bottle and held it aloft.

"Abe sent you a bottle of gin," I yelled, hoping I wouldn't hear a shell being jacked into the chamber.

It worked like magic. Out of the cabin popped a fellow who looked like he came straight from central casting: A big gnome with a white beard, wire-rimmed glasses, an old slouch hat, a rain jacket with a hood, wool shirt, jeans and boots as slumpy as the hat.

Turns out he was a cordial fellow glad to have company, even if it was a reporter, providing the scribe was carrying a bottle of gin. After inviting me in to take a seat at a small table, he grabbed an old rag and wiped out a chipped cup, sloshed it half full of gin and shoved it in front of me.

He then filled another cup to the brim, took a gulp and told me to fire away. I turned on my tape recorder. Digital recorders were not yet readily available, you understand.

Born July 10, 1896, Montana-reared Robert Clayton Cutler had lived some three decades along the creek, after homesteading in Homer, Alaska, where he met and married a school teacher named Margaret Richardson. His wife had taught school in the Last Frontier's remote villages for nearly a quarter of a century, beginning in 1924. The couple moved south to Oregon where she worked as a librarian until she died in a car wreck in the spring of 1954 near Gearhart, a seaside hamlet where the couple operated a chicken ranch just south of Astoria. Her twin sister, Elizabeth Richardson Childs, taught literature, including the works of Shakespeare, at what is now Southern Oregon University in Ashland during the late 1920s, according to her son Herb Childs. In fact, when Angus Bowmer, considered the father of the regionally famous Shakespeare Festival in Ashland, came to that fair town in 1931, he took over Elizabeth's old job. I bring this up because I didn't want you to think the old miner was wholly uncivilized, despite his protestations to the contrary.

"I wouldn't have lived ten minutes over in that civilized country," Bob told me, referring to his life after his wife died. "They'd have to put me in jail to keep me there."

For him, "town" was Kerby where he got his grubstake and visited his brother twice a year.

"When I first come here, this country was full of deer," he observed. "But Kerby got all settled up and they got to shootin' everything they could kill."

After declaring that Kerby had become a burgeoning metropolis, he drained his cup. I took a sip of what I can only imagine kerosene tastes like. But it wasn't so bad once my tastes buds became totally numb. In any case, my face quickly became frozen into a foolish grin.

Besides, his colorful tales of mountain life made up for the bad booze. Take the time a rattlesnake nailed him, laying the miner up for two weeks. The snake didn't survive.

Then there was the stormy night the miner broke his right leg just below the knee.

"See, the wind was blowing my stovepipe over," he said. "I clumb up there and put the stove pipe back on. I started backing down to the edge of the roof there and just got a'hold to the ladder when the darn thing broke. I hit the only rock there with my leg.

"Well, I jumped up real quick and fell down just as fast," he added. "That leg just folded up." Folded up as in the tibia snapping like a bread stick just below his knee. Having broken my fibula, the smaller of the two leg bones between the knee and the ankle, the thought of the resulting pain of snapping the tibia in such a fashion makes me want to upchuck. Being a wuss, I went to the hospital where a doctor straightened it out and installed a metal plate to keep it plumb. What's more, I insisted they put me under before the surgeon picked up his carving utensils.

The old miner wasn't so fussy. Accustomed to fending for himself, he crawled inside his cabin and hoisted himself upon his four-poster bed.

"I tied my leg to the corner of that bed there," he said, pointing to the old bed in the one-room cabin. "Then I pushed myself back and pulled until I got 'er straight."

Taking another gulp of gin, he no doubt noticed the grimace on his listener's face.

"Oh, I done all this quick, see, that way it didn't hurt as much," he said. "I done a fine job of fixing it up." He pulled up his right pant leg, revealing a shin that was somewhat straight. He didn't appear to have bothered with socks before putting on his ankle-high hiking shoes.

When I left him, he was in fine spirits, having consumed much of the bottle and shared his life story. He never found the mother lode, although he assured me it was out there.

He died of natural causes a few years later, leaving the world poorer without his rich character. Like Si McKee, he was buried near his cabin. If there is an afterlife, I like to think that Elijah, Si and the hermit on Josephine Creek are somewhere swapping colorful mountain tales, some of which may even be true.

TWENTY-FOUR

The Lure of Gold

L IKE THE SOURDOUGHS BEFORE THEM, the Fattig brothers carried a gold pan while wandering into canyons and along streams in the Madstone country. If they didn't have a gold pan handy, a frying pan would do the job, thank you.

"Back in the mountains, we found enough gold to live on," Alfred said. "There is still gold back there. I don't think they will ever find it all. There was gold in all those creeks.

"Now, you see that black sand, that's a pretty good indication you're getting near gold with your pan," he added. "I looked for gold a lot, but I was a better hunter than a gold panner, that's for sure."

Looking back over seventy years to those distant mountains, he did find what he believed was a sizeable strike. While the brothers found a bit of gold in the Chetco River drainage, it was high in the Baldface Creek drainage that Alfred discovered what he insisted to his dying day was the mother lode.

Unfortunately for those who are interested in finding precious metals, his memory was too vague to provide much direction. It had been too long since he had hiked those rugged trails.

But he talked about a trail, now lost in time, which took hikers from O'Brien into that upper Smith River drainage.

"Only I would leave the trail on top of the coast range to go to the right and go until I got close to the first peak," he said, apparently referring to a mountaintop known as Chetco Peak which rises to 4,660 feet above sea level.

A very crude map he drew from memory nearly half a century ago indicated the area he found gold in the spring of 1918 was just south of Chetco Peak and on the east side of Doe Gap. The map, little more than chicken scratch, is misleading since it places geological features in different locations than you would find them on the modern national forest map. For instance, Alfred's map incorrectly places Chetco Peak about four miles west of Doe Gap. Yet his map correctly shows the Smith River drainage falling away to the south of the peak. Just as he recalled, a series of small seasonal streams do cut into the ridge leading to the peak.

If you had become crazed by the lust for gold and followed his faulty map, someone would have one day found your bleached bones down some rocky ravine. Like the remains of miners of yore, your bones would be stuffed inside a hastily dug hole and covered with dirt. Remember, the mountain etiquette prevails on these lonely mountains where the wind wails and the coyotes howl.

Allowing his map and memory were a little sketchy on how to locate his find, Alfred Fattig insisted his gold discovery could be found again by a determined seeker of the precious metal.

"You just follow the top of the range through the woods to Chetco Peak," he said of reaching the site where he found gold. "I am not sure of this but I believe it is the last little dry creek before you get to the peak. It couldn't be more than the third dry creek from the peak. Of course, all them creeks up there all run dry in dry season."

Although that description was mighty vague as to the exact location of his would-be gold strike, the events leading up to his discovery were still nailed down in his mind.

One spring evening in 1918 found him camping alone along the unnamed stream. He estimated he was about two miles from Chetco Peak, indicating he was probably in the far upper reaches of the Baldface Creek drainage.

"I camped right beside the little creek early in the spring when there was enough water for camp use and to pan a little," he said. "While I was waiting for water to boil for coffee, I panned some dirt right out of the hole where I got coffee water. I got gold the first pan.

"It was round gold, just as round as marbles, not flake stuff," he continued. "You can find gold most any place in gold country but not gold like that."

He would return to the site a few years later, this time packing a six-foot sluice box with an intention to test the gold potential of his discovery.

"It took me two days to pack that sluice box in there," he said. "That was late in the fall but there wasn't enough water. I planned to go back in the spring while there would still be a little snow on the ground and I would be sure of enough water."

As fate would have it, he was never able to return to the site where he left his sluice box.

"Of course, it would be rotten now," he observed. "My old camp might still show up—rocks from the fire. I do remember my campfire wasn't more than about twenty feet from where I got the gold. I know other places but that is the most likely place for it to turn out good."

In his honor and in keeping with naming other lost gold discoveries in the West, the site will hereafter be known as "Uncle Alfred's Lost Golden Marbles Mine." I think it has a nice ring to it.

While the brothers toiled hard for what little gold they found while on the lam, some folks were just plain lucky in making a strike.

"I knowed a man who found gold with his bare hands once," Alfred said. "He was wading in the water, fishing. The bottom of that stream was awful slick. Well, he slipped and put his hand out to catch himself on the bank and put his hand in a pocket with $1,500 in it."

Even allowing for a miner's predilection for embellishing old tales, there is likely a nugget of truth in the story the fellow told Alfred. In any case, he couldn't recall the name of the stream, telling Alfred only that it was somewhere in the Smith River drainage. Even by Texas standards, that is a lot of country, much of which is nearly perpendicular.

Back in those days, if you were fortunate enough to strike it rich, rich being relative among those grubbing for gold, that didn't mean you got to keep your hard-earned gains. About the time Uncle Alfred's Lost Golden Marbles Mine was initially found, two bandits found their mother lode in the Boswell mine near Holland, the hamlet in the Illinois Valley.

The *Daily Courier* reported that on the evening of May 2, 1918, miners Robert Boswell and his son, Robert Boswell Jr., were melting down their gold a few miles east of Holland when two masked men, both armed, stepped out of the brush. Ordering the Boswells to throw up their arms, the bandits bound and gagged the miners, tying them to a nearby tree, the paper reported. The robbers then went to work melting the gold into bars, it added.

Before the night was over, the robbers had mined some $6,000 in gold bullion from the Boswells, the paper noted. The bad guys then disappeared into the night.

Young Boswell, who was later able to untie the bonds that held him, then free his father, had noticed that one of the robbers had a portion of his index finger missing from his right hand, a clue that would later aid authorities in identifying the culprits. Ten days later, Sheriff George W. Lewis arrested R.W. DeWitt, a sometimes miner living in a shack about a mile from the mine. His partner in the crime, identified as J. F. Howell, absconded with the gold, DeWitt told Lewis. DeWitt escaped from the Josephine County jail that July, remaining at large until he was recaptured on Jan. 8, 1919, in Salt Lake City. Unfortunately, young Boswell would never live to see the felon punished. Drafted into the Army shortly after the robbery, he was sent to France where he died in late October of 1918, just two weeks short of the armistice, the *Courier* reported.

Aside from Uncle Alfred's alleged gold strike high in the Baldface Creek drainage, the Fattig brothers never found much gold. They discovered small pockets of gold north of Chetco Peak, and were told by an old miner about precious metal being mined in Broken Cot Creek which cascades down a ravine cutting into the northeast flank of the mountain.

While at the Madstone cabin, the brothers panned throughout the upper Chetco River drainage, Alfred recalled. Although gold was scarce, they discovered metal they couldn't identify.

"We found some mineral that we never did find out what it was," Alfred said of mining near the cabin. "It was as soft as lead but could not be melted in a forge. It could be mashed between our teeth but could not be melted with coal in a forge. When you get it panned down, you can rub the fine stuff with your thumb and the black will rub off and leave a grayish color, something like lead.

"Now, I'm not trying to start a mineral rush," he cautioned, adding he didn't know if the mystery metal was worth anything. "A man would be foolish to start out to look for it unless he just wanted an excuse to go into those mountains."

The brothers concentrated on panning for gold. After all, the heavy yellow material was money in their pockets.

"All of them little stores in the Illinois Valley used to buy gold and we sold our gold to them the same as other people did," Alfred said.

However, they usually took their gold to general store owner John Wittrock in Kerby, he added. The two would bring their gold in to be weighed, then receive payment in supplies. They also received cash for the gold, providing there was any coming after the supplies were purchased.

It was Wittrock's store that had been threatened after the owner initially refused to fly an American flag to demonstrate his patriotism during the war, he noted. "He was a good man," Alfred said. While he didn't volunteer any information about Wittrock's relationship with them, it is conceivable their friend would have tipped them off when authorities were in the area looking for scofflaws, including two brothers who had dodged the draft.

Although the younger brother laid claim to having found a big strike, although it quickly became lost again, the elder brother had the gold thumb when it came to mining. A blurb in the Feb. 10, 1934 edition of the *Daily Courier* offered testimony to his mining skills.

"Forty nuggets taken in two days from the sluice box at the junction of Canyon and Josephine creeks six miles west of Kerby were brought to Grants Pass Friday by Paul Fattig," it read. Since that was nearly two decades before I was born, the nugget bearer would obviously have been my father.

"His brother, Charles, has mined property covering about twenty acres, for the last eight years, with moderate success until he made a rich find last week," it read. "One of the nuggets brought here was worth $65 and, combined with the second largest, two of the gold lumps were equal to $107. Beside the remaining 38 nuggets was fine gold estimated at $40."

Keep in mind this was 1934 when gold was bringing in only $35 an ounce. That means the largest nugget was nearly two ounces, a lump that is worth more than $2,600 in today's market since an ounce is going for a little more than $1,300 as I type this.

The nuggets came from the Royal Crown mine, a placer claim our dad owned along Josephine Creek upstream from where gold was initially discovered back in the early 1850s. The story hints that Uncle Charlie was the main miner in the operation but Dad, being more gregarious, was the fellow who went to town to cash in on any gold unearthed.

TWENTY-FIVE

Surrender

WHILE THE FATTIG BROTHERS HID OUT in the mountains, the world outside was rapidly evolving, even in rural Oregon. Consider a small item in the Oct. 3, 1918 issue of the Grants Pass newspaper.

"The day of the woodsman with the Big Ax may soon be over, if a new tree felling machine comes into general use," the *Courier* announced. "The new machine is run by a small motor. It will cut through a trunk 30 inches in diameter in a few minutes. Its saw is a chain with links of six teeth each…"

The chainsaw swiftly came into general use, antiquating the powerful ax wielder and misery whip operators of old. In the Oregon logging woods, the rhythmic chunking sound of an ax striking the trunk of a tree and the grating noise of the two-man crosscut saw was replaced by a screaming machine spitting oil and fumes. The industrial revolution had arrived. Instead of taking hours to cut down a large tree, a skilled timber faller could cut down dozens in a day. But the mechanism came with a price. While a bad swing from an ax could easily slice open a leg, the new machine in the hands of a careless operator could amputate a leg in a second. Although the new-fangled machine harvested a few legs, it greatly increased the ability of humankind to log forests. The pros and cons of cutting large swaths across national forestland are still being debated today.

More important than changing technology was the fact that, in little more than a month after the *Courier* wrote of the chainsaw, the First World War would be over. While the brothers continued to hide out in the mountains, they were being forgotten by everyone except their immediate family and those few authorities who kept a list of WWI draft evaders in Oregon. Veterans were returning home and starting families, getting on with their lives. The world was moving on.

After hunting deer within a day's walk of the cabin for more than a year, the brothers had thinned the ranks of the local ungulate population. Too often hunting trips were now ending with the brothers tightening their belts and hiking back to the cabin. They hungered for the fragrance of their mother's fresh homemade biscuits wafting out of the kitchen, for the gentle sounds of voices from the porch on an evening, for the feel of a soft bed at night. They were tired of the mountains and weary of each other.

For the brothers, the remote mountains had become the heart of darkness of which Joseph Conrad so eloquently wrote, a place where the quiet, once embracing, now smothered them like a shroud. The mountains which earlier felt protective now felt like prison walls. The lean diet of meat with basically no vegetables was also taking its toll, giving them scurvy-like symptoms. Lacking vitamin C, they suffered from swollen and bleeding gums. As Alfred noted, Charlie had already pulled out several teeth and the ones remaining were hurting him, something that did not turn him into Mr. Congeniality. Alfred's teeth were also bothering him. Both suffered stomach ailments, problems no doubt exacerbated by both bad food and poor hygiene. For those few times when hunting was good, they had eaten too many meals of venison without benefit of any spices. If a guest dropped in for a dinner of stewed venison, he would have noted the cuisine tasted remarkably like jerky boiled in water. And he would have been right. Fine cuisine it was not.

It was in the fall of 1919 that the brothers, facing another cold, wet winter, laid their options out on what passed for a table. The clear October nights offered shooting stars in the heavens above and frost on the valley floor. The wind carried a shivering chill from the north.

Mother Nature was already using a broad brush to paint the broadleaf maple leaves a bright yellow.

"We got to talking one night around the fire," Alfred said. "We knew the war was over. We wondered how they would treat us if we turned ourselves in. Charlie, he first brought up the notion of going in and giving himself up. He was tired of the hills."

A misanthrope he may have been, but Charlie had apparently just about had it with mountain life. The fact the brothers couldn't abide each other no doubt also fueled his discontent.

"He wasn't no mountain man by a long shot," Alfred observed, reiterating a common theme when it came to describing his often ill elder sibling. "If I hadn't been with him, he'd have starved to death for sure."

Although the younger brother was also weary of their hermitage, he had other concerns when it came to returning to face the music. One issue was Charlie's communications with the outer world, letters he would mail during their resupply trips.

"Now, I'm going to tell you just as straight as it was," Alfred said. "Charles, he had written a lot of dirty letters to different newspapers that had been sticking up for the war. He had vengeful ways."

The letters weren't sent to local newspapers, he said, noting they were mailed to distant publications such as the *Kansas City Star.* They learned of the pro-war stances taken by papers like the Kansas City publication because stories from those papers were often carried in local papers the brothers picked up while on a resupply mission, he added. Scribbled under candlelight in their cabin, the letters were filled with anger at the world, Alfred said. They were mailed surreptitiously when they dropped into places like Kerby, Waldo or Crescent City, he added.

"When he brought up this notion to give himself up, I thought to myself that with those letters he had written to different people about that war, well, I knowed they'd handle him pretty rough," Alfred said. "But I didn't say nothing about it to him."

Never very close, the brothers had become like a bickering couple who could no longer stand the sight of the other, let alone talk about their feelings to their cabin mate. But that night, with the embers dying in the fire, they quietly agreed to part company. Early the next morning at the tail end of October in 1919, nearly a year after WWI ended, Charlie Fattig shouldered his pack and headed to the outskirts of civilization, intent on finding work in a gold mine along Josephine Creek just west of Kerby. He planned to work for a while before turning himself into the authorities, he told his brother. Exactly when he was going to surrender was left up in the air. What was not in question was that their union, born out of necessity, had dissolved. They were on their own.

With the war over and his willingness to hide out in the mountains waning, Alfred Fattig was ready to face his punishment. He was weary of the immense solitude that he felt now covered the wilderness like a dark cloud. While he still loved the wild country, the hunger for human contact had grown too strong and the silence too big. Civilization with its softer side of life was beckoning. He was tired of gnawing on jerky as tough as rawhide and eating what he prayed was a wild carrot. The pacifist would have probably killed for a slice of apple pie. For the whole pie, a serial killer would have emerged.

For the ensuing eight months after his brother left, Alfred Fattig wandered the mountains alone. Seldom did he meet anyone along the trail. If he did see strangers in the distance who did not look like miners or trappers, he ducked into the brush and let them pass without greeting them. In short, he had gone native. But the life he had dreamed of as a youngster living like an Indian in the wild had lost its luster. Like Tom Sawyer on Jackson's Island, he grew weary of the wilderness. When he ventured from the cabin, he would sit around his campfire at night, thinking about the folks back home. Thanksgiving of 1919 brought little to be thankful for. And Christmas day found him searching for peace of mind. At times, he must have considered taking his life and very well may have acted on that had it not been for his strong faith.

He would not have been the first overwhelmed by the solitude and trying conditions. A page 22 article in the Jan. 2, 1898, edition of the *Oregonian* newspaper in Portland reported on the actions of one fellow who could no longer stand the strain imposed by the unrelenting loneliness.

"William Hyde, who went to Chetco, Curry County, from Grants Pass, and had been engaged thereabouts as a trapper, in a fit of despondency concluded that life was not worth living, and, taking his gun from behind his cabin door, placed the muzzle of it under his jaw and blew the top of his head off," the article reported in grisly detail. "The suicide occurred Monday evening, the 20th of December, and the dead man was found soon after the fatal shot was fired. His lifeless body was found in a sitting position on a trunk, the head resting on the weapon which had inflicted the deadly wound. Hyde left a widow and four children in Josephine County."

Like the trapper, Alfred Fattig had created a hell of his own making. He was so lonesome he even missed his elder brother, something he would never have anticipated. The silence was deafening, the immensity of the forest incomprehensible. Yet he continued to hold out, reluctant to return to civilization which now represented freedom from his mountain confinement.

But even the warming days of spring with budding leaves and blooming flowers failed to lift his sinking spirit. The nature that he had once found so captivating was no longer wonderful to behold. The mountain man was tired of hunting, tired of fishing, tired of following the lonely trails. For him, the love affair with Mother Nature was over. His boyhood infatuation with wilderness was gone.

By summer, Alfred Fattig decided it was time to face the wrath of Uncle Sam. His brother had already left and was working as a gold miner.

When he left the Madstone cabin, he literally hung up his old rifle, the one with which he slew the buck with the strange stone in its belly.

"I just got full of killing of any kind," he said. "I hung up my gun in our cabin on the Chetco. I heard later it hung there for almost three years. I didn't care if somebody packed it off or not. I was sick of hunting."

One can't help noticing the irony of a pacifist packing a rifle during his peaceful opposition to war but giving it up when heading back to rejoin a society which largely supported the war. It was one of several head-scratching incongruities in the unusual life of Alfred Fattig.

With his gear on his back, he left the Madstone cabin—sans his trusty rifle—early in July of 1920 and climbed the rocky ridge overlooking the upper Chetco River. He stood there for a moment, looking back down on the cabin with the shingled roof. He could see the river's clear water and hear the rapids racing over the boulders. He could not help but feel a heavy weight on his heart, not knowing when or if he would be returning to the Madstone country. These mountains had been his home for some three years. Now he must make peace with a world in which he had refused to wage war.

He turned on his heels and hurriedly walked down the Madstone Trail he had followed many times before to the Little Chetco River. He had miles to go. He followed the river upstream to a point where he could begin the long hike up the ridge leading to Canyon Peak. Upon reaching a high shoulder of the peak, he hiked around to Babyfoot Lake where he spent the night. The following morning found him hiking down Canyon Creek to Josephine Creek where he stopped at the mine where his brother was working. He was glad to see his brother, not because of brotherly love, but because he wanted to talk to authorities before his brother caused a problem for them both.

"I knowed if he went in there first, why, we'd both get twenty-five or thirty years in the penitentiary," Alfred said. "We had seen newspapers where certain ones had got twenty-five and thirty years. I figured we stood a better chance if I went in first and talked to them."

With Charlie agreeing that the younger brother would go to the authorities first, Alfred no longer followed the remote mountain trails to avoid people. He marched boldly north on the old stage road, then up along the Applegate River toward the Fattig farm. He stopped and talked to everyone he met en route, whether he knew them or not. He was no longer Albert Barnes. He was Alfred Fattig, returning home at long last. Although he may have looked a bit rustic, he did not stand out among the miners and farmers using the old wagon road.

Like Rip Van Winkle, he found changes had taken place since he went into hiding. For instance, Congress had passed the 19th Amendment to the U.S. Constitution in June of 1919 and would ratify it on Aug. 18, 1920, giving women the right to vote. Alfred's mother would be able to vote for the first time that November. The world had entered the Roaring 20s. With the war behind them, Americans were ready to kick up their heels. Unfortunately for the non-teetotalers, they wouldn't be doing it with legal booze since Congress also enacted Prohibition on Jan. 19 of that year, a law that stayed on the books until 1933. Indeed, he returned to civilization in turmoil.

But he did notice a marked difference from the pre-war modes of transportation: there were now more motorized vehicles bounding along the road. He stepped aside when an automobile rumbled past but caught a ride with an old farmer in a wagon heading past the Fattig place.

"I knew 'em—he shook my hand," he recalled. "I was back home."

Embraced by his parents, he ate his first meal in years in which he wasn't constantly looking out the window. He was at home and at peace. But after a few days of eating his mother's cooking—he particularly loved her baked beans which were served with a homemade biscuit floating in the bowl of juicy beans—he traveled into Jacksonville, the county seat.

The day was July 22, 1920. It was an eventful one, according to the front page of the Grants Pass paper: American financier William Vanderbilt died in Paris; U.S. Sen. Warren G. Harding would accept the Republican party nomination for president at its convention in Marion, Ohio; and the Grants Pass Park Board ladies announced a rummage sale. It was also the day draft dodger Alfred Fattig would try to surrender to authorities.

That's right. He would try but didn't initially have much success. He stood before the stone steps leading up to the main entrance of the Jackson County courthouse in that picturesque little town. The thought of entering the imposing brick building must have been an unnerving experience for one who spent the previous three years in small cabins and makeshift shelters. Taking a deep breath, he brushed off his clothes and walked into the solemn chambers of District Court Judge G.A. Gardner.

"After I got through telling him my story, he says he wasn't looking for people like me," Alfred recalled with a chuckle. "That may have sounded strange but everybody wasn't for that war."

More to the point, a judicial decision regarding draft dodging wasn't in Gardner's bailiwick. It was a federal case. But he was an officer of the law. He told the scofflaw to go home to the family farm and wait until he could summon federal marshals from Portland. The wheels of justice were beginning to turn.

"Now, I wasn't scared," Alfred cautioned his listeners. "I was ready for whatever was ahead."

He was at peace. He was tired of life on the run. He decided to rest at home and visit friends until the marshals paid a visit.

"The marshals, they come for me when I was visiting some of my people," he said. "I had told them where they could find me. Well, I was on the other side of the Applegate River that day. The main road was over the other side."

The two marshals had to cross a swinging bridge to reach the man who had dodged the authorities for three years.

"Anyone wasn't used to it, why, it'd swing to beat the band," Alfred said. "It just teetered and swung. You had to grab the sides to keep from being pitched over. I crossed over and looked back. They hadn't even started. I had to wait for them on the other side. They didn't like crossing that bridge."

He laughed at the memory of the nervous marshals tiptoeing across the bridge while grabbing the rope rails with a death grip. The crossing was over a rocky area but the water was low, he noted, adding, "There wasn't really anything for them to fret over."

This coming from a fellow accustomed to negotiating narrow mountain trails winding along cliffs or along the edge of a roiling river, either of which could mean death to someone stumbling off the path. In comparison, the swinging bridge over the Applegate was a walk in the park.

The marshals took him to the Jackson County jail in Jacksonville where he spent the night after having what he recalled was a surprisingly good meal. Of course, stewed road kill would have been a refreshing repast after his mountain meals. The next morning, on July 26, 1920, he and the two marshals boarded a train in Medford bound for Portland where he would be tried in U.S. District Court.

"I just wanted to get it over with," he said. "I wanted it done."

In closing this chapter, I can't resist offering up yet another quirky coincidence linking my world with my uncle's, albeit tangentially, something we can toss in the six degrees of separation bin. Back in April of 2013, I wrote a lengthy feature article on the 100th anniversary of the shooting of popular Jackson County Sheriff August Singler who was killed during a shoot-out with a wanted man on April 23, 1913. For the article, I interviewed his seventy-one-year-old granddaughter who later gave me one of the cards he had printed for his successful 1912 election as sheriff. When he was elected, his first ever campaign, by the way, his wife Rose took the job of cooking for the county jail inmates.

After her husband was killed—he shot the criminal to death before perishing—Rose continued to cook meals for the inmates, a job humanely provided by the county to help her and their eight young children survive. She was paid thirty-five cents a meal, including the tasty dinner she served Alfred Fattig. August D. Singler, a singular hero in my book, is believed to be the first sheriff in Oregon killed in the line of duty, according to the Oregon State Sheriffs Association.

If you are a National Basketball Association fan, you may also recognize the surname. Medford-native Kyle Singler, who was playing for the Oklahoma City Thunder at the time of this writing and previously played for the Detroit Pistons, is one of August Singler's great-great-grandsons. He was a star at Duke University when the Blue Devils won the 2010 NCAA championship. It appears straight shooting is a genetic trait in the Singler family.

TWENTY-SIX

Facing Judgment

D URING THE TRAIN RIDE NORTH, ALFRED FATTIG watched the Oregon
countryside roll past. It was the first time he had been on a train
since he was a youngster riding west with his parents and siblings around
1900. But he wasn't full of eager anticipation this train ride. Sitting next
to the marshals with his wrists in handcuffs, the twenty-five-year-old
must have worried he may be spending the next twenty-five years or so
in prison. The train steamed through the Rogue Valley, stopped at Grants
Pass to unload passengers and pick up a few, then continued north into
the rolling hills, past Roseburg and on into the wide Willamette Valley.

Up in Portland, regular readers of the *Oregonian* would have noticed
a little blurb in the morning paper on July 27, 1920.

"Alleged Draft Dodger Surrenders," read the headline. "Alfred Fattig,
alleged draft evader, surrendered himself to the sheriff of Jackson County
yesterday, according to word received by Charles Reames, assistant
United States attorney," the article stated. The writer was apparently
unaware the draft dodger had bypassed the sheriff for the judge in this
case. Then again, Alfred had spent the night at the sheriff's barred abode
in Jacksonville before heading up to Portland.

"Fattig is said to have registered and then disappeared," the article
noted. "Charles Fattig, a brother, has been indicted by the grand jury on
a similar charge."

Chances are most readers would have given the article short shrift. Other than offering an unusual surname, it gave no details that would have garnered interest. They would jump to news of more import. There was a follow-up on the death of American financier William Vanderbilt a few days earlier in Paris. Harding was already starting to campaign for the general election. A few wildfires—they called them forest fires back then—were popping up around the West.

But they would have doubtlessly read an above-the-fold front page *Oregonian* article on July 29, 1920. "Slacker Lives 3 Years in Forest," read the headline. "Alfred Fattig Is Driven Out by Solitude," cried one subhead. "Oregon Hermit Surrenders," shouted the next subhead. "Scruples Against Killing Cause of Flight," concluded yet another subhead.

"Living on deer and bear meat, wild honey and huckleberries for three years, and with only half a dozen shells of ammunition remaining, Alfred Fattig, draft evader, could stand the solitude of the Siskiyou mountains no longer," the article began. "He surrendered to the sheriff of Jackson County and yesterday in Portland told his story to Charles W. Reames, assistant United States attorney.

With his brother, Charles, Alfred Fattig disappeared in the mountains after filling out his draft questionnaire in 1917, according to the article.

"Alfred has led the life of a nomad and when he separated from Charles last fall, he became a wandering hermit until the very sound of his own voice scared him," the article added. "Alfred has no idea where Charles has gone. Their miserable existence palled on Charles more quickly than on Alfred."

At this point in the article, an editor added yet another subhead, "War Would Have Been Easy." A WWI combat veteran wounded in action would have begged to differ. It must also be observed that Alfred was playing fast and loose with the truth when he told Reames he had no idea where his brother was.

"We didn't want to kill anyone," Alfred told Reames, according to the statement. "We were brought up to believe that killing isn't right, so rather than go to war and kill people, we preferred to hide out in the mountains. It has been a terrible experience. The Army would have been heaven compared to it. No one told us that because of our conscientious objections to killing we could have been assigned to non-combatant service."

Keep in mind the reporter did not interview the defendant but was relying on a statement written by Reames. There is no question the assistant U.S. attorney cleaned up my uncle's verbiage here and there. For instance, the phrase "non-combatant service" would have never passed the lips of Alfred Fattig. It simply was not in his vernacular. While he was intelligent, he was an uneducated man who survived on his gut instincts when he was in the mountains. Although he had let it be known he was opposed to war when filling out his draft card in June of 1917, he had neither the wherewithal nor the knowledge of where to turn to pursue formal conscientious objector exemption status.

"When we decided that we could not be soldiers because of our principles against killing, we prepared for fleeing to the mountains," the statement continued. "We took clothing, salt, matches, weapons and ammunition. I forget how many pairs of shoes I carried, probably half a dozen. I had 1,000 rounds of ammunition. We carried a prospector's pan and pretended to be prospectors when we occasionally met prospectors or miners in the mountains, which wasn't often."

Interjecting once again, I have to observe it was highly unlikely he carried 1,000 cartridges, given the bulk and the weight of that many shells. Nor would he have referred to them as "rounds." That term is military jargon, not something a hunter of that era would have used.

But that is getting overly fastidious. Let us get back to the statement furnished by Reames.

"Once since we left I returned home," Alfred told the man who would prosecute him. "I saw my mother in February, 1918, and then went back to the mountains. About Christmas time in 1918 we heard from an old miner that the war was over."

To butt in once again, Alfred apparently did not want to implicate anyone who may have helped him during his years on the run. In his later account with Jim and I, he noted our paternal grandparents brought the brothers supplies quite a few times.

"Always we kept moving, summer or winter," the statement stressed. "We never remained more than two weeks in one spot. We each had a small tent and a sleeping bag, and once in a while we found an abandoned cabin which would shelter us. We ranged in the mountains around Indian Creek and the Clearwater country and kept high up in the Siskiyous except in winter when the snows were terribly deep. We never tried prospecting; it took all our time trying to keep alive."

The Clearwater country apparently referred to the upper Chetco River drainage. He clearly didn't want authorities to know precisely where the draft evaders had spent considerable time. You will notice the Madstone cabin is not mentioned in the statement. It seems that Alfred wanted to keep the cabin a secret, perhaps because he wanted to return to it one day and naively thought no one would stumble upon it. Contrary to the statement, they had indeed panned for gold, even earning some income from that endeavor. It seems Alfred wanted to keep secret areas where he had found gold-bearing ground.

"It was always a case of trying to get food," the statement said. "We killed and ate deer and bear and grouse. We trailed wild bees to their trees for honey and we ate berries. A few times, we got a little coffee from some store in a little settlement, but mostly we drank only water. We got a little cornmeal once or twice.

"The diet of wild game was monotonous," it added. "We had to keep eating fresh meat, without bread or vegetables, and it affected our constitution, but we kept going. We cooked our meat with the grease reduced from fat taken from bear and deer. Always we had to avoid discovery. We never built a fire when within five miles of a settlement except at night, for fear the smoke would be seen, and when we used a fire we placed it where it would be concealed."

At this point, Alfred told Reames his brother had decided the previous fall to leave and go somewhere to work. He doesn't mention the fact they could no longer stand the sight of each other.

"I decided to keep in the mountains, alone," Alfred stated. "All through the winter in the Siskiyous, with deep snows, 1 lived alone, and had to hunt and fish to keep supplied with food. Lonesome? It was awful! I never heard a voice for long periods of time, except my own, and the sound of my own voice startled me. I wouldn't go through the experience again for any sum of money. My hair grew long, but I kept it reasonably short by cutting it myself. I had a razor and kept shaved."

You can imagine his haircut was not something that would catch on in the salons of New York City. However, at this juncture, as he had clearly stated, appearances were not foremost in his mind.

"Finally it got so I simply couldn't stand it any longer," the statement read. "You keep thinking about your condition and you almost lose your mind. I wanted civilized food. I wanted to be with people and, above all, I wanted to get back and help my mother and father, who are getting old. And so I came out and surrendered. If officers had found me I wouldn't have resisted them at any time during the long hiding-out.

"Yes, a man can keep himself alive for an indefinite period in the mountains of Oregon, but we're too far advanced here for a man to live the life of a hunter alone," his statement concluded.

My uncle was no dummy. He knew full well that a grim portrayal of his years in the mountains could only help reduce the punishment. Yet he didn't have to embellish his experiences very much. He had endured some tough times.

The now-defunct *Oregon Journal* newspaper in Portland also carried a July 29 front-page story as well as a photograph of the draft dodger. Imagine a mug of the extremely talented actor Tim Blake Nelson as one of the main characters in the 2000 movie, *O Brother, Where Art Thou?* and you are in the ball park. Alfred's mug looked like the product of Aunt Mom and Uncle Dad.

However, because it was an afternoon paper, it was able to add the sentence handed down, something the morning *Oregonian* did not include in its coverage that day.

"Shirker Who Fled Gets Nine Months," read the *Journal* headline above Alfred's photograph.

"During the three years Alfred has lived the life of a hermit in the woods, existing on deer and bear meat, huckleberries and wild honey," the story read. "Because he only had six shells left and because his body was becoming so weak on account of the lack of food other than meat, Alfred decided he would surrender and pay his penalty.

"He is unable to eat today because his stomach is so weak it will not stand solid food," the article continued. "Prisoners in the jail gave him the first real haircut he has had for three years. He took along scissors and endeavored to cut his own hair whenever it got long enough to bother him."

Curiously, it added that, "His hearing is impaired a little, as he has been away from all noise." The writer did not explain just why a person's hearing would suffer because of silence. Perchance his ears weren't exercised enough?

As in the *Oregonian* piece, the *Journal* quoted Alfred as telling authorities the he did not know the whereabouts of his brother. "Federal officials are endeavoring to find his brother," the *Journal* concluded. Again, Uncle Alfred was being a wee bit deceitful since he knew full well how to track him down.

"Fattig was raised in the Dunkard church and claims his religious beliefs prompted the act," the *Journal* article concluded.

The *Portland Telegram*, another defunct newspaper, also got into the act with its own page one article on July 29. "Hermit Draft Evader Must Go To Prison," read the headline. "Man Who Hid In Mountain Fastnesses Three Years to Avoid Army Draws Nine Months' Term," added the subhead.

One paragraph found in this report but not included in the other articles was that a fellow named John S. Drake, who had failed to register for the draft, had been sentenced that day to one year in the county jail.

It also fleshed out a bit more of the hardships the scofflaw faced while hiding out. "I lost twenty pounds in the mountains, and now I suppose I'll lose fifteen more," Alfred said, apparently referring to lean meals he expected in the jail term ahead.

Alfred Fattig's day in court began in the morning of July 29, closed for a short lunch break, then concluded early that afternoon. Alfred pleaded guilty to the charge of violation the Selective Service Act of 1917. Specifically, he failed to answer his draft call on June 10, 1918.

The defendant "willfully failed and refused to appear and submit to physical examination as to his fitness for military service under an act of Congress approved May 18, 1917," according to the federal court records kept in the Seattle office of the National Archives. The defendant had been duly notified of his responsibility to report for the military draft, Reames told presiding Judge Robert S. Bean.

Uneducated and alone, Alfred Fattig stood before the court and told them why he had decided to evade the draft. He didn't recall being nervous, despite never having been in court before, let alone federal court in the largest city in the state.

"They wanted to know if I wanted a lawyer," Alfred said in the 1988 interview in Texas. "I told them I would tell my own story. I told them just how I felt."

His story was one of opposing war, of refusing to fight against his fellow man in a far-off land.

"They wanted to know where my brother was," he said. "I told them I couldn't tell them where he was, only where I left him."

That was true since Charlie Fattig was on the move when the two brothers parted, he explained.

"The prosecutor said he would like to come down and go hunting with me some day," Alfred said. "They all let me know they thought that I didn't belong in jail."

Still, the law was the law and he knew he would be serving time. Yet Judge Bean gave him what appears to have been a light sentence in the form of nine months behind bars in the Multnomah County jail at Rocky Butte just outside of Portland. His earnest demeanor coupled with his apparent innocent attitude along with the fact he had voluntarily walked out of the wilderness to give himself up no doubt worked in his favor. The attitude most folks had at this point that they were ready for the war to fade into history probably didn't hurt.

Stories on the draft dodger's surrender and sentence were printed in papers throughout the nation. City dwellers in the Big Apple read it when the *New York Tribune* ran the story on page two on July 30, 1920.

In Texas, the *El Paso Herald* ran a short front page article on July 29.

"Loneliness Drives Draft Fugitive From the Oregon Hills, Hiding Place for Three Years, To Jail Cell," read the three decker headline with a Portland dateline.

"Three years of wandering in the all but deserted mountains of southern Oregon in efforts to escape a charge of evading the selective draft were ended today with Alfred Fattig, a 25-year-old farmer, in jail," the article read. "He surrendered, he said, because the loneliness which became unbearable. During his wanderings, the meat of wild animals and berries has been his principal means of subsistence. Fattig and his brother, Charles, fled to the mountains in 1917 because of conscientious scruples against war."

It added that the brother had not yet been apprehended. The *San Antonio Express* ran the same story on July 30, albeit inside.

In Grants Pass, the *Daily Courier* carried a short story on its July 29 front page under the headline, "Draft Evader Given Jail Term Sentence."

"Alfred Fattig, the Jackson County draft evader who surrendered last week, after three years in the Siskiyous, today received a sentence of nine months in the county jail," the paper reported in a wire story which carried a Portland dateline.

The weekly *Jacksonville Post* in Jacksonville also ran the story on its front page on Aug. 7.

"Alfred Fattig, draft evader from Jackson County, Oregon, has surrendered to authorities at Portland, after having lived in the woods on wild animals and berries," the short article read.

In Medford, the *Mail Tribune* ran a front page article on July 29 under the heading, "Alfred Fattig Draft Evader Gets 9 Months."

"Alfred Fattig, alleged draft evader from the Applegate country in Jackson County, who for the past three years has lived the life of a hermit in the Siskiyou Mountains in southern Oregon today appeared before federal judge Bean and pleaded guilty to a charge of draft dodging," read the report. "He was sentenced to nine months in the county jail. Alfred Fattig is well known in the Applegate district and for many months eluded federal officials searching southern Oregon for draft dodgers. According to reports Fattig recently appeared in the

Applegate Valley fully armed and dressed in a suit of buckskin of his own making."

You have to chuckle at the image of a wild man wearing buckskin clothing and a rifle over his shoulder striding along the road bordering the Applegate River. However, Alfred already told us he shed his buckskins shortly after trying them out. He also left his rifle back at the cabin, he noted.

Doubtlessly, he must have encountered plenty of negative reaction to his decision to fly the coop instead of reporting for the draft. Certainly the fact Jonas and Harriett Fattig moved to the Illinois Valley after Alfred was released from jail speaks volumes about the reaction they received from local folks. For instance, consider the "Ye Smudge Pot" column written by Arthur Perry which ran on page four in the July 30, 1920, edition of the *Mail Tribune* in Medford. The column could be described as a snide reflection of the news of the day.

"Mr. Fattig, of the local quota of draft evaders, wails in the *Portland Telegram* to wit: 'I lost twenty pounds in the mountains, and now I suppose I'll lose fifteen more,' he declared this morning," Perry wrote. "This is too bad, but some of those who did what he was supposed to do lost arms and legs and their lives. He should be reimbursed for loss of fat and sleep."

Although Rocky Butte was a county jail, it held federal prisoners who served hard time. After donning his drab prisoner uniform, Alfred quickly found himself pounding rocks in the quarry on the east side of the butte. During the late summer, the rock quarry baked like an oven.

"It was a rock pile," Alfred said. "After I got my sentence, I asked to go to the rock pile. I figured I'd rather work than sit around. I asked to go there right away. I wanted to be out of doors."

It was not a pleasant period is his life. The food was bland at best. A slice of stale bread and a bowl of weak soup was common fare. "It sure wasn't food to break rock on by any means," he said. "Now that was hard work. But they treated me good. None of them guards ever held it against me for not joining the war."

Before his sentence was up, he was made a trustee and eventually transferred to the city jail in Portland where he spent the remainder of his sentence. Thanks to good behavior, he was released just seven and one-half months after being locked up.

He found the world was changing. As you have read, Harriett Viola Fattig could now vote, thanks to Congress having ratified the 19th Amendment on Aug. 18, 1920, giving women the right to cast a ballot. But they couldn't legally celebrate with liquor: the country had gone dry with the ratification of the 18th Amendment which prohibited the sale of alcoholic beverages with an alcoholic content greater than 2.75 percent. Then again, Grandma Fattig did not condone booze.

Upon his release he took the train back down to the Rogue Valley, returning to his parent's home near then Applegate River. Although he was ostracized by many for his anti-war stance, particularly those who had lost a friend or loved one in the war, he also had supporters who figured he had paid his debt to society. In many respects, his world must have been very much like today's political animosity between Democrats and Republicans where sullen silence is the best we can offer each other. Each side knew they were dead right and the other was dead wrong. To avoid confrontation, he kept a low profile, working on the farm, visiting friends on occasion and fishing the river when the mood struck. But he didn't go hunting as he once did. He had his fill of hunting for a while.

But there was something gnawing at him, something he knew he had to do. Finally, in January of 1922, he decided to visit his elder brother at a mine on Josephine Creek. A letter from a fellow named Charlie Hooper, aka Charlie Fattig, had divulged his whereabouts.

"Nobody knew I was going," Alfred said. "I rode a bicycle from the Applegate to the mine. Nobody knew I was going to see him."

He found the hardrock mine easy enough and walked up to see his lean brother outside the adit (horizontal tunnel), examining some rock he had just brought out of the mine in a wheelbarrow. Charlie offered a friendly greeting which, given his taciturn ways, was tantamount to a bear hug and a kiss on both cheeks. Charlie's mining partner, who was aware of their draft dodging ways, was also friendly.

As it happens, the two miners had just a few days earlier had a close brush with death at the mine. The two had just stepped out of the tunnel into daylight to examine some rock they had moments earlier broken away from the wall with picks. That's when they heard the rumble of the tunnel caving in deep inside the mountain. Had they been inside, their bodies would have still been under the mass of rocks when Alfred arrived.

"The whole earth came down," Alfred said. "That was a close call."

Too close, for the older brother it seems. He was ready to listen to his younger sibling about the prospects of going to Portland to turn himself in to authorities. Alfred convinced him that if he would surrender on his own volition, the chances were good he would receive a minimum sentence at Rocky Butte. Tired of living a life of constantly looking over his shoulder, Charlie agreed to accompany his brother to Portland. He may have seen the collapse of the cavern roof as a warning it was time to go pay his debt to society.

Oregon rain poured down on a gray day outside of the federal courthouse in Portland on Feb. 11, 1922. Inside, Charlie Fattig, accompanied by his brother, was standing before Judge Bean who must have felt a sense of déjà vu. The defendant doubtlessly was more than a little apprehensive. A bench warrant had been immediately issued for his arrest and a $1,000 bail issued, a sum the brothers could not pay given the fact draft dodging was not a money-making enterprise. Charlie faced the same charges Alfred encountered eighteen months earlier, according to court documents retained by the National Archives office in Seattle. Like his brother, he had violated the law after refusing to report for the draft in June of 1918, the document said.

As his brother had done in July of 1920, Charlie Fattig pleaded guilty and made a brief statement why he had disobeyed Uncle Sam. Like Alfred, Charlie spoke of his belief that war was wrong. But the elder brother did not have the same easy way with words as his brother. Nor was there as much interest by newspapers in the second mountain man as there had been for the first. The novelty had worn off. Judge Bean gravely studied the second draft-dodging brother for a moment before announcing the sentence.

For the penalty, let's turn to the *Oregonian* newspaper of Feb. 12, 1922.

"SLACKER GETS 9 MONTHS," announced the headline of the small article buried inside the paper. "Fattig Follows Brother From Mountains to Cell," the subhead added.

"During the next nine months, Charles Fattig, draft evader of Jackson County, will languish in jail," the story reported. "After having spent several years in the mountains back of Medford, Fattig yesterday followed the example of his slacker brother, Alfred Fattig, and gave himself up. He was sentenced by Judge Bean in the federal court. The brothers evaded the draft in 1917 and disappeared into the mountains. A short time ago Alfred, weary of the cold and hardships of his seclusion, gave himself up. He received a nine-month sentence."

There was no big splash on the front page of Oregon's leading newspaper. It seems there was little interest in another story about a wild man emerging from the mountains to face the punishment civilization was waiting to mete out to him for refusing to become a warrior. Then again, the elder brother didn't have the natural charisma of the younger sibling. Yet it is likely that Alfred having broken the legal ice in the federal court in Portland in 1920 helped his brother when it came to the penalty phase of evading the draft.

Charlie was relieved by the light sentence although he wasn't too keen about going to jail, Alfred said.

"I tried to make it easy for him," he said. "I went to visit him a couple of times when it got hard for him. He couldn't take it like I could."

Thus ended the Fattig brothers' flight into the southwest Oregon mountains to avoid the military draft of World War I. They paid with years of hard living in the wilderness followed by a jail sentence, albeit a relatively light one. Perhaps the biggest price they paid was being spurned by society. While they had their supporters, they would be shunned by others, particularly by those who had lost a loved one in the war. The family would move to the Illinois Valley to begin life anew.

TWENTY-SEVEN

The Family Rift

A CENTURY HAS PASSED SINCE THE FATTIG BROTHERS defied Uncle Sam by refusing to report for compulsory military service and march off to World War I. As we have seen, there was little support for draft dodgers back then, just as there would be if military conscription is ever reinstated. Yet the brothers were periodically resupplied by family members when their grub ran low. To put it into today's parlance, the family had their backs. That support was clearly orchestrated by Jonas and Harriett Fattig who were both staunchly opposed to war based on their religious beliefs.

That is not to say there weren't feelings of conflict and doubt within the family. For instance, our father was eleven when American doughboys began fighting in France. Like most young boys, he likely felt his heart swell when he saw a young man in military uniform bidding his family farewell before catching a train in Medford on the first let of his journey to the battlefields in France. Even out in the Applegate Valley, he would have faced ridicule by other farm boys razzing him for having two brothers too cowardly to fight. Those catcalls would invariably turn into fisticuffs at times. The notoriety brought by the brothers' draft evasion prompted Jonas and Harriett to sell their Applegate farm and move to the Illinois Valley in 1921. The move occurred when one son was fresh out of jail and another was about to serve his time. The Illinois Valley remains a remote part of Oregon even today, but was even more isolated when the 20th Century was young and full of promise. The family needed a fresh start.

Seeking a new beginning is one thing; walking away from the family forever is quite another. When Alfred left southwest Oregon in 1927, he did not return. Ever. He never spoke to his siblings for the remainder of his life, a period of more than sixty years. However, he did maintain a letter-writing correspondence with his sister. What triggered the irreconcilable split among the brothers? Why was there no rapprochement? What happened?

Like the sword of Damocles, those bundled questions have hung over my head ever since my childhood when I began wondering about the family rift. When Dad died in 1961, it had been more than thirty years since he had seen his brother Alfred. As a third-grade student mulling over that fact, I knew an hour waiting for noon recess on a warm spring day could move at a glacial pace. Three decades seemed like an eternity. Even then, I wanted to know the cause of the Big Bang that triggered our family's great divide. As an adult more than half a century later, my interest has not wavered. I figure discovering the cause of the schism could shed some light on who we are, where we had been as a family and where we are going.

If you would kindly humor me once again, we are going to venture back into the family closet one last time and rummage around to see what we can find out about these eccentric folks and the family feud. You may chuckle at some of their idiosyncrasies but keep in mind the weird ways of your Great Uncle Ichabod and Great-Great Grandmother Martha may have been just as wacky. In an attempt to shed my biases, I'll try to peek into the closet from a journalistic perspective without taking sides. Just be aware the words anyone chooses ultimately lean one way or another, reflecting the built-in prejudice that comes with using any language, be it written or spoken.

Obviously, all families have their squabbles. These days they are often over politics or religion, although the two are often indistinguishable. Another point of friction may surface when one sibling takes a path leading away from the footsteps dutifully followed by generations of his or her forbearers. A case in point: when I told my twin after I got out of the Marines that I was going to college on the G.I. Bill, he was visibly upset. "You can't do that!" he retorted. After all, the Fattigs dwelling in the mountain valleys of southwest Oregon did not go to college. From his perspective, I was getting a tad uppity. Perhaps even a little supercilious as those snooty professorial wordsmiths are wont to say. Thus began a deteriorating relationship between me and my siblings. I was the first out of our gene pool to swim upstream to college in living memory. While I was far from an outstanding college student, I like to believe my decision not to accept the familial status quo opened some doors heretofore closed to us. My children as well as Jim's are largely college educated, the presumptuous little twits. Come to think of it, my brother George also spent a couple of years in college, although he retained a semblance of decency by never earning an onion skin and staying the hell away from journalism. After all, having one sibling stumble down that dark path into the Fourth Estate was shame enough for several generations.

In all seriousness, the divide between Alfred and his male siblings was deep and wide, one that could not be bridged by a hug and simple apology. As evident in our Wonder years, both Charlie and our father were ever alert for Alfred's return. A tiny tiff it was not.

Nor was it directly related to the Madstone years. When our father spoke of the cabin and his brothers' anti-war stance, it was with obvious pride. The man who hung a pine slab in our Kerby house with the words "Life is a struggle but not a warfare" written on the wooden plaque had no issue with their decision to refuse to go to war. He knew patriotism was more than donning a uniform and strutting in lockstep. He understood it sometimes meant mustering up the courage to tell the emperor when he is wearing no clothes. His brothers didn't tell Uncle Sam his posterior was exposed, of course. They simply didn't hang around to watch him prance around buck naked.

We already know the two draft evaders did not get on well. Their personalities collided well before they began suffering Madstone cabin fever. With his cantankerous attitude seasoned with a large dose of defensive pessimism, Charlie saw his cracked cup of life as half empty and leaking. But Alfred's solid mug of optimism was half full with the level rising. The elder brother generally disliked people while the younger one leaned toward the gregarious. The fact one was an atheist and the other a staunch Christian certainly didn't help matters. But their personality clashes in themselves would not have caused the unforgiving rift. It was obviously much deeper.

While there is no smoking gun pointing to the cause of the ultimate umbrage, my interviews with those close to the immediate family and my research into what few records are available indicate it was rooted in two principal issues. One was the relationship the three brothers had with their father; the second was the ancient custom of the eldest son inheriting the estate, a tradition known as primogeniture.

Let's examine the parental relationship first since it set the scene for the family fissure.

Unequivocally, Uncle Charlie and our dad did not get on well with their father. Jonas was a strict authoritative figure and a hard worker who did not tolerate others who failed to mirror his ways. Anecdotal evidence provided by folks who knew him plainly demonstrates that fact.

Previously mentioned Glenn Smith who was reared near the Fattigs in the Applegate Valley knew my grandparents and my father who was just two years his senior. When I asked him about his childhood memories of my dad, he looked at me for a moment before replying, apparently wondering whether he should be candid. He decided to leave the bark on his words.

"Well, while the rest of us boys were doing chores, milking cows and what not, your dad was always out hunting and fishing," he said. "He didn't have to work at home like the rest of us. He had an easy life as a kid in the Applegate. Your grandmother babied him."

To borrow an expression from our Brit friends across the pond, I was gobsmacked. That revelation did not square at all with the tales Dad told of a childhood of toil and going without in the Applegate Valley. If Glenn Smith's recollections were spot on, and there is no reason to doubt him, our father's formative years in the Applegate Valley were largely ones of relative leisure. As the youngest in the family, he was apparently pampered by his mother who was still grieving over the loss of daughter Besse Bell. It seems she protected him from his stern father who would not have been too pleased by what he would have seen as mollycoddling. His stern attitude may have been intended to counter her tender ways. In Dad's defense, perhaps he escaped the farm whenever possible to avoid punishment in the form of chores from the unforgiving family patriarch.

As with all children, I only knew my father as an adult. I can attest he was a hard worker before he lost his leg, and strived to work even after losing body parts. But the next time your father tells you of his childhood toils, of having to walk a mile to school in the snow, barefoot mind you, take it with a liberal sprinkling of salt. It is simply dear old dad taking his poetic license out for a stroll.

Uncle Charlie was known for having a generally frail condition his whole life long, not for being a stout worker. It is likely that Jonas, a tireless worker down on the farm, pushed the elder sibling to become more of a hale fellow, causing a deep and permanent resentment.

On the other hand, brothers Charlie and Paul may have also been right about their descriptions of their father being a bullying bible thumper. Judging from what they said about him, he certainly came across as being as solemn as a sermon and sterner than a Marine drill sergeant.

While neither the eldest son nor the youngest was the light of their father's eye and they reciprocated his displeasure in kind, Alfred clearly adored their father. Like Jonas, he was also a hard worker who didn't tolerate those who could not carry their share of the load, according to those who knew him. During our visit with him in Texas, the fair-haired son spoke with pride of his father's work ethic, unbreakable heartiness and hunting skills. He could not say enough nice things about Jonas Fattig.

The brothers' sister, my Aunt Laura, who never had a bad word to utter about anyone, doted on their mother, often speaking of her kind and gentle ways. She said little about their father beyond noting he was stern and worked hard. Her silence in regards to him being warm and fuzzy may be more telling than her endearing words about her mother.

Based on that scenario, most family behavior experts would shake their educated heads and conclude the Fattig nuclear family of that generation met the textbook description of being dysfunctional. No argument there. Still, the family unit was a microcosm of the state of Jefferson, that mythical region of southwestern Oregon and northwestern California known to be unruly and itching for a fight. For many families in the region during that era, being dysfunctional was the only way for them to function at all. Certainly in this odd situation in which a family counselor would have to dig deep to find a comparable case in a thick textbook, a flawed family was better than no family.

However, children are supposed to love their parents. OK, if Adolf Hitler spawned children, they would have had justifiable reason to want to exterminate their ruthless nut job of a father for the good of humankind. But Jonas was no mass murderer, no cruel despot. For instance, he never employed corporal punishment to punish his children for misbehavior at a time when such flogging was the norm, according to Aunt Laura. Again, Jonas merely seemed to be a stern taskmaster with little patience for offspring who didn't share his puritanical work ethic.

No one alive today can tell us about the Fattig family and the inner life on the farm they worked for a quarter of a century in Holland, the tiny community in the Illinois Valley. But we can peek over the shoulder of Grayce Lewis Hudron who was born on Dec. 26, 1916, in the Lewis family ranch house in that farming community.

"I was born up on the old ranch just up the road, about a quarter of a mile from Grandpa and Grandma Fattig's place," she told me in a 2005 interview. Although she has since passed away, at the time she was still living in Holland on property she and her late husband, Joe Hudron, bought in 1940. She was the descendant of pioneers, including the Holland family who founded the hamlet in the late 1800s. Her husband, the maintenance man at Illinois Valley High School while I was a student in the late 1960s, was a good fellow who patiently put up with our juvenile shenanigans.

Although Grayce had no memories of the WWI years and the local reaction to the two older brothers' draft evasion, she was able to shed light on the Fattig family and its unusual ways in the 1920s. What's more, the tiny lady was a real hoot: friendly, funny and quick as a buggy whip.

"Now, Grandma Fattig was a good cook—I ate at their farm many times," she said. "Your grandma and my mother [Katherine] all belonged to the garden club. They'd all fix lunch when it was their turn to entertain. Your grandma made the best sweet buns I ever had. Oh, my gosh, they were good."

Harriett Fattig, with her children grown, all but adopted the friendly little neighbor girl. She cooked baked beans to die for, Grayce said.

"I always found a way to eat at the Fattig house when she made those wonderful beans," she said. "She would fill your bowl, then place one of her biscuits—they were so light they would almost float away—in the bowl and let it soak up a little of the juice before serving it to you. It was heavenly."

Grandpa Fattig didn't have refined eating habits, she said.

"First of all, everything—and I mean everything—went together on his plate," she said. "Meat and potatoes and gravy and vegetables, everything. If there was dessert, it was piled on there, too. Then he'd chop it all up together."

She stopped talking to chuckle at the memory of Jonas industriously mixing his food together before wolfing it down. The sickly-looking dish must have looked like something someone had just upchucked. As one with a weak stomach, I would not have eaten much had my grandparents lived longer and invited me over for dinner.

"It just irked Grandma Fattig to no end," Grayce said of Jonas' eating habits. Yet the family patriarch would shrug and retort it was all going to the same place, she noted.

"But he was a good man, not a mouthy man at all," she added. "Jonas, he never swore. I can still hear him visiting with my dad. The closest he ever came to saying 'God!' or 'Damn!' or 'Hell!' was 'Goll!' And that was when he was really upset. 'Goll!' he'd tell my dad."

The Fattigs were advocates of the Dunkard faith who prayed before their meals, she recalled. While piety was apparently the path preferred by the parents, it has been demonstrated the eldest son never followed in his father's verbal footsteps when it came to avoiding swear words. However, Alfred was a practitioner of cuss-free language, at least in the autumn of his life.

Harriett was a short lady who was always ready to help a neighbor, Jonas was tall and lanky with a drooping mustache and just as accommodating when someone needed a helping hand, Grayce said.

"They were good neighbors," she said. "That Jonas, he could outwork anyone."

Come harvest time, her father, James Lewis, would invariably turn to the lanky neighbor with the curious eating habits.

"In those days, when they would do the threshing of the grain, two or three neighbors would stack the grain loose, then the wives would cook the lunch and dinner," she explained. "My dad thought he couldn't thresh without Grandpa Fattig and E.N. Cooke. That E.N. Cooke was a horse man. E.N. never touched a whip to our old team, Babe and Dan. It was all horses in the early days."

That would be Edwin Nathan Cooke, a short but stout man who would become my maternal grandfather. The two men who worked side by side on the Lewis ranch never had any inkling they would one day share a bond through blood relatives in the form of grandchildren. Unfortunately, like our paternal grandparents, the easy-going and well-liked E.N. Cooke died before my siblings and I were born.

Had Grayce been a few years older, she could have also been related. She freely admitted to have been smitten by our father as a young girl.

"He used to say 'poppycock' when he thought something we said didn't ring true," she said. "We girls thought he was so worldly. To us, he was quite the dapper gentleman."

But it was a local young lady three years her senior named Lorena Coffey who stole the dapper gentleman's heart. After our future father married Lorena, the two made their home in the Fattig farmhouse, Grayce recalled.

"Lorena was loved by everybody," she said. "She was a wonderful person. And she just loved horses."

Grayce remembered the grim day in 1935 when Lorena, then twenty-four, died of childbirth in an upstairs bedroom of the Fattig farmhouse.

"On the day Lorena died and the hearse came to the house to pick up her body, her horse in the pasture next to the house kept whinnying," she said. "When the hearse went down that long driveway, her horses ran after it, whinnying, all the way to the end of the pasture. It was so sad. Your father and grandparents were devastated. We all were."

Grayce and Joe Hudron, who came west from the heartland to serve in the Civilian Conservation Corps in the Illinois Valley, would be married on Oct. 12, 1935. Their first car was a 1929 Ford roadster with a little rumble seat which took them to local dances, she said.

"Joe and I, we went in for the fiddlers," she said. "That's my kind of music. There's violinists and then there's fiddlers. I'll take the fiddlers every time."

The young couple would kick up their heels over at the nearby Bridgeview Grange hall where Jonas Fattig fiddled before he grew too old to play, she said.

"It was also where your father and Lorena used to go," she said, later adding, "Yes, the Fattigs had a lot of memories here, some good and some bad."

The fact Jonas fiddled indicates the old workhorse must have let his hair down and kicked up his heels once in a while. Moreover, the anecdotal evidence indicating our father and his first wife attended those dances shows our grandfather and his youngest son shared some happy times.

The last time I saw her, Grayce presented me with one of those good memories. It was a tiny teapot, the kind that holds two demitasse cups of tea. Its pearl porcelain has an iridescent patina that seems to glow when reflecting light.

"That was your Grandma Fattig's—she gave it to me when I was a little girl," she said. "She was a wonderful lady. Your grandma handled that very teapot. I want you to have it now."

I had a lump in my throat when she gave me the teapot my grandmother once cherished. Grayce was ten years old when Harriett Fattig bequeathed the teapot to her in 1926, some ninety years ago as I write this. It is the only item our family today has from the Fattig farmhouse in the Illinois Valley. Whether the teapot came from the Applegate Valley or even Kansas, we will never know. To match it, I would have to track down the old fiddle my grandfather once played in barn dances in the Applegate Valley and later in the Bridgeview Grange hall in the Illinois Valley. Fat chance, but I keep checking out old fiddles when we visit an antique store in the region. Perhaps I'll one day find a battered fiddle with the initials "JF" scratched on the chin rest.

Ultimately, as with all couples who have the fortune to grow old together, the good memories Jonas and Harriett Fattig made and shared would come to an end. As they aged, they could no longer work the farm they loved.

It was in their Holland farmhouse that Harriett, Jonas' wife and partner for fifty-one years, died on Jan. 18, 1940. Born in northeast Kansas on Oct. 28, 1872, she was sixty-seven.

She had been a teenager, a mere seventeen, when they were married in Beaver City, Nebraska, in 1889. Born in Iowa on Jan. 22, 1858, some three years before the first shot was fired in the Civil War, the *paterfamilias* was twice her age when what in effect would become the two family plow horses became hitched. They had worked hard to carve out a life together, first farming on the Greats Plains before migrating west to Oregon around 1900. After he first worked as a laborer in Ashland for a few years, they took up a 120-acre homestead in the Applegate Valley in 1907. They proved up on the land in 1913, meaning that Uncle Sam granted them the deed to the land. That would be the cash cow they sold to buy the Illinois Valley farm. They had lost one daughter but four of their children grew to adulthood. To the hilt, they had backed their two sons who balked at serving in World War I. By most measures, they had a full life together.

With Harriett's death, the fire in Jonas' belly flamed out.

"Grandpa was lost without her," observed Nanine Anderson Nichols in a 1989 interview. You may remember her as another denizen of Chapter Nineteen, my cousin who was born in the Fattig farmhouse in the Applegate Valley on Valentine's Day in 1915. "Of course, he was in his eighties by then. He could no longer work the way he used to. He didn't know what to do with himself."

Charlie Fattig, who had been living on the Fattig farm where he had been raising fir seedlings to sell to the U.S. Forest Service, assumed control of the estate not long after his mother died, she said. However, she did not know just when that occurred; noting only that it was just a few years after Harriett died.

What we do know is that Jonas Fattig was not doing well by the mid-1940s. On one fine Sunday afternoon he strolled buck naked amongst a flock of church ladies out on a picnic near the family farm in Holland, startling them like a brace of nervous quail surprised by an old hound dog, according to Nanine, confirming family lore which I had heard since childhood. While a medical professional may have determined he suffered from senile dementia, according to the family's considerably less than professional diagnosis, the elderly gent had become as ringy as a church bell in his doddering years.

It was shortly thereafter that primogeniture kicked in. The patriarch could no longer lead the family, much less be responsible for the farm. It could be Uncle Charlie was keen on wresting control of the family farm from his father. It may very well be that he felt it was his responsibility. We will never know the truth, naked or not. By this time, Alfred had already been gone for two decades. And our dad apparently had no claim to the land. As for Aunt Laura, she was already married with children and did not factor into the equation, given the custom in that time and place of female siblings not having a voice in the matter. Parenthetically, our daughters today would not tolerate such backwards and unfair traditions.

What we do know is that the eldest son, both by family custom and law, had the right to do as he pleased with the property in those distant days. With roots tapping back into early Western civilization, the accepted tradition allowed the first-born male child to inherit the entire estate, excluding other siblings.

According to records I obtained from the Oregon state hospital in Salem, the old farmer was committed to the state asylum in April of 1947 by Charlie S. Fattig. Jonas was eighty-nine at the time. At the time his father was committed to the state hospital, the eldest son had already sold the family farm and purchased a store and gas station at the base of Hays Hill just south of Wonder, Nanine recalled.

To slake your already nearly satiated appetite for southern Oregon geography and history, the geological feature and Fort Hay a few miles to the south were named after a pioneer named Hay. Fort Hay, a farm house turned into a makeshift fortress during a skirmish in the Rogue River Indian War of 1855-56, morphed into a stage stop called Anderson Station. The local community was originally dubbed Anderson before being renamed Selma. Actor John Wayne developed a fondness for the region while filming the blockbuster movie *Rooster Cogburn* in 1974 along the Rogue River and kept his horses in Selma at the old Deer Creek Ranch which he co-owned. History doesn't record whether the Duke visited Waters Creek. If he did, he likely kept his Winchester handy, it being bear country and all.

Included in Jonas' medical records were copies of two Western Union telegrams. One was from the hospital staff to Charlie Fattig, then living in his little cabin in Wonder. It notified him that his father had died Sept. 17, 1947, and requested he wire back with funeral instructions.

"In regards to remains of Jonas Fattig am leaving to your disposal," our uncle shrugged in the terse reply via telegram. It was heartless, to say the least.

The medical records listed the cause of death as "bronchopneumonia." The folks in the white coats added his clinical diagnosis was "senile psychosis." They also noted that he was extremely sad, and that he did not know why he was locked up in what he must have felt was tantamount to a prison. Jonas Fattig died alone, far from family or friends.

Her mother was very upset by what happened to their father, Nanine said.

"Mom always felt it was wrong the way Grandpa was treated and the way he died," she said. "She also felt like she should have gotten something from the Fattig place in Holland. She hated the way it all happened. But there wasn't anything she could do about it. It was just the way it was done in those days."

Nanine also divulged a characteristic about Alfred Fattig which may have explained some of the antagonism among the brothers.

"Alfred had a terrible temper when he was young," she said. "Grandma used to try to curb his temper. That caused friction between him and her. Grandpa didn't really get after him."

Upon finding out from his sister what happened to their father and the family farm, Alfred was furious, she said.

"I don't know if he ever threatened to do something to Charlie but he may have," she said. "I do remember Mom saying he was very angry."

Being the only sibling who farmed, Alfred may have figured he deserved to inherit the family farm. As the only sibling close to his father, he must have been intensely upset upon learning the family patriarch died alone. But Alfred had been gone from Oregon for twenty years. Like his sister, he didn't have a say in the way it unfolded.

In a related development, Charlie acquired the acreage along Waters Creek in Wonder while he owned the store. According to a warranty deed dated May 27, 1946, local residents Earl and Thelma Martin sold the property to Uncle Charlie for one dollar. The Martins, who owed him a large bill for groceries and gas, gave him the property in lieu of cash, our mother said. It is interesting that the curmudgeon otherwise known as Uncle Charlie, on Oct. 28, 1948, gave the Waters Creek property to our father for the sum of $1 and "other valuable consideration," according to another warranty deed signed by both brothers. That would have been a little more than a year after James Bridger popped into the world.

While presenting the property to the youngest brother sounds like a magnanimous gesture, I suspect our uncle had an ulterior motive. After all, he wasn't exactly known for his charitable ways. I believe Uncle Charlie, never a fighter, wanted Dad to be on hand in the event Alfred returned to settle what he rightly felt was a shoddy treatment of their father. It is very likely the elder brother wanted the younger brother around for protection.

Charlie operated the store for several years before quitting the retail business, a profession that he was wholly unequipped to face each day. As you have seen, he was not a people person. Having sold his store, the WWI draft dodger retreated to his little cabin along Waters Creek and glared out at the world filled with damned varmints.

By any standard, Jonas Fattig was treated poorly as he approached the end of his life. Of that, there can be no doubt. Nor is there any question the elder brother's treatment of their father must have made Alfred fighting mad when he learned of it back in Texas through his sister. He was very fond of his father and did not get on well with Charlie. It is conceivable that Alfred threatened his older brother with a sound throttling or worse. It is also likely our father would have sided with the older brother as owner of the Waters Creek land whose acquisition was indirectly connected to the Holland farm and their father.

Again, there is no question the eldest brother was within his rights to sell the property. He was simply following a centuries-old custom. His sister may have felt slighted but she had no legal grounds to pursue. Besides, knowing her, she would have suffered in silence. As for Alfred, not only did he have no legal standing to interfere but he was also out of the picture.

Yet the scenario I laid out leaves a bad taste in one's mouth. Perhaps there were other mitigating circumstances we don't know about. All who knew the gospel of it are long dead. Like those who have gone before, the answers belong to the ages.

TWENTY-EIGHT

Madstone Legacy

C LEARLY, WORLD WAR I, HERALDED AS THE WAR to end all wars, failed to live up to its epithet. A little more than two decades after the last shell was fired in WWI, the world would explode into another brutal global conflict, one which inflicted yet more death and destruction. Before nuclear weapons shook the globe to end four years of fighting in World War II, some 405,400 young Americans would lie dead on foreign soil. If you read the introduction to this book, you may recall that roughly 116,500 Americans died in WWI during the little more than one year we fought in that conflict. In both wars, roughly 100,000 Americans were killed each year. That is a staggering annual price to pay for the collapse of civilization.

As I write these words, the world is in upheaval. Thanks to the deadly mix of religious zealotry, cultural clashes and nationalism, blood flows throughout the Middle East, terrorism periodically explodes in Europe and has reared its evil head on our shores. When the terrorists take a rare holiday, the smoke of war can invariably be found drifting up somewhere around the planet. Some are simply this week's coup in a third-world country; others are seemingly endless conflicts carried through time by generation after generation. Meanwhile, arms merchants continue to grow fat on the bounties of war while the victims—the wounded, the homeless widows and orphans—struggle to survive. Only the dead no longer suffer. Humankind is always itching for a fight; gray-haired leaders ever ready to send youth off to die in the latest cause célèbre. The cycle continues. To slightly rewrite the 1960s folk song, when will we ever learn?

In the year 2017, some fear our nation is coming apart at the seams as our domestic political infighting reigns supreme. Indeed, the United States of America at times seems to be nothing more than warring factions united only by anger and resentment for those with differing points of view.

Yet the last military draft was in December of 1972 with the authorization of Uncle Sam to require military induction expiring on June 30, 1973. Since then our military has been all volunteer, unless you consider activating National Guard units for overseas deployment to be a type of military draft. On the other side of that coin, the citizen soldiers volunteered to wear the uniform. In any event, registration for the Selective Service System officially ended on April 1, 1975.

Alfred Fattig was quick to observe that political leaders promised the first global war would be the last war. He had bristled at my suggestion some felt it was a just war in an unjust world. Nor was he impressed with my contention that some past wars needed to be fought, just as there will be wars in the future which we cannot avoid. My awkward addendum that warfare could certainly be reduced was received with the shake of the head it deserved.

"We was wrong?" he thundered, his dark eyes flashing with anger. "That war wasn't sensible in the first place. There was people killing each other. I don't care where you are a'killing people, it's murder. Anyone who can't figure that out, why, they don't think much."

Even at ninety-six, he remained defiant. After all the years that had elapsed since WWI, resentment lingered towards those who had chastised him for evading the military draft. For a few minutes, he was silent, unwilling to engage in conversation.

"War is plumb out of my line," he said softly after a moment. "There is nothing honest about war."

He reiterated he had no regrets he took to the mountains to avoid serving in the war. When he faced the wrath of Uncle Sam, he paid his debt to society, he offered.

"I don't know how it would have turned out or where I'd be," he said when asked how his life would have been different had he answered the draft call in 1917. "I've always been glad that I did what I done."

He also felt he was able to reduce his jail time by surrendering to authorities and explaining his rationale. "It could have been years instead of months in there," he said.

But he wondered aloud why organized religion wasn't more supportive of pacifists in WWI and in subsequent wars.

"The churches were a lot to blame," concluded the devout Christian. "Most of them didn't stick up for anyone who didn't go to war. I'd just like to ask some of them church members what they considered murder. Now, I don't claim to be the best man on earth. We all make mistakes. It don't matter how hard we try. Likely we're wrong more than we're right. I just done my best to be truthful. A lie is a bad thing to fool with. There is nothing in a lie but a lie."

Following the war and their incarceration, the two brothers were shunned by some in southern Oregon for their pacifist stance. No doubt there were ugly instances which caused his parents to move from the Applegate Valley to the more remote Illinois Valley. But the surviving brother chose not to reflect on those incidents. Instead, he focused on the more pleasant memories.

After serving their jail time, the brothers worked together on a mining claim known as the Cedar Bar Mine on the west bank of Josephine Creek near the confluence of Canyon Creek. It was just downstream from the mine that gold was first discovered in quantities that brought hordes of miners to the region in the early 1850s. The discovery was made by a group of miners who had failed to hit pay dirt in the '49 California gold fields.

"There was a lot of gold in the Illinois Valley," Alfred said. "I expect there is still a lot there. But it is hard work, digging for gold with pick and shovel."

They were accustomed to the hard labor, thanks to the big rocks they broke into little rocks at Rocky Butte. But they had found the world they once knew had changed from the time when they first hid out in the mountains.

For instance, there weren't as many people living in the local communities as there had been before WWI. Residents in Grants Pass, who had literally given its first-born to the war effort, found that many of those who marched away never returned. The 1920 census revealed that only 3,151 people lived in the community, a substantial drop from the 3,897 counted ten years earlier. Many of the "soldier boys" had failed to return, the *Daily Courier* lamented, adding they were apparently attracted to the city lights.

In 1927, fed up with the shunning he received from society, Alfred Fattig began a self imposed exile from the region he had grown to love as a young man. He first traveled north to the Alaska Territory where he lived for several years before heading to the Deep South.

"When I left Oregon, there weren't no place you could go that hadn't been disturbed by people," he said. "In Alaska, you could go way back in the mountains where no man had ever been. Animals weren't afraid of a man."

He spent the Great Depression in southeast Alaska, trapping and mining for gold. Wandering alone, he trapped and hunted—the Madstone years were far enough away for him to regain his love of hunting—throughout the Alaskan southeast although he made the Ketchikan area his home base.

Come winter, he watched the Northern Lights finger paint a colorful light show overhead. Early summer brought rain and clouds of swarming mosquitoes.

"I was pretty near a wild man when I was in Alaska," he said. "I laid out in the mountains there at night. I had nothing to lose but my own life. If I lost it, there was nobody to worry about it. I was just one. I liked my own company and the wild animals, the thick timber and the rivers and lakes. I liked to sleep outdoors among the wild animals. I was a savage when I had to be. Guess I was kind of a lone wolf."

The lone wolf met his match in Arkansas. It was there he encountered

Leota Titus, the lady who would become his wife on Dec. 26, 1944. The couple moved to Texas where he farmed and helped raise her six children from a previous marriage.

But peace continued to elude him. It was not far from the land he farmed for some four decades that President John F. Kennedy was assassinated in Dallas on Nov. 22, 1963.

Alfred did not see himself as a profile in courage. He would tell you he was a simple man simply following his conscience. Despite spending long months in the wilderness, often by himself, he felt he was not alone in his opposition to war as a solution to conflict.

"A lot of people was against that war," he said of WWI. "War ain't no good. People are beginning to realize that now."

Again, recent history would argue against that statement but it was largely true when he spoke those words in the late 1980s.

Largely unchanged is the wilderness that is the Madstone country. The remote mountain canyon remains a timeless place, a place where years are not counted. It is just as wild and wooly as when the brothers first ventured into that rocky yet beautiful terrain a century ago. You see hawks soaring overhead and hear their piercing cries when the river rapids or the wind whistling up the canyon isn't drowning out all other sounds. There is an occasional large pile of bear scat along the Madstone Trail and browsing deer often peek at you from behind an azalea bush.

But the trail is little used by humans today, except for intrepid hikers. Although I'm far from intrepid, I've hiked in there twice, and each time was barely able to stagger back to what passes for civilization. Fortunately, my right leg is lame so I can falsely blame it for my wheezing and whining hike out.

As you have read, the Madstone cabin is gone, razed by fire. But there is a Forest Service sign marking its location. When I was last in there some thirty years ago, a couple of fire-blackened cedar logs could be seen where the cabin once stood. A chimney made from a hydraulic mining giant lay near a pile of rocks which was apparently part of the smokehouse. There were bits of pottery, broken glass turned purple from age and square and round nails, some rusted through. A rusting blade of a shovel could be seen, along with an old file and a rusting hinge. Sturdy tools that were solid and seemingly everlasting in Alfred's day were returning to the earth.

Yet there were also a few spent .40-65 Winchester shells amid the debris. Did one once house the black powder and bullet that killed the forked-horn buck carrying the madstone back in 1918? The only answer you'll hear is the constant chuckling of the Chetco River in the distance. Of course, the 1894 Winchester that Alfred left hanging on the wall when he left the Madstone country was likely taken by a cabin visitor not long after he abandoned the site. Back then, it was permissible to take items from an abandoned cabin just as Alfred had cannibalized other deserted cabins to build the Madstone cabin. Call it borrowing. However, those cabins are now part of the region's history so don't even think about taking anything from the old sites.

For the past half century, the nearest river Alfred would have seen was the Red River flowing through northeastern Texas. The reddish-brown water of the Red was a far cry from the Chetco, he allowed.

"The deep pools in the Chetco were so clear you could see every little rock in the bottom," he said, noting it was like looking into a swimming pool.

When Jim and I met him, Alfred already knew about the cabin having burned. Our brother Charles had hiked into the upper Chetco in the early 1980s, becoming the first member of the family to see it since Alfred had left the mountains. In his letters to Alfred, Charles had let him know the cabin was gone.

"I felt pretty bad when I heard about it burning down," Alfred told us. "I figure that was my fault."

The reason, he explained, was that he built the smokehouse adjacent to the main cabin, creating a fire hazard. It wasn't until after the interview that I learned the cabin may have been the victim of a wildfire or a careless visitor, not poor planning.

"I wish that old cabin was still standing there," he said. "I put in a lot of years on those rocky old trails."

Once again, he was a young man, hiking the mountain trails embedded in his memory. Perhaps he was standing on the ridge overlooking the cabin, watching a wisp of smoke drifting up from its chimney.

"I could still fish and hunt for bee trees," he said when he returned to the present. "I don't suppose I could pack in an old buck like I used to. But I wouldn't want to kill them anyway."

As hunters, most Fattigs in our little circle no longer go out and slay wild creatures. My eldest brother, the one the alert reader will recall in Chapter Two killed a bear when he was only ten, allows that he is no longer interested in big game.

"I tapered off my hunting trips when my kids started college and I had to increase my work hours because of the added expense and I never really got back into it," he explained in the summer of 2016. "Now I have a more 'manly' hobby. I take pictures of moths that have faces designed on their backs and wings. Every morning I go out around the pool and look for them. I guess I am much easier amused now than in my younger years."

Although I was never the hunter on par with Jim or Alfred, although it could be said I got the biggest buck for my bang, I understand why our uncle hung up his rifle. Killing for food or your survival is one thing; killing for a trophy or just to prove you can take something's life is quite another. I was reminded of that early in September of 2016. A doe with big brown eyes and her little spotted fawn had been hanging around our garden fence on our property in the Applegate Valley just a few miles from where Jonas and Harriett Fattig homesteaded. One morning she hobbled up with her left rear leg dangling. It appeared someone had shot her. Whether it was a juvenile with a rifle or a shot gone awry we will never know. What I know for certain is the doe and fawn will have a difficult time surviving the winter. There is little we can do to save them. May there will be a special place in hell for someone who would shoot a doe while her little spotted fawn looks on in bewilderment. If such an act had occurred in Uncle Alfred's presence, his pacifism could have very likely turned to deadly fury.

While the wilderness may have not changed much, the settled land and culture he knew in his youth have been dramatically altered. There are an estimated 10,000 folks now living in the Applegate Valley. On warm days when the thermal winds are strong, the great wings of a hang glider launched from nearby Woodrat Mountain soar silently overhead like a modern-day Icarus attempting to flee Crete. Hang gliders often float over the land where the Fattig farm once stood. The old house is long gone. The working farm has been swallowed up by gentleman ranches.

Gone, too, are all the family members he knew since childhood. While visiting him in 1988, I showed him a black and white photograph that included his mother, sisters Laura and Bessie Bell Fattig, his little sister who died at age six in Ashland in 1904. Tears formed in his eyes as he looked at Bessie's image, one he hadn't seen for more than sixty years.

"That must have been taken pretty near her death," he said as his gnarly fingers gently held the photograph. "This little girl here…"

His voice trailed off as he looked through watery eyes at her image.

"These two kids, way back then, we often had to stay by ourselves," he said of his sisters. "We used to get together and sing. Since she left, I've never tried to sing. Never. She was just a little girl when she died."

The old man paused again, lost in his memories of the funeral on the hillside overlooking Ashland.

"That was the worst day of my life," he said. "I told myself many times that if she had lived I would have had a good friend. But she lays up there on the hill all alone in a grave."

She is no longer alone. In 2006, my wife and I acquired the unclaimed cremains of Jonas Fattig from the Oregon State Hospital in Salem and buried the canister alongside Bessie's remains in the Hargardine Cemetery in Ashland. Father and daughter are now together.

"I never wanted to be at home when any of the rest of the family died," Alfred said. "I never was."

The only other family member buried in Jackson County is Jacob Fattig, his paternal uncle who died in 1922. He is buried in the Jacksonville Cemetery.

"That was my daddy's brother who came out to Oregon," he observed. "Outside of him, I can't ever remember meeting any of his kin folk."

In the senior center in Gainesville, Texas, Alfred Fattig rested his hands on his cane as he reflected on his long life. His nation had been in three major wars—World War II, Korean War and the Vietnam War—since he dodged the military draft. Indeed, it would fight two more wars since we met, both of which seem to refuse to die. Of course, the weapons of World War I, while deadly to those who fought in the trenches, seem obsolete today.

"I don't know how the world is going to turn out," he said. "Anyway, I'll be over the river before many more years."

To the very end, he did not retreat from his philosophical opposition to fighting in World War I. Even after nearly a century of studying life, he figured we had a ways to go.

"I've always believed I was right," he said. "We got to learn right from wrong."

The last time I saw our uncle, my brother Jim and I were walking down the hall away from his room in the senior center in Texas. We had already shaken his hand and said our good-byes to him and his family. Just as we reached the end of the long corridor, I glanced back. Alfred was standing in the doorway to his room, watching his kid brother's sons walk away. He silently held up his right hand and slowly waved a final farewell. I responded in kind.

Rest in peace, Alfred Fattig.

ABOUT THE AUTHOR

C ONTRARY TO WHAT HE SOMETIMES tell folks with tongue held firmly in cheek, the author wasn't actually raised by wolves in the wild. But it is true his grandparents homesteaded in Southern Oregon, and that he and his siblings, like their father and his siblings, were born and reared in the region where they all ran rampant in the mountains, making wolves exceedingly nervous. After an uneventful hitch in the Marine Corps and what he describes as a less than stellar scholastic performance at the University of Oregon, he managed to obtain a degree in journalism. Over the subsequent decades, he was able to convince more than a dozen newspaper editors from Alaska to California to hire him, decisions which he hopes did not leave a permanent blemish on their careers. Upon retiring to become a recovering journalist at the end of 2013, he immediately fell off the wagon and started writing books. *Madstone* is his second non-fiction book. He lives happily with his wife, Maureen, in a restored cabin not far from his grandparent's original homestead with a menagerie of adopted fierce creatures.

www.hellgatepress.com

CPSIA information can be obtained
at www.ICGtesting.com
Printed in the USA
LVHW081543251121
704451LV00015B/801